gamify your
classroom

Colin Lankshear and Michele Knobel
General Editors

Vol. 71

The New Literacies and Digital Epistemologies series
is part of the Peter Lang Education list.
Every volume is peer reviewed and meets
the highest quality standards for content and production.

PETER LANG
New York • Bern • Frankfurt • Berlin
Brussels • Vienna • Oxford • Warsaw

MATTHEW FARBER

gamify your classroom

A FIELD GUIDE TO GAME-BASED LEARNING

PETER LANG
New York • Bern • Frankfurt • Berlin
Brussels • Vienna • Oxford • Warsaw

Library of Congress Cataloging-in-Publication Data
Farber, Matthew.
Gamify your classroom: A field guide to game-based learning / Matthew Farber.
pages cm. — (New literacies and digital epistemologies; v. 71)
Includes bibliographical references and index.
1. Educational games. 2. Educational technology.
3. Learning. 4. Lesson planning. I. Title.
LB1029.G3F37   371.33'7–dc23   2014037497
ISBN 978-1-4331-2671-0 (hardcover)
ISBN 978-1-4331-2670-3 (paperback)
ISBN 978-1-4539-1459-5 (e-book)
ISSN 1523-9543

Bibliographic information published by **Die Deutsche Nationalbibliothek**.
Die Deutsche Nationalbibliothek lists this publication in the "Deutsche
Nationalbibliografie"; detailed bibliographic data are available
on the Internet at http://dnb.d-nb.de/.

Author photo by Amy Roth

CONTENTS

ACKNOWLEDGMENTS

This book would not have been possible without the support of many people. I would like to express my gratitude to the New Jersey City University Educational Technology Department, specifically my "Leaducator" cohort and my doctoral graduate professors Laura Zieger, Christopher Shamburg, Cordelia Twomey, Christopher Carnahan, and Leonid Rabinovitz. I am grateful to my series editors, Michele Knobel and Colin Lankshear, for their faith in my vision. Thanks also go to the staff and administration at Valleyview Middle School and the Denville Township Board of Education, as well as my student playtesters. On a more personal note, I would like to thank my wife, Laura, for her patience throughout the duration of this research, my curious son, Spencer, and our playful dog, Lizzie. A special thank you is extended to my parents, Gary and Judith Farber, as well as my wife's parents, Virginia Fisher and Frank Fisher.

INTRODUCTION

In 2012 the Joan Ganz Cooney Center at Sesame Workshop published results of a study about games in the classroom. Five hundred kindergarten through grade-8 teachers participated. The questions were about game-based learning knowledge, integration, and comfort. About 12% of the respondents reported that they had received training about computer-based games while in a teachers' college (Millstone, 2012). Most teachers said that they had learned about educational games on the job, from colleagues, social media, or journals—not in formal training or college (Millstone, 2012).

Right now there are hundreds of millions of dollars—from the government, universities, and private foundations—in use researching the efficacy of using games for learning. The Cooney Center's report led me on a quest to interview people at the forefront of game-based learning. What I discovered was a small circle of passionate people. In January 2014 I asked Kurt Squire, co-founder of the Games + Learning + Society Center, about the community of game-based learning advocates. He said, "We all want to make learning engaging for kids, and some aren't being served well. That's why we're here."

I wrote this book to share what I have learned about using games as an educational tool. I am a "boots-on-the-ground" classroom teacher. I teach middle school social studies in New Jersey, and I am also a doctoral candidate in Educational Technology Leadership at New Jersey City University, where I am an adjunct instructor. Additionally, I write regularly about game-based learning for Edutopia, George Lucas's educational foundation.

Much of this book draws on my experiences implementing games with my students. Research brought me to the New York City headquarters of BrainPOP, Electric Funstuff (developer of the award-winning *Mission US* games), the 11th annual Games for Change Festival, and the game-based school Quest to Learn. I have advised the Institute of Play, designer of the Quest school model, and I am a member of the GlassLab Teacher Network. In the 2013–2014 school year, my students tried several games for learning, such as *Minecraft*, *Do I Have a Right?*, *SimCityEDU*, and *Historia*. We also played many nondigital games, including the argumentation challenge, *Socratic Smackdown*. By the end of the school year, one class started calling themselves "the Beta Testers!"

I use games to deliver content, to build skills, and for review. You could call my teaching style "game-inspired learning." Sometimes I don't play games with my students at all. Regardless of your teaching discipline or grade level, whether you are a pre-service teacher or veteran educator, my hope is that this book will engage and reinvigorate the way you teach and how your students learn!

New Media Literacy & Games

There is project-based learning, problem-based learning, inquiry-based learning, and even zombie-based learning (honest! Zombies can teach about geography! http://www.zombiebased.com). Now there is game-based learning. Video games are popular and kids love them, so maybe teachers should teach with them? I know, it sounds crazy.

In the heyday of arcade video games, everything depended on a player's quick reflexes. Reacting too slowly could doom Pac-Man's survival. Computer-based games have undergone a lot of advancements in the past 40 years, including the addition of adaptive engines that scale up to a player's ability. Modern games can be used to teach abstract concepts such as the laws of physics, systems thinking competencies, social and emotional learning, collaborative team building, spatial reasoning, problem solving, and many other real-life skills. In a sense, *all games are educational*. After all, you need to learn a game to master it!

Games are considered to be "new media" (as opposed to more "traditional" media, such as books or the theater). I interviewed digital media scholar Henry Jenkins about where games as new media fit into the context of school. We spoke in May 2014. Jenkins published several books on the topic, including *Textual Poachers: Television Fans & Participatory Culture* (1992), *From Barbie to Mortal Kombat: Gender and Computer Games* (1998), and *Convergence Culture: Where Old and New Media Collide* (2006), as well as white papers for the MacArthur Foundation about digital media literacy. Among other organizations, he cofounded MIT's Education Arcade, with Kurt Squire, to "prototype how games could be used in learning." Jenkins has been featured on PBS's *Digital Nation*, and even testified in front of Congress about the misunderstandings about violence in video games.

It is helpful to remember that movies, cable television, Google, YouTube, and other technologies that now are used for teaching also have had their educational validity questioned. Jenkins was prompted to write a blog post in 2006 about misunderstandings about video games, "Reality Bytes: Eight Myths about Video Games Debunked." Common misconceptions included:

1. The availability of video games has led to an epidemic of youth violence.
2. Scientific evidence links violent gameplay with youth aggression.
3. Children are the primary market for video games.
4. Almost no girls play computer games.
5. Because games are used to train soldiers to kill, they have the same impact on the kids who play them.
6. Video games are not a meaningful form of expression.
7. Video game play is socially isolating.
8. Video game play is desensitizing. (Jenkins, 2006b)

Data supported Jenkins's points about who actually plays video games. The proliferation of casual gaming on smartphones (e.g., *Angry Birds*, *Candy Crush Saga*) diversified the population of digital game players. Furthermore, social media has made the act highly participatory (e.g., *Farmville*, *Words with Friends*). The Entertainment Software Association, the lobbyist organization that runs the ESRB (the Entertainment Software Ratings Board, the rating agency for games), reported that today's gamers are, on average, 31 years old and have been playing for 14 years (2014 Essential Facts about the Computer and Video Game Industry, 2014, p. 3). 48% of players are female

(2014 Essential Facts about the Computer and Video Game Industry, 2014, p. 3). I asked Jenkins about what has changed since his "Eight Myths" post. He stated that the blog post took just minutes to write and has lingered on longer than he had expected. Often it comes up in the discourse, especially when senseless tragedies such as the Sandy Hook Elementary School shooting in 2012 are blamed on gaming (in that case, Wayne LaPierre, the head of the National Rifle Association, pointed the finger at the gaming sector). Almost all children play video games, many of which contain violence. But correlation does not imply causation. Jenkins continued:

> Every time we have a Sandy Hook we're back to the debate about game violence. On the gender front, there is probably greater equity from girls and boys playing games, especially if you factor in casual games, but the stereotypes culturally around female players still persists as a very active problem. I think we've made some progress in educators getting to play games and see it as valuable in their classroom, thanks in part to the MacArthur Foundation's Digital Media and Learning initiative, and a few other things. When I talk to teachers, the kneejerk response is that children should be doing homework and not playing games. These myths are not as deeply rooted in the culture, but we still revert back to them when pushed on questions. They're questions we must engage with closely and critically moving forward.

Game-based learning scholar James Gee wrote an online article about *Grand Theft Auto* demonstrating new media bias. He stated, "In a mission, the player must sneak into a parking lot and, unseen, plant a bomb in the trunk of a car and leave the scene without doing damage to the getaway car. Our intuition about content-driven media tells us that this is about a crime but the task could be changed to placing flowers in a loved one's car without being discovered, and the problem and its difficulty would be the same" (Gee, 2010). In other words, gamers care more about mechanics of play than the narrative thread. In *Theory of Fun for Game Design* Raph Koster shared a similar view. He wrote that players do not see actions as morally wrong; rather, "they see a power-up" (2005, p. 85). A simple solution to alleviating new media bias is for parents to play video games with their children.

No matter how much research points to the benefits of utilizing games as a teaching tool, the teacher is still the gatekeeper of how lessons are delivered in his or her classroom. In January 2014 I spoke to Shula Ehrlich, learning designer at the Institute of Play, about what is the key to making game-based learning integration more widespread. For game-based learning to catch on, Ehrlich believes that teachers simply need to see how engaged students become. "It takes one successful experience, one teacher seeing a game in a classroom and seeing how it transforms learning," she said. "We have teachers coming in skeptical; they see games as waste of time and the need to just hit standards. After one successful experience, they turn around. All teachers have the capacity to become game designers."

Book Overview

Writing this book gave me the opportunity to interview several leaders in the game-based learning sector. I share the history and backgrounds of many influential people. Many of the designers, developers, and academics I spoke with are true artists in their field, devoted to bettering learning. All of the interviews occurred between January and July 2014. I was fortunate enough to speak with the following designers, developers, and academics (listed alphabetically):

- Richard Bartle—Professor of Game Design at University of Essex, and creator of the Bartle Player Type Theory
- Sue Bohle—President of the Serious Games Association
- Jim Bower—Founder of *Whyville*
- Asi Burak—President of Games for Change
- Seth Corrigan—Research Scientist for Learning Analytics for GlassLab
- Zoe Corwin—Research Assistant Professor at University of Southern California
- Chris Czajk—Thirteen/WNET, Co-developer of the *Mission US* history games
- Nicole Darabian—Decode Global, developer of *Get Water!*
- Bernie DeKoven—Author of the influential book *The Well-Played Game*
- Jim Diamond—Center for Children and Technology
- Shula Ehrlich—Lead Designer at Institute of Play for Quest to Learn school
- Noah Falstein—Chief Game Designer at Google
- Tracy Fullerton—Chair of the Interactive Media & Games Division of the University of Southern California School of Cinematic Arts, Director of the Game Innovation Lab
- James Gee—Mary Lou Fulton Presidential Professor of Literacy Studies, Division of Curriculum and Instruction, Arizona State University,

and author of *What Video Games Have to Teach Us about Learning and Literacy* (2003, 2nd ed. 2007)
- Alan Gershenfeld—Co-founder of E-Line Media
- Emily Goligoski—Mozilla Foundation's Open Badges Initiative
- Marientina Gotsis—Research Assistant Professor at University of Southern California
- Claire Greene—Co-founder of the Sandbox Summit
- Spencer Grey—Electric Funstuff, designer of the *Mission US* history games
- Erin Hoffman—Game Design Lead at GlassLab
- Katya Hott—Researcher at BrainPOP and #edtechbridge Twitter chat co-moderator
- Steve Isaacs—Middle school video game design teacher, and a BrainPOPstar and #edtechbridge Twitter chat co-moderator
- Rex Ishibashi—CEO of Originator children's mobile apps
- Henry Jenkins—Provost Professor of Communication, Journalism, and Cinematic Arts, a joint professorship at the Annenberg School for Communication and the School of Cinematic Arts at University of Southern California
- Santeri Koivisto—Co-founder of TeacherGaming (*MinecraftEdu* and *KerbalEdu*)
- David Langendoen—Electric Funstuff, designer of the *Mission US* history games
- Jocelyn Leavitt—Co-founder of Hopscotch coding apps
- Allisyn Levy—Vice President of BrainPOP's GameUp
- Karina Linch—Senior Vice President of Product Management at BrainPOP
- David Liu—COO of Knewton adaptive learning
- Jessica Millstone—Educator Fellow at the Joan Ganz Cooney Center at Sesame Workshop
- Jill Peters—Executive Producer of Children's and Educational Media for Thirteen/WNET; co-developer of *Mission US*
- Leah Potter—Electric Funstuff; designer of the *Mission US* history games
- Scott Price—Games and Education Project Manager at BrainPOP
- Kate Reilly—Product Manager at E-Line Media for *Historia*
- Toby Rowland—CEO and founder of MangaHigh

- Katie Salen—Co-author of *Rules of Play* (2003); founder of the Institute of Play and Quest to Learn
- James Sanders—Presidential Innovation Fellow; co-founder of ClassBadges
- Jesse Schell—Professor at Carnegie Mellon University; author of the textbook *Art of Game Design: A Book of Lenses* (2008); CEO of Schell Games
- Simeon Schnapper—CEO of Youtopia
- Lee Sheldon—Author of *The Multiplayer Classroom: Designing Coursework as a Game* (2011); Associate Professor in the Department of Communication and Media Games and Simulation Arts and Sciences at Rensselaer Polytechnic Institute
- Valerie Shute—Educational Psychologist and Research Scientist at Florida State University
- Wendy Smolen—Co-founder of the Sandbox Summit
- Abby Speight—Senior Product Manager at Zynga.org
- Kurt Squire—Associate Professor at University of Wisconsin–Madison, and Director of the Games + Learning + Society Center
- Bill Tally—Education Development Center's Center for Children and Technology
- Robert J. Torres—Senior Program Officer at the Bill & Melinda Gates Foundation
- Chloe Varelidi—Mozilla Foundation's Open Badges Initiative
- Krishna Vedati—CEO of Tynker coding apps
- Dan White—Co-founder and Executive Producer of Filament Games
- Joseph Wise—Co-director of the PlayMaker School, Los Angeles

The intent of this book is to serve as a "field guide" to help you navigate best practices in game-based learning. I have included practical advice on game implementation, no matter what level of experience you have. Each chapter of this book is divided into sections and concludes with lesson plan ideas, games to play, and additional Internet resources. The point is to create as useful a book as possible. I have tried my best to assure that the links in this book are as up to date as possible. Of course, the Internet changes rapidly, and some links may not remain active after this book's publication date. Nonetheless, I encourage you to learn by doing, exploring as much as possible, online and from other texts.

Just about every lesson plan idea can be aligned to a state's standards or Common Core State Standards. Because some games are tools, not just content-drivers, I did not always specify standards. For example, the building-block game *Minecraft* can meet a variety of math, science, and social studies standards, depending on what the student is learning in the environment. I also share links from online lesson plans, many of which contain specific state and Common Core standards. My hope is that you will integrate games for learning, and not be overwhelmed by "the next big thing." Start by adding in a few per games year. After time, you will see an engaged student population intrinsically motivated to learn!

· 1 ·

GAMES FOR LEARNING

Humans have been using games and stories to teach for thousands of years. Developmental psychologist Jean Piaget based his theories of constructivism ("learn by doing") on his observations of children playing marbles. Learning theorist Lev Vygotsky and educator Maria Montessori also wrote about childhood games. Games provide a social construct and structure to deliver meaning to activities.

Video games entered schools around the same time as desktop computers. I still remember playing *Oregon Trail* on an Apple II computer when I was in 7th grade. Over the years, games and computer became more sophisticated. To understand how we got to where we are today, it helps to review the ups and downs of past initiatives. For many, the term "educational games" calls to mind boring experiences that focused on content over delivery. In this chapter, I review the so-called edutainment era as a way to frame what to look for in a game—and what to avoid.

James Gee is the Presidential Professor of Literacy Studies at Arizona State University, as well as the co-founder of the Center for Games and Impact. In 2003 he first published *What Video Games Have to Teach Us about Learning and Literacy*. In it, he connected problem-solving skills to skills used with commercial video games. The book included a set of "Learning Principles" about what games can teach. For example, the "Probing Principle" connected the trial and error one does while exploring a virtual environment to the methodology of scientific experimentation (2007, p. 105). Gee's research and findings have been very influential in game-based learning circles, and are cited throughout this book. I highly recommend reading further into Gee's research, including his article "Good Video Games and Good Learning" (2005).

I interviewed Gee in April 2014. I wanted to learn more about game-based learning best practices. Much has happened in the decade since Gee initially published his observations. I asked him what ways games have expanded into learning spaces. He said, "The area has expanded [more] than anything anyone could have predicted." He explained how he led a group from the University of Wisconsin when they attended an American Education Research Association conference. At the time, it was the only presentation on game-based learning. Now there are dozens. Gee continued:

> The expansion of it has been surprising. To me it has expanded in two ways. A lot of people want to rush out games for school simply to be able to make a profit. They design their games for the schools we have: skill and drill and teacher accountability to tests. They design their games to be standalone things, by themselves. None of that was what I proposed. What I proposed was not to put games in school, but to put the type of learning and teaching games do in school—with games, and with everything else. I wanted to create a new paradigm of learning in school. I wanted to change the way school works. I don't want to stress skill and drill—I want to stress problem solving, complex and critical thinking.

Gee is describing two different interpretations of game-based learning. One is content driven, supporting the current culture of high-stakes assessment and rote learning. The second interpretation uses games to present authentic problem sets for children to collaborate on and reason out together, often by taking multiple approaches. Solving a math problem to kill a zombie is drill-and-skill rote learning. Having a conversation of physics concepts such as velocity in the slingshot game *Angry Birds* can promote higher-level discussions. The focus of this book is game-inspired and quest-based learning, to integrate "good" games into meaningful learning.

From *Mancala* to *Kriegspiel*

Games have been entertaining and teaching humans for thousands of years. It is hardly a trend! People are finally connecting the dots from play to learning.

Many classic board games have roots hundreds—if not thousands—of years old. Ancient games were used to reinforce belief systems, strategize, and apply a practical use of mathematics. I use board game history as a talking point when teaching middle school world history. The study of "what dead people did" seems more relatable when you picture people playing and interacting together, not just signing famous documents and saying really important things. Think about classic games such as China's *Go!* and *Mahjong*, Japan's *Shogi*, as well as parlor games including *Chess, Checkers, Poker*, and *Bridge*. Why are they still popular in today's digital age?

Jane McGonigal's best-selling book *Reality Is Broken: Why Games Make Us Better and How They Change the World* (2011) detailed the ancient Greeks' fascination with *Mancala*, a game that used sheep's knuckles as dice, which provided a diversion to Herodotus's people during long periods of starvation (McGonigal, 2011, pp. 5–6). *Mancala's* objective was to capture the opponent's game pieces across the board. It was also played throughout the Middle East region. Versions can still be purchased at most toy stores today.

Senet is one of the earliest games on record. It was discovered within the tombs of the Egyptian pharaohs buried thousands of years ago (Piccione, 1980). The name *Senet*, or "passing," referred to death, when one meets the sun god Ra. Paintings showed the game on a checkered board with small moveable pieces. It was played both for skill and to reinforce religious beliefs (Piccione, 1980). King Tut was buried with four game sets (Piccione, 1980). Perhaps the boy king needed something to do in the afterlife!

Snakes and Ladders—better known to Americans as Hasbro Gaming's *Chutes and Ladders*—originated in India several hundred years ago. It reinforced tenets of Jainism such as karma. The board was often decorated with more snakes than ladders to subtly illustrate that it is more difficult to do good than evil. *Snakes and Ladders* was eventually brought to England in the Victorian Age. Its appeal and popularity transcends world cultures, probably because the game board is heavy on illustrations and contains little text. It is now so ingrained in Western culture that it is often parodied in the cartoon *SpongeBob Squarepants*, renamed "Eels and Escalators."

Strategic board games were popular across Europe, too. The simplest may have been *Nine Men's Morris*, a precursor to *Tic-Tac-Toe* (Boyle, 2013). Digital versions can be found in Apple's App Store or online, and even as a "mini-game" in *Assassin's Creed III*. One of the more complicated games to emanate from Europe was *Kriegspiel*. Basically a 19th-century variation on chess, it was "devised as an educational game for military schools in the eighteenth century" (Poundstone, 1992, pp. 37–38). One could argue that it was a pre-cursor to modern-day war simulations, more advanced than the board games *Risk* and *Stratego*. The Prussian army obsessively played it (Poundstone, 1992, pp. 37–38). Some battles in the Russo-Japanese War and World War I were attributed to tactics from the game (Poundstone, 1992, pp. 37–38). *Kriegspiel* and *Poker* eventually inspired mathematician John von Neumann to devise game theory (detailed further in Chapter 2).

Video Game Mania!

Many of the earliest video games were made by academics to entertain other academics—the few who had access to large, mainframe computers. In the 1950s, computers with cathode ray displays were programmed to play simple games. Alexander S. Douglas created OXO (1952), a simple *Tic-Tac-Toe* game, and William Higinbotham, at the Brookhaven National Laboratory, made *Tennis for Two* (1958). The first popular video game, which spread on college campuses throughout the 1960s, was the spaceship game *Spacewar* (1961).

The first commercially successful video game is considered to be *Pong* (1972). Basically a simple paddle-and-ball tennis emulator, *Pong* was an instant success. It marked the first time televisions became interactive, "transforming viewers into players, permitting them not to just watch a media image, but to play with it" (Salen & Zimmerman, 2003, p. xiv). It was originally created for the Magnavox Odyssey home gaming system in 1972 and then was ported to coin-operated arcade machines.

Similar to pinball, early video games often were played in public places. The hardware and monitors were stored in wood cabinets and the games usually cost a quarter to play. This time period, from 1979 to 1983, is often regarded as the classic era of arcade video gaming. Early games were designed to entertain and turn a profit. Arcade games were played in short bursts, with little to no instructions required (Dunniway & Novak, 2007, p. 30). Simply pop in a quarter and click the buttons until the game ends. Then, repeat. Popular titles included *Space Invaders* (1978), *Pac-Man* (1980), and *Donkey Kong* (1981).

The goal of the immensely popular *Pac-Man* was to navigate a maze, eat-ing white dots while being chased by ghosts. *Pac-Man's* significance extends beyond its status as a cultural phenomenon. It was also among the first games to feature a "cut scene," or short, narrative sequence between completed levels. Cut scenes serve as a reward, as badges and achievements do in today's games. They also give players a moment of reprieve and relaxation from non-stop action. *Donkey Kong* pushed game storytelling further. Exploits of Mario's quest to save the princess have been copied innumerable times, even today. The popularity of the documentary *King of Kong* (2007), about the high-scoring champions of *Donkey King*, and Disney's animated *Wreck-It Ralph* (2012), attest to the nostalgia arcade games elicit.

After the video arcade revolution, console games found a place in our homes. Console home video game systems refer to the external box and controllers that hook up to a television. Modern examples include the Nintendo Wii, the Sony PlayStation, and the Microsoft Xbox. Engineer Ralph Baer is credited with inventing the console system in 1968. His "Brown Box" used a set of transistors and could play multiple games (Baer, 2005). In 1970 Magnavox purchased the rights to sell the device, and encased it in plastic. The original version does not look all that different from the so-called next-gen (next-generation) systems of today. Baer went on to create other computer-based toys and inventions, including the electronic memory toy *Simon* still sold today.

While not the first home system, Nolan Bushnell's Atari 2600 (1977) brought console gaming to most of America's living rooms. (Apple's Steve Jobs began his career as one of Bushnell's early employees.) The Atari 2600 could plug into any television; the game cartridges were sold separately. Activision, founded in 1979 by former Atari programmers, became one of the first video game software companies. To this day, Activision (*Guitar Hero*, *Call of Duty*) and Electronic Arts (*Madden NFL*, *Mass Effect*) are two of the biggest publishers of third-party gaming content. (Former Apple employee Trip Hawkins founded Electronic Arts in 1982.) Nowadays, smaller studios often design and develop games, and then larger publishers such as Activision and Electronic Arts distribute them.

Due to a crowded market and lackluster sales of titles that were rushed to market, the video game business crashed in 1983. Atari reportedly filled a landfill with unsold *E.T.: The Extra Terrestrial* game cartridges. (Excavating the landfill was the topic of a 2014 documentary that confirmed the game's mass burial.) The 1985 release of the Nintendo Entertainment System home console (known as Famicom in Japan) turned the industry around. This system featured a (then) cutting-edge 8-bit processor. Popular titles included *Super Mario Bros.* (1985), a classic "side-scrolling" adventure, and

The Legend of Zelda (1987). Nintendo's legendary Shigeru Miyamoto created both. Nintendo positioned itself as rescuing the home video game market by enforcing strict standards such as its Nintendo Seal of Quality. Similar to Apple's business model, Nintendo created a walled garden of vetted games. In the early 1990s competitor Sega released the 16-bit Genesis home console system. The competition between Nintendo's Mario and Sega's Sonic the Hedgehog—nicknamed the "console wars"—was fierce. Sega became Nintendo's chief competitor by targeting games for older children. The result was that consoles became less like toys and more a way for digital content providers (e.g., Sony) to enter people's living rooms. (The complete story of Nintendo and Sega is told in Blake J. Harris's 2014 book and documentary *Console Wars: Sega, Nintendo, and the Battle that Defined a Generation.*) The 1990s also saw the growth of handheld games devices such as Sega's Game Gear, Nintendo's GameBoy, and the PlayStation Portable.

Faster microchip processors led to console and PC games that featured more realistic graphics. First-person shooter games that arm the player with an array of violent weapons, including *Wolfenstein 3D* (1992), *Doom* (1993), and *Goldeneye 007* (1997), became instant bestsellers. Controversy followed soon after. Most notorious was *Mortal Kombat* (1992), which encouraged players to "finish" their opponents with final, gory deathblows. (The gore was tuned down in the Nintendo version; blood was displayed in greyscale.) *Super Mario 64* (1996) was less controversial. It was among the first games to feature a 3D world that let the player control the "camera"—the point of view that appeared on the screen (Dunniway & Novak, 2007, p. 22). Other 3D games followed, including *The Legend of Zelda: Ocarina of Time* (1998). As a result, today's console game controllers have two thumbsticks (small joysticks for your thumbs), one to move for the onscreen avatar and one to control the camera. PC games usually use the mouse or trackpad to control viewpoint; arrow keys or WASD keys control the game's action.

Violence in video games can be misunderstood. It is often a device intended to advance a storyline. Furthermore, violence isn't exclusive to games. It is prevalent in "traditional" media, too, from books to film. Senate hearings prompted by parental concerns occurred in the 1990s. This eventually led to the creation of the industry's self-regulating Entertainment Software Rating Board (ESRB). As with the introduction of film ratings in the early 1970s, the rating of video games led to an increase in content targeted to adults (e.g., the films *Midnight Cowboy* and *The Godfather*, and the game *Grand Theft Auto*).

Mobile apps, such as those found in Apple's App Store, do not apply for ratings. Apple has its own parental warning system.

The new millennium enabled gamers to connect via Internet-ready consoles from Microsoft (Xbox) and Sony (PlayStation), as well as by personal computer. People could now play cooperatively, helping one another to advance. A new genre emerged—massively multiplayer online role-playing games (MMORPG), where players play in large groups via remote servers. Popular titles included *World of Warcraft* (2004) and *Star Wars: Knights of the Old Republic* (2003). New technology also meant that designers could create more immersive virtual worlds with high-definition graphics. The *Tomb Raider* series' female protagonist, Lara Croft, solved puzzles and explored exotic locales. So-called open-world games (e.g., the *Grand Theft Auto* series, the *Assassin's Creed* series) allowed users to explore and choose which "missions" to play. This type of story unfolds in a nonlinear, self-directed fashion, and is often from the third-person or over-the-shoulder perspective. The Internet enabled independent game publishers (or "indies") to join the marketplace via digital download distribution (e.g., Valve's Steam platform for PC and Mac, Xbox Live Arcade, PlayStation Network).

By 2007, video gaming had become quite complex, alienating new users. A case in point: the introduction of Sony's PlayStation 3 controller, with seventeen buttons! A game on Xbox or PlayStation can take up to 50 hours to fully complete. Enter the Nintendo Wii. It not only introduced the concept of motion-controlled gaming, but also brought casual gamers into the market. PlayStation next offered motion gaming via its Move controller. Microsoft further innovated by introducing the Kinect camera capture system, which turned the player into the controller—no buttons needed. Dance and workout games for each of these platforms became popular.

Mobile platforms such as Apple's iPhone and iPad, and Facebook, the social media giant, brought even more casual gamers into the fold. The prototypical touch screen game, or "killer app," was the physics-themed slingshot game *Angry Birds* (2009). Zynga popularized social gaming games with *Farmville* (2009) and *Words with Friends* (2009). Social games can be played asynchronously: Draw a picture with *Draw Something* (2012) and then check later in the day to see if your friend guessed what it was. Casual, social games do not always follow the "win, lose, or tie" paradigm of traditional, competitive games. People may play in a semicompetitive, virtual environment with the goal of simply "liking" other's actions rather than winning (Kim, 2012b). They may also seek only to collaborate with others (Kim, 2012b).

The Edutainment Era

Educational games have a reputation of poor design. Many games were rushed to market and placed educational content ahead of game mechanics. This is akin to watching a movie that is all exposition and contains little action or entertainment value. You wouldn't give a student a boring book to read, so why do the same with a game? To understand today's successful learning games such as *SimCityEDU* and *Mission US* (both discussed in later chapters), let's review the problems of the past. This period still casts a long shadow over learning games in schools.

Oregon Trail was an innovative game that showed the promise of what an educational game could deliver. It was developed in 1971 and sold in 1974 by the Minnesota Educational Computing Consortium (MECC). It was one of the first games designed specifically for schools. The game used interactives and simulation to teach children about the hardships of travelling cross-country in 19th-century America. The game was originally played on the Apple II computer. The fail state (what happens when you lose) displayed a message that has joined the popular lexicon: "You have died of dysentery." Iterations of *Oregon Trail* still exist on Facebook and on mobile devices. There is also a zombie-themed parody, *Organ Trail* (2011).

Following the success of *Oregon Trail*, many other for-profit publishers began to design "edutainment" (a portmanteau of "education" and "entertainment") games. More computers in schools during the 1980s meant more educational games would come to market. In 1983 Electronic Arts published M.U.L.E., an economic simulation game about colonial survival on a new planet. Beginning in 1985, Broderbund Software published *Where in the World Is Carmen Sandiego?* In this geography game, Carmen travelled the world solving mysteries. The Learning Company, founded by three teachers and a game designer from Atari, focused on language arts skills (Shuler, 2012). It published the *Reader Rabbit* series. *Math Blaster*, basically *Space Invaders* meets arithmetic problems, came next. This is the classic "chocolate-covered broccoli" game, where the mechanics (shooting spaceships) had nothing to do with the concept it was delivering (math). Other edutainment titles evolved over the years, including *Mavis Beacon Teaches Typing* (1987) and games found on *Fun Brain*. Many of these games relied on simple, "drill-and-skill" mechanisms adapted from early arcade game design principles, such as pattern recognition and hand-eye coordination. Corporate consolidations by Mattel and Vivendi, coupled with changes in consumer demand, eventually ended the era around the turn of the millennium (Shuler, 2012).

Serious Games

Serious games are used to teach or train in schools or in professional development classes. They may involve a simulation of a problem in a workplace scenario. Clark Abt first coined the term "serious game" in his 1970 book, *Serious Games.* He wrote about strategy board games used by the military. As mentioned earlier in this chapter, the Prussians played *Kriegspiel,* a chess variation, to train for the battlefield. One of the most played modern military games of all time is *America's Army* (2002). Businesses use serious games, too. For example, *Everest Manager* (2013) teaches team building.

The Serious Games Association aggregates educational training games. It curates titles for kindergarten through grade 12, higher education, business, the health care sector, and government institutions. I spoke to Sue Bohle in April 2014 to learn more about the organization. She is the founder and president of the Serious Games Association. Bohle started in the video game business in the 1980s, with Atari—just before its business model imploded. A decade ago, specialized organizations emerged, such as Games for Health, founded by Ben Sawyer. The Game Development Conference, for commercial developers, included "serious games," but it took a "stepchild approach" to them in comparison to its bread-and-butter business—entertainment games. Bohle explained to me that there was a push for serious games to have its own conference. The Serious Play Conference, launched in 2011, is a forum for stakeholders to come together. In 2014 the Conference moved to the campus of the University of Southern California. The University has an interdisciplinary approach to game development throughout the entire school, including in its communications, education, and medical departments.

In addition to the conference, there is the *Serious Games Directory.* Bohle described how it came out of a need expressed by a school administrator who attended one of its conferences. The directory is still being developed; currently it includes schools where consultants can take courses for training with serious games. Its website is also an excellent place to search for resources. Click on the "Award" tab to see a list of effective games, viewable by entry year. The games are peer rated and include well-received titles such as *Dragon Box* and *Quandary,* both discussed later in this book.

Because serious games are designed to teach and train, I wondered how gameplay could potentially interfere with the delivery of content. I asked Google's Noah Falstein, because serious games were part of his design background. We spoke in May 2014. He also was a keynote speaker at the 2014

Serious Play Conference. Falstein had worked for 17 years at LucasArts, 3DO, and DreamWorks Interactive. His credits included *Indiana Jones and the Fate of Atlantis*. Following LucasArts, he grew interested in serious games, or, as Falstein called them, "games with purposes beyond entertainment." As a consequence, he worked on a lot of educational titles, including *Hungry Red Planet*, a children's nutrition game funded by a National Institutes of Health (NIH) grant. Falstein shared an experience about a game that encouraged children to continue chemotherapy treatments. His example is valuable when considering how to construct game-based lessons. Falstein explained:

> There was a game I did with Hope Lab called *Re-Mission*. It helped kids with cancer understand their treatment. It used the fiction of a little nanorobot in your blood-stream fighting cancer cells. At first they [NIH] wanted to make everything look realistic. One of the problems is that, on microscopic level, healthy cells and cancer cells don't look different at all. Only the nucleus may be different. Accuracy is important, but we weren't teaching microbiology. We were teaching teenagers why they should care about chemotherapy. The concept was more important than the literal depiction. A study eventually showed that the game encouraged people to take their chemotherapy therapy.

Falstein's point is that sometimes it can be acceptable for serious games to sacrifice details when delivering a message. "What's critical from a designer's standpoint is a clear way to distinguish what is factual and what is part of a game fantasy," he continued. "Effective games have some of both. People can pick up the information later once you get them interested, but you can't get them interested by dry information alone." This is another important take-away from an experienced, serious game designer. Falstein uses games as a starting point for learning. In other words, students shouldn't just play serious games; the activity requires teacher-led reflection to enable real-world connections.

Games as Art

Games, like other media, evoke emotions. The most obvious feelings players have are fun, happiness, or frustration. But can games make us cry? Are games—like books, paintings, music, and photography—art? Can a player experience a deeper range of emotions from play?

Shortly before his death, film critic Roger Ebert took the hardline stance that games could never be considered art. Critics of Ebert suggested that he play the video game *Flower* (2009), designed by Jenova Chen. *Flower* is told from the point of view of a dreaming flower. Others recommended Kellee Santiago's TED Talk about art and games (see the link at the end of this chapter; Santiago worked with Chen at Thatgamecompany). Ebert did not agree. He wrote, "The difference between art and games is that you can win a game" (Ebert, 2010). I asked Tracy Fullerton, Chen and Santiago's graduate professor, about games as art. We spoke in March 2014. She called Ebert's view "too rigid." (Fullerton collaborated with artist Bill Viola on his art installation *The Night Journey*.) In his book *Video Games and Learning*, Kurt Squire also disagreed with Ebert. He wrote, "Independent games like *Flower* show that games are capable of expressing a range of emotions, but developers may need to go around the mainstream to do it" (2011, p. 216).

Brenda Brathwaite's nondigital board game *Train* (2010) is an example of a nondigital game presented as art. Like *Monopoly* and *Life*, it was packaged in a box. The difference was that there were broken shards of glass mixed in with the yellow pegs, cards, and pieces. The cards, called Terminus, represented concentration camp locations. The game's objective was not revealed until midway during play. Brathwaite told *The Daily Beast* that she intended to "make a game about complicity, and so the rules drop the player not in the shoes of a Holocaust victim but a train conductor who helped make the Nazi system run" (Craire, 2010).

In March 2012 the Smithsonian American Art Museum debuted its "radical" new exhibit *The Art of Video Games*. The exhibition was interactive; visitors could play the games, including *Pac-Man* and *Mass Effect* ("The Art of Video Games," 2012). The museum was among the first to "explore the forty-year evolution of video games as an artistic medium, with a focus on striking visual effects and the creative use of new technologies" ("The Art of Video Games," 2012). The Museum of Modern Art in New York City followed in 2013 with a video game exhibition. Its collection ranged from *Pac-Man* to *SimCity* to *Portal*. The museum selected the collection based on "visual quality, elegance of the code and design of playing behavior" (Indvik, 2013). One could argue that early arcade games have become ingrained in the American popular cultural landscape (e.g., "retro-gaming" in Disney's 2012 hit film *Wreck-it Ralph*). *Flower* was eventually added to the Smithsonian American Art Museum's national collection, in December 2013. In an interview, museum director Elizabeth Broun told *The Verge* that the museum has an "ongoing commitment to the study and preservation of video games as an artistic medium" (McCormick, 2013). As far as the Smithsonian is concerned, video games are art.

Machinima is another artistic medium for games. "Machine cinema" enables anyone to use game worlds to tell stories. There are even machinima film festivals. *Anna* (2003) was one of the first notable films. Its story "deftly employs pathos to engender an emotional relationship between the viewer and the life and death of a single flower" (Luckman & Potanin, 2010, p. 141). Tools and applications for student-created machinima will be discussed in Chapter 11.

There was a time when photography ("anyone can take a picture!"), movies, and television weren't considered art. In 1961 Newton Mino, Chairman of the Federal Communications Commission, famously called television "a vast wasteland." I think viewers of *Breaking Bad*, *Mad Men*, and *House of Cards* would disagree. The debate may stem from the growing pains of being an immature medium that struggles to be taken more seriously.

The new millennium brings with it the next wave of video games. Game design as a college major is growing in popularity. Similarly, in the 1960s many universities from New York University to the University of Southern California opened film schools. Graduates of those programs included Steven Spielberg, George Lucas, Francis Ford Coppola, and Martin Scorsese. They ushered in a new era in cinema. Think of how the movies of the 1970s such as *Jaws*, *Star Wars*, *The Godfather*, and *Taxi Driver* were different than films in the 1950s and 1960s. Perhaps current design students will do the same, elevating the craft by bringing more emotional depth to game experiences.

Bringing Games into Classrooms

Although there is over a half of a century of research regarding games and learning, significant barriers to adoption still persist. Most of the people I interviewed expressed a "disconnect" between game developers and classroom implementation. Textbooks and educational websites continue to refer to review quizzes as games. Dan White, co-founder of Filament Games, explained, "There are too many interactives that try to pass themselves off as learning games; they are really dressed up flashcards." As a result, teachers become confused about which games (if any) to implement. White pointed out a "literacy gap with teachers who cannot discriminate between the 'drill and kill' and quality gameplay delivery."

Erin Hoffman, lead designer at GlassLab (*SimCityEDU*), explained the struggle to get "good" learning games into students' hands. We began speaking in January 2014. She remarked how confusing the education market is. She explained, "What competency should you be teaching? What standard? How are you going to get it to them? How is the school going to find out or buy the product? Who are the gatekeepers that will let you into it? Do you try to sell directly to parents? It's super hard to get the game into the hands of an 11-year-old middle school kid. It has to look enough like a game, they talk to their friends about it, and then they ask their parents if they can have it. There are a lot of gates."

The 11th Annual Games for Change Festival, which took place in the spring of 2014, featured a panel called "Turning Fantasy into Reality: Building Games that Schools Need." It was led by *Education Week*'s Kevin C. Bushweller and featured game scholar Constance Steinkuehler, E-Line Media's co-founder, Alan Gershenfeld, and Carnegie Mellon's Jesse Schell. To my dismay, no teachers were represented on stage. Some of the discussion still hinged on the persistent supposition that teaching hasn't changed in decades. Student-centered, cooperative, and project-based learning is quite pervasive. One would be hard-pressed to find a pre-service teacher these days who is being trained as a lecturer. In May 2014 I asked Gershenfeld, one of the panelists, to elaborate on his comments at Games for Change. He explained that he was taking a "global position." He elaborated:

> Some people in game-based learning believe in magic algorithms. It's just a piece of the puzzle. Building large app stores is another piece, too. I think there are going to be a new publishing mechanism that are going to create powerful spaces for technology-mediated, inquiry-based learning in a blended environment that's going to be part of longer trajectories—in school, out of school, across multiple grades, reinforcing certain dispositions. I see new structures that will involve not just one company designing it all, but structures with multiple companies participating. Broadly speaking, games and inquiry-based learning are going to have the bones and core pillars to make that happen. But it is not a game. It's just an approach.

Gershenfeld points out that there are certain drivers from games—and other digital media—that can be harnessed to engage learners. These observations echoed James Gee's view that students shouldn't just play games, but learn from them. The true challenge—or art form, as Gee explained to me—is matching the learning objective to a game. Shoehorning a math problem into an otherwise fun environment is awkward. When properly implemented, games for learning can have astonishing results. Toby Rowland, CEO and founder of the adaptive math game portal MangaHigh, explained to me the potential game-based learning promises. We spoke in February 2014. "You'll see some eyes light up, doubtful in the beginning, but they get into it," he said. "When you can grab a student's interest at some level and they can build confidence, it's easier to extend that confidence into other topics. I mastered this topic using game-based learning; perhaps I am not as bad at this hard subject as I thought I was. Maybe I should extend and try something else."

Studies about the educational merits of games stem from just a handful of organizations and leaders, including James Gee, Henry Jenkins, futurist Marc Prensky, and Katie Salen, co-founder of the Institute of Play. In February 2014 I asked Salen about why games are still considered an afterthought in teachers' colleges and kindergarten through grade-12 classrooms. She gave me a hopeful response. "The interesting thing to me about the field is that it is moving forward really fast in terms of the changing of people's attitudes," she said. "Eight years ago was a totally different state of mind. Even last year people had assumptions that they don't anymore, like you can never bring a console game onto the classroom. Nowadays, it's okay. The speed of time a person's mind can be changed can be rapid." Nonetheless, bringing games into classrooms can still be seen as tacked on, similar to how other educational technologies are sometimes misappropriated. Salen elaborated, "The add-on thing is really interesting when it is not the central experience, like a novel. It's always an exception to play a game."

What facilitates adoption in the organizational structure of a school? Is it teacher skill level and style? Is the learning game adaptable to different environments, like 40-minute bell schedules? In February 2014, GlassLab's Seth Corrigan briefly explained the history to me. Methods of easing adoption barriers on an institutional level date can be traced back to the 1947 publication of *Frontiers in Group Dynamics*, from Kurt Lewin. Organizations have "channels" that funnel through new ideas. Lower one or two barriers at those channels and a change can take hold. Streaming video first seemed impossible; now it is commonplace. Subscription models (e.g., Discovery Streaming) and free options (e.g., YouTube, TeacherTube), in conjunction with interactive whiteboards and school Internet connectivity, came together to make that possible. The change just didn't spontaneously happen. Kurt Squire expressed hope in digital distribution as a way to alleviate logistical problems. It is certainly easier to play a game in a web browser or on an iPad app than it is to purchase licenses and ask the informational technologist to install software. It was certainly easier for me, as a classroom teacher, to have students play games on BrainPOP, because it worked in Google Chrome. Perhaps games can find a way from marginalization to full integration.

At Games for Change, Jesse Schell stated that administrators—specifically, principals—who were born after 1965 grew up with video games, and therefore would be open to integrating games and learning. I noticed this tipping point when I requested extra technology to run the *SimCityEDU* pre-release. Of course, a perceived embrace of games by younger administrators may be misreading educational leadership; successful principals sometimes take a hands-off approach. Gershenfeld pointed out research from the Cooney Center that showed that older—not younger—teachers were actually more open to games. More experienced teachers saw the need to further engage students.

Many educational technology tools offer teachers free or deep discounts. Furthermore, Web 2.0 tools often enable educators to create and manage virtual classrooms. Examples include Glogster's interactive digital poster creator and Prezi's online presentation application. One reason for this is that teachers are marketing a product when they incorporate it into a learning experience. My former students downloaded Animoto's slideshow app for iPhone after we used it for projects. Video games, however, do not need this additional sales push. Games are much more commercially viable when compared to their Web 2.0 counterparts. As a result, there are fewer free and discounted video games for schools.

In January 2014 I had the opportunity to interview Jessica Millstone, the Education Fellow at the Joan Ganz Cooney Center. Unlike Sesame Street, which was co-created by Joan Ganz Cooney, the Cooney Center focuses on upper elementary through late middle school students. Millstone is also an instructional technology adjunct professor at Bank Street College of Education. She has worked with Common Sense Media, an informational website for parents. "We find that teachers don't know what is a game," she said. "Teachers have trouble distinguishing a game and an interactive. Our research is on how teachers choose a game, where they go to find out about games, and the logistics about the way a game changes a classroom. How do you take a beginner to the next step, iterating it to make it better and better?"

The Cooney Center launched *GamesandLearning.org*, funded with help from the Bill & Melinda Gates Foundation. The site features original stories, as well as aggregated news. The purpose is to provide a centralized place for investors and developers to find out about educational games. Millstone explained, "It's hard for game makers to know what's happening in the class-room because the classroom is a closed environment. We need to have a bridge between the two worlds." Issues linger regarding how to bring games into formal teacher education (both pre-service and graduate-level), profes-sional development, and workshops. Much needs to be done to make game-based learning more embedded in the training of teachers.

Whereas commercial video games are targeted at children, learning games must be appealing to both teachers and students as end users. Looking at a teacher-inclusive model, it becomes obvious that the teacher needs to be engaged in the ideas of games in the classroom. To scale games for school use, there must be teacher demand, as well as professional development training and support. Millstone next shared a story about attending the Games for Change conference about 5 years ago. Impactful games were introduced; how-ever, no one mentioned the teacher's role. Millstone told attendees, "You're not getting it into the classroom unless you go through the teacher. The teacher is the bridge."

Conclusions and Takeaways

People have been learning with games for thousands of years. Gaming, both paper-based and digital, has endured and become ingrained in pop-ular culture. Like any new media, it has its growing pains, which itself is a teachable moment. Bringing effective games to students has many barriers. Teachers may see play as frivolous, while students may be biased against learning games in school. The business world embraces serious games and simulations.

Lesson Plan Ideas

Game Critic: Preview articles on Game Informer magazine's website and have students write their own reviews of their favorite video games. The reading level may be higher than you think! This project meets Common Core State Standards for English language arts. Common Core State Standards for English language arts apply. Game Informer—http://www.gameinformer.com

Kriegspiel: A free digital download for Mac and PC from Alex Galloway of New York University—http://www.r-s-g.org/kriegspiel. This game can be used to meet social studies standards, including the Russo-Japanese War and World War I.

Games

America's Army, the U.S. Army's serious recruitment game—http://www.americasarmy.com

Argument Wars, a "serious" Supreme Court argumentation game—https://www.icivics.org/games/argument-wars

Everest Manager, corporate team-building serious game. Works as a classroom icebreaker activity, too—http://www.everestmanager.com

Government in Action, a serious civics game—http://www.mhpractice.com/products/GinA

Muzzy Lane, serious game developer for the corporate, health care, and education sectors—http://muzzylane.com

Oregon Trail, the original and in many ways quintessential educational video game—http://www.oregontrail.com/hmh/site/oregontrail

Organ Trail, parody of *Oregon Trail*—http://hatsproductions.com/organtrail.html

Pac-Man, one of the games that ushered in the "golden age" of arcade video games—http://www.thepcmanwebsite.com/media/pacman_flash

Pong, the simple tennis game that started the video game revolution—http://www.ponggame.org

Spacewar, emulator of the first video game, playable in a computer browser—http://www.masswerk.at/spacewar

Resources

Anna, the award-winning machinima film—http://youtu.be/bKEr5RRKoO4

Are Video Games Art?, Kellee Santiago's TED Talk—http://youtu.be/K9y6MYDSAww

Art of Video Games exhibit at the Smithsonian American Art Museum—http://americanart.si.edu/exhibitions/archive/2012/games

Board Game Geek, the ultimate non-digital gamer community—http://boardgamegeek.com

Board Games with Scott, a blog from Scott Nicholson, game design professor and author of *Everyone Plays at the Library: Creating Great Gaming Experiences for All Ages* (2010)—http://www.boardgameswithscott.com

Common Sense Media, a web portal to advise parents on appropriate digital media—https://www.commonsensemedia.org

Joan Ganz Cooney Center at Sesame Workshop—http://www.joanganzcooneycenter.org

Joan Ganz Cooney Center's *GamesandLearning.org* portal—http://www.gamesandlearning.org

Entertainment Software Association (ESA), the game industry's lobbyist organization. It also hosts the annual E3 Conference and manages the ESRB Ratings System—http://www.theesa.com

Essential Facts about the Computer and Video Game Industry, a free document from the Entertainment Software Association, with facts and figures about who plays digital games—http://www.theesa.com/facts/pdfs/ESA_EF_2013.pdf

Gamasutra, the online magazine about trends in game development, including in education. Every year *Gamasutra* hosts the Game Developer Conference (GDC)—http://www.gamasutra.com

Game-based learning blogs on Edutopia—http://www.edutopia.org/blogs/beat/game-based-learning

GameInformer magazine, popular game magazine at a surprisingly high reading level—http://www.gameinformer.com

Gaming Can Make a Better World, Jane McGonigal's TED Talk—http://www.ted.com/talks/jane_mcgonigal_gaming_can_make_a_better_world

Gaming for Understanding, Brenda Brathwaite's TED Talk—http://www.ted.com/talks/brenda_brathwaite_gaming_for_understanding.html

James Gee's *Good Video Games and Good Learning*—http://gamesandimpact.org/wp-content/uploads/2012/02/GoodVideoGamesLearning.pdf

Joystiq, video game news—http://www.joystiq.com

The Night Journey, the art installation from Bill Viola and Tracy Fullerton—http://www.thenightjourney.com/statement.htm

Play, Play, Learn, a website from Christopher Harris, co-author of *Libraries Got Game: Aligned Learning through Modern Board Games* (2010), is an excellent blog to follow. Harris is also a regular contributor to the *School Library Journal*. His site links many board games to Common Core State Standards—http://playplaylearn.com

Polygon, online magazine that covers the gaming industry, as well as the designers, players, and related conferences—http://www.polygon.com

Project New Media Literacies—http://www.newmedialiteracies.org

Serious Play Conference—http://www.seriousplayconference.com

· 2 ·

WHAT ARE GAMES?

Is *Minecraft*, which is basically a digital version of LEGO, a game or a digital toy? Or is it both? There are several definitions for what a game actually is. This chapter features a brief discussion of Johan Huizinga's and Roger Caillois's mid-20th-century definitions, leading up to Jane McGonigal's more recent interpretation. I asked some leading experts including Richard Bartle, Bernie DeKoven, Jesse Schell, and James Gee for their input and interpretations about requiring students to engage in supposedly fun activities. Surely you can't tell a group of children, "Have fun! By the way, your grade depends on it!"

Game design has more to do with human behavior than coding. It can be defined as "the process by which a game designer creates a game, to be encountered by a player, from which meaningful play emerges" (Salen & Zimmerman, 2003, p. 80). Much of the field grew in the 1990s through the 2000s without intersecting with the learning sciences. There were, of course, a few exceptions, but they were far and few between. To master a game requires learning the rules and the system. Looking back, the parallels become more obvious.

Game design is a growing academic discipline. Rather than coding and programming, it applies human behavioral psychology to create fun experiences. This chapter takes a close look at the theory and makes connections to practical classroom applications. To play a game—or better yet, to win a game—takes a level of mastery. It can be said, therefore, that all games teach.

The following sections break down how games function as interconnected systems. The approach, known as "systems thinking," is ingrained in the mission of the Institute of Play's Quest schools. Katie Salen, founder of both the Institute and Quest, discussed the approach with me when I interviewed her in February 2014. Games model real-world systems, which can help make learning concepts more relatable. The ability to discern how parts interplay—like characters in a novel, weather patterns, or cause-and-effect patterns in history—is a 21st-century career skill. The section includes strategies and tips to implement systems thinking in your classroom.

This chapter also reviews the basics of game theory and its applications to game outcomes, as well as modern economic theory. Mathematicians during the Cold War used games to model human behavior. In what came to be known as game theory, researchers created scenarios to interpolate how nations would react in standoffs. John von Neumann and John Forbes Nash (famously portrayed by Russell Crowe in the movie *A Beautiful Mind*) both consulted for the RAND Corporation during the height of tension between the United States and the Soviet Union.

Defining Games

As mentioned in Chapter 1, games have been used to teach people's shared cultural history for thousands of years. Modern research about play and games dates back to the early 20th century, alongside the burgeoning fields of child psychology and human behaviorism. Almost all of the modern-day discussions of games are rooted in the essays and observations from Johan Huizinga and Roger Caillois. Both were among the first to connect the significance of structured play to childhood development.

In 1938 Johan Huizinga published *Homo Ludens* (Gr., "Man the Player"). Huizinga, a Dutch historian, wrote about play as a competitive act, as well as how play promotes socialization. He recognized that humans—like other animals—engage in playful activities. For example, cats hunt toys around people's homes as practice for tracking down live prey; moose battle one another with their antlers to practice combat skills. His treatise was more philosophical than psychological, discussing the process more than the need for play.

Huizinga introduced an important concept known as the "magic circle"— the place where play occurs. He wrote, "The arena, the card-table, the magic circle, the temple, the stage, the screen, the tennis court, the court of justice, etc., are all in form and function playgrounds, i.e. forbidden spots, isolated, hedged round, hallowed, within which special rules obtain. All are temporary worlds within the ordinary world, dedicated to the performance of an act apart" (1938/1955, p. 10). Sometimes known as a playspace, the magic circle is where people engage together in games. Basically, it is "where the game takes place" (Salen & Zimmerman, 2003, p. 95). It can be a game board, a field, a bridge table, or even a multi-user virtual environment. Game tokens, from the thimble in *Monopoly* to video game avatars, serve to draw the player into the magic circle (Salen & Zimmerman, 2003, p. 96). The magic circle remains significant to developers of virtual worlds, discussion forums, and massive open online courses.

In 1961 French anthropologist Roger Caillois published *Man, Play, and Games*. He defined four types of games: *agon*, representing pure competition; *alea*, where the player choice depends on random variables or luck; *mimicry*, for acting, singing, and role-playing; and *ilinx*, the thrill from being in motion (I have a 3-year-old son and can attest to his joy at spinning around endlessly in circles!). Caillois described his four domains of play by drawing on everyday examples. He wrote, "One *plays* football, billiards, or chess (*agon*); roulette or a lottery (*alea*); pirate, Nero, or Hamlet (*mimicry*); or one produces in oneself, by a rapid whirling or falling movement, a state of dizziness or disorder (*ilinx*)" (Caillois, 1961/2001, p. 12). In 1990 psychologist Mihaly Csikszentmihalyi posited that each of Caillois's sets of game activities serves to keep people happy, fulfilled, and positively balanced. As we will see in the following chapter, Csikszentmihalyi's theory of optimal psychology is very influential in game—and learning—design.

What is a game can sometimes be hard to pin down. In the book *Rules of Play*, Katie Salen and Eric Zimmerman analyzed several definitions of games. They concluded that a game is a system in which "players engage in an artificial conflict, defined by rules that results in a quantifiable outcome" (2003, p. 80). In *Reality Is Broken*, Jane McGonigal broke down games into overlapping components. She wrote that all games share four common characteristics, interconnected into a working system. McGonigal's components of games include:

1. A goal
2. Rules
3. A feedback system
4. Voluntary participation. (2011, p. 21)

All games, including competitive sports, adhere to the above definition. Take bowling, for example: There is an achievable goal (anyone, even a novice, can throw a strike); rules (two throws per turn; the play is turn-based); feedback (a leaderboard is displayed in tabulating everyone's scores); and the unspoken agreement to participate and follow the rules. With my social studies students, I connect games to the election process. You run for office (the goal to becoming president is 270 electoral college votes), and there are rules to follow (the media is watching!), feedback (polling), and, of course, participation—our government is a participatory democracy. The magic circle is the United States map, with each state worth a different number of points, based on population. The presidential election is a winner-take-all, red-state-vs.-blue-state, zero-sum game.

Voluntary Participation

When students are told to engage in game-based learning, are they voluntarily participating? I suppose this is more of a philosophical question, but one worth addressing. After all, can you force children to have fun in a game you designed? Isn't it like dragging a kid kicking and screaming to baseball practice? As we shall see, to effectively implement play in the classroom, a degree of freedom must exist.

Bernie DeKoven is one of the foremost experts of play. He wrote several books on the topic, including the highly influential *The Well-Designed Game* (1978). His writing was significant to the "new games movement" in the 1970s (he was also quoted several times in Salen & Zimmerman's *Rules of Play*). When I spoke to DeKoven in April 2014, I asked him whether teachers could assign play and games for learning. I got a terse response: "No." He then elaborated, "Game-based learning goes against that [play]. Play-based learning says, 'Do what's fun for you,' which means kids may not be learning what's on the curriculum or directly relating to the curriculum." Allowing children to discover through play, especially in today's high-stakes testing environment, is a tough sell for schools that adhere to a standards-based curriculum. DeKoven believes that teacher-led (or top-down) games curtail the natural learning that play delivers. "If it [game-based learning] is prescribed and kids have to do it, you won't get the kind of play you need for kids to learn from it," DeKoven continued. "The best, most effective way is if kids want to play the games on their own free will. For me, play is freedom."

In March 2014 I asked Richard Bartle whether students could effectively play a game if they are obligated to do so. Bartle is a legendary game designer and a professor at the University of Essex in the United Kingdom. He explained that engaging with a game doesn't mean that the participant is necessarily playing. He stated, "[Students] have a choice whether to 'play it' or whether to 'work it.' If the game is fun they'll play it. If it's not fun, then they'll work it, so you do have a choice." Bartle used a disconcerting game of chess as an example, just to drive his point home. He said, "If a person likes chess, it wouldn't matter if he or she were forced to play—even at gunpoint." As an extreme, think about how children "tributes" were forced to compete in Suzanne Collins's *Hunger Games* books. "If you get a group of people together and they don't want to play [a game], they'll work it," Bartle continued. "Any advantage of the gainfulness and of the playfulness is gone." He proposed a straightforward solution: Teachers should look for games that are fun for everyone to play. The component of putting fun first is natural for game designers, but not for teachers. If the goal is to engage learners, then educators should take notice to what drives game design.

My quest to define game-based learning as a voluntary activity came to a conclusion after speaking with games and learning academic James Gee, in April 2014. He gave me a detailed and lengthy response. Because his response mirrors much of my intended vision for this book, it is worthwhile quoting in its entirety. He said:

First of all, I don't care at all about a definition of a game. I don't mean to produce one. Even in the commercial industry, there are many, many different types of games. It's been so controversial whether *The Sims* is a game or not. But nobody cares. Will Wright [creator of *The Sims*] didn't care when he took his billion dollars to the bank. What we're talking about is learning that is inspired by games. We're not talking about learning that always has to be a game. Good games set up learning and how to teach. We want to take those principles. To me, it's not game-based learning or game-inspired learning. It is taking principles from games and extending them across multiple platforms, multiple tools, and multiple forms of participation—one of which happens to be games. I know it's been a fetish for people who try to find the definition of games. Many of these people are inspired by a notion of play, or play is the magic circle, and if you add any external goals you've destroyed the play. I don't believe in the magic circle. What I believe is, if the child is motivated enough—motivated intrinsically— then it [the activity] becomes like play. He is not doing it for the external factors; he's not doing it for extrinsic reward piece. [When] children and animals are playing, they are learning. And when they are learning, they are playing. Learning is an appetite for human beings. When you put it in school and make it boring and decontaminated, then of course you kill that appetite. It's like when you give people bad food. The fact of the matter is that when you trigger the human instinct of learning—and this is true of adults, not just children—you're triggering a deeply satisfying thing. When people learn something new and they gain mastery, they are profoundly satisfied. The issue is how do we get engagement by an affiliation, not whether we call it play or call it a game. There's a big debate about whether *Minecraft* is a toy or a game. Who gives a damn once it's made a billion dollars, when it captured the imaginations of millions of young people into design and architecture? What can be gained by having a definitional war over it? Is eBay the largest multiplayer game in history? What we want to say is, "What's the interactivity? What's the engagement? What are the values?" Let's ask important questions, not trivial questions like what's a game.

Gee wrote *What Video Games Have to Teach Us about Learning and Literacy* (2004) to examine what educators can learn from effective, well-designed games. This book intends to continue that conversation. Yes, free play is important. Sometimes, using games in the classroom is appropriate. Creating fun and engaging, student-centered activities should be the goal of every teacher. Keep in mind that not every concept needs to be taught with a game; rather, adopt the techniques that games do well (like stories, games are better at teaching whole concepts; do not use games to teach dates, facts, or other rote information).

Game Mechanics

When I read about "gamification mechanics," points, badges, and leaderboards seem to be the focal point of discussion. Each of those elements, however, has more to do with feedback than play. Game mechanics, sometimes called core mechanics, usually pertain to the actions of play. Mechanics I detail in this section pertain to those that draw players into the magic circle—the interconnected system that is a game. Like physical mechanics (think: cogs, wheels, and sprockets in a watch), game mechanics set play in motion. A game's core mechanics can be defined as "the essential play activity performed again and again in a game" (Salen & Zimmerman, 2003, p. 316). The mechanics in baseball are hitting, throwing, and catching. In *Angry Birds*, the mechanic of angles occurs when a player's finger pulls back on the slingshot. Eating dots is the mechanic in *Pac-Man*. Some games use the mechanic to deliver a message.

MDA: *A Formal Approach to Game Design and Game Research* was an influential paper published in 2004. In it, the authors compared games to other consumable media (e.g., books, theater, film). The M is for "Mechanics—the particular components of the game, at the level of data representation and algorithms" (Hunicke, LeBlanc, & Zubek, 2004). (The *D* represents "Dynamics," or what changes in the system during play, and the *A* stands for "Aesthetics," the physical appearance of a game and its components.) Games often have multiple mechanics that overlap and require players to build certain skills. There are similarities to Lev Vygotsky's Zone of Proximal Development methodology, in which skills are scaffolded until mastery is reached.

Mechanics include "anything a player can do in a game, such as moving, jumping, shooting, fighting, or driving" (Dunniway & Novak, 2007, p. 5). Different chess pieces have different properties—rooks and bishops, for example, are restricted in their movements across the board, and chess players take turns in rounds. *Rock-Paper-Scissors*, for another example, involves bluffing and guessing. Game mechanics that lend themselves to learning include judging, arguing, voting, trading, guessing, contending with time constraints, and engaging in role-play simulation.

Implementing game mechanics, with appropriate educational objectives, can make learning more engaging. It can serve to reinforce skills and content the same way symbolism and imagery help with storytelling. *Pox* is a simple board game in which "infected" red poker chips need to be surrounded by "vaccinated" blue chips. *Pox's* mechanic teaches about vaccination circles. In this case, the mechanic serves a dual role: as a player's actions and as a device to carry a message, similar to symbolism in literature. After all, isn't it more effective to teach about democracy with students voting in a mock election than with a PowerPoint lecture?

Game mechanics, like Bloom's Taxonomy of Higher Order Thinking, are designed using action verbs. In April 2014 I asked James Gee to explain the "design grammar" of game mechanics. "Games are built on verbs, not nouns," he said. "That's what a game mechanic is, depending on the action you take." In a game, you are doing something. You are taking an action that has consequences to the system and to other players. Gee elaborated, "The power of a game is matching the game mechanic to the content. And the content of game mechanics is problem solving. When you get a beautiful mechanic that fits perfectly with the problems you are solving, it is genius. A good example is *Dragon Box* [reference link at the end of this chapter]. It's teaching algebra, and the mechanic is balance and the content is solving equations. It fits perfectly. It's not a matter of picking the perfect mechanics. It's how do we get really good marriages between the mechanic and the problem solving set. That's an art."

Educational game designers are different than their commercial counterparts. Rather than simply choosing a fun mechanic, such as chasing or hiding, they must consider learning objectives. A game becomes chocolate-covered broccoli when the mechanic doesn't fit with the content. In many edutainment games, the learning is presented as an obstacle for students to solve in order to progress. Not only does this turn an activity into a chore, it makes the learning into something the student has to—rather than wants to—do. "There isn't an answer on what mechanics you ought to use or can use," Gee continued. "In fact, we should invent new mechanics and new verbs. It's really finding the best matches with the content. The content of the game cannot be seen as inert facts because the game is based on verbs. The verbs have to match to an activity, and the activity is what you do in the game."

"Chocolate-covered broccoli" games are easier to produce than innovative activities. They can be derivative in nature, with learning content sprinkled in. They may be engaging for a few minutes here and there, but not long term. This is why I am leery of large, comprehensive learning platforms that promise dozens of games for every content area. Answering velocity formula questions in order to shoot an alien seems more educationally straightforward than using *Angry Birds* or billiards to teach physics concepts in an authentic, situated setting. For many teachers and administrators, content-specific games seem like an easier sell. Gee concluded that he advocates "getting really beautiful games—where the content and mechanic are well married—and then putting it into some sort of learning system." In other words, create a project-based learning activity, perhaps with stations around the classroom, and present authentic problems for children to solve. Learning is more than just playing and games. The point of game-based learning is to deliver instruction, not to become the instruction.

Joe Bisz, an associate professor of English at the City University of New York's (CUNY) Game Network, classified simple and complex game mechanics. Bisz's webpage (referenced under "Resources" at the end of this chapter) illustrates how to apply game mechanics in teaching. He linked activities to James Gee's Learning Principles, as well as futurist Marc Prensky's Engagement Principles (Prensky coined the terms "digital native" and "digital immigrant"). Examples of complex mechanics that work in school included Challenge-and-Switch, in which students answer questions incorrectly, and then trade to see who can figure out what went wrong, and Collecting-and-Creation, a mechanic that involves dissecting and trading words and sentences (Bisz, n.d.). Other mechanics pertained to role-play. Complex mechanics can be applied to studying, too. Rather than flashcards, Bisz recommends *Concentration*, the memory matching game, *Classify the Pieces*, a sorting game (the mechanic is present in BrainPOP's *Sortify*), *Cut-Ups*, using scissors to scramble information, and *Find-the-Clue*, an inquiry-based discussion activity (Bisz, n.d.). For more ways to integrate game mechanics to teaching, I highly recommend purchasing a deck of cards Bisz created called *What's Your Game Plan?* It can be used by one person or with a roomful of teachers at a workshop to help educators brainstorm ideas. (See the link under "Games" at the end of the chapter; there are free downloadables as well.)

Game design is really about the player's experience. If you feel frustrated or pressured by time in a game, it was likely intended to trigger that emotion. In March 2014 I asked Carnegie Mellon's Jesse Schell about mechanics that work best for educational settings. He first recommended reading *New Traditional Games for Learning: A Case Book* (2013), research from teachers who used nondigital games in the classroom. The book covers studies of what did and didn't work, including how live-action role-playing (LARPing) games can be used to engage students.

Schell said that he hesitated to use competitive situations in the classroom. "It rewards people who need the least help and punishes those that need the most help," he said. Instead, Schell recommended using a narrative to frame authentic learning, emphasizing intriguing stories. Schell gave me a teamwork example about firefighters in an emergency situation simulation. "People like solving problems together. Cooperative challenges with a point work the best." If this sounds to you like problem-based learning, you are right! Schell continued:

> One of the biggest things a teacher may overlook—one of the greatest powers of games in the classroom—is the ability of a game to introduce a teachable moment. A lot of game designers are creating educational games that are striving to replace the educator. What they should be doing is augmenting the educator. Games are great at creating teachable moments. Games are terrible at knowing they have successfully delivered the teachable moment and then filling in the right information at the right time. But instructors are great at that!

One of the objectives of Schell's firefighter simulation was to usually set up a situation where students would fail. Upon failure, the instructor could then say, "You failed because you didn't use this simple four-step methodology. Let's talk about what you should have done." According to Schell, the biggest power of games in education is to create that conversation. "When you've done the game right, students ask questions in their minds," he concluded. "That means they want to learn."

In my practice, I have found that it is essential to integrate game mechanics in almost all student projects and activities. Match a mechanic with a learning objective. Not every activity I teach is a game; however, every lesson attempts to involve a game-like mechanic. I also bring students into the equation, asking them which mechanics I employed in a particular lesson—and why. This is another way to employ "game-inspired" learning in an activity that is not quite a game.

When I spoke to Google's Noah Falstein, in May 2014, I asked him to me give an example of how mechanics can drive instruction. "As a consultant it drove me crazy," he said. "People would want the wrong things. They would say they wanted a game teaching the history of the American Revolution. Then they would say, 'My son loves *World of Warcraft*, so can we use that and put in some American Revolution content in there?'" In Falstein's opinion, teaching with games only works when it is matched with other traditional methodologies. He continued, "It is a bit of an art and a science to match the mechanic to the subject of what you are trying to teach. Games are not good at teaching lists of facts. I'm not sure there is any good way; it's dry and rote. They are good at teaching about relationships, allowing people to step into the shoes of another experience." Falstein recalled learning from playing simulation games. He said:

> I remember playing a version of *Civilization* when resources were first added. I had a big country and we were at the point where we just discovered oil. Oil deposits showed up on my map, but there weren't any in my country. But there was a big one in a small country adjacent to mine. I was ignoring this country because it was small and innocuous. I was thinking, "It's small and I can put together an army and go and grab it; the other countries will get angry, but I'm wealthy enough and I can give some money and appease them." All of a sudden, I realized that this is what Saddam Hussein was thinking about Kuwait. It's an eerie feeling running this country, and I found myself rationalizing why I would expand my country. Would the country I took over want to be part of my country? It gave me the feeling of how leaders of countries can talk themselves into missteps or things seen as either infamous mistakes or great, bold moves that unify the country.

Any experienced educator will tell you that there is no universal single way to teach everything. Falstein recommended a "combined arms approach," using games, traditional lectures, and books. Kurt Squire's research, where he used the game *Civilization* combined with class discussions about the book *Guns,*

Germs, & Steel (1999), recommended the same approach. Falstein finds this model to be equitable. "It is a good tripod to discuss the rise and fall of civilizations," he said. Matching game mechanics with learning objectives, while mixing in books and teacher-led reflection, is a key to effective game-based learning.

Playing by the Rules

Rules describe a game's mechanics. They limit play to the structure of the game. Game designer David Parlett classified different types of rules. Of note are house rules, laws, social mores, and the rules you hang in your classroom (2005). (Like a game, school has rules—granted, they're not as much fun as *Twister!* Students know when to change classes and how to answer multiple-choice questions.) If games didn't have rules, then an interactive activity would be simply be free, or open, play.

Many games teach the rules and goals during play. For example, the player learns during, not before play that *Pac-Man* cannot touch pink ghosts, but can eat blue ghosts. This is the essence of constructivist learning. Some (or most, depending on who you ask) students tune out when teachers review directions. Children are used to learning constructively by playing games, whether on the playground or on a tablet. Perhaps lessons should reveal themselves the same way.

Games as Systems

"Systems thinking" is a way of viewing the world as a series of interlocking connections. It is the study of how components interconnect, as well as how those relationships fit within other systems (Senge, 2006). The smallest interconnection is a feedback loop (feedback is one of the components of a game). Game designers always view a game as a system: The goal, rules, feedback, and participation all interconnect. Change one element and the entire dynamic is different. Weather is another example of a system. It is comprised of evaporating water, rain clouds, and precipitation.

James Gee wrote that games offer something unique, because they "encourage players to think about relationships, not isolated events, facts, and skills" (2005, p. 36). You can't take the feedback of a game, such as awarding a badge, and add it to student work and call it a game. If the goal is to create a game out of schoolwork, all parts of the game system must be present and functional. Like educational technology, gamification should never be an add-on. Games should be presented as complete, functioning systems.

As a social studies teacher, I am accustomed to teaching cause and effect. The world is comprised of complex and dynamic systems (Senge, 2006, p. 70). If one person—or nation—takes an action, it has a consequential effect; other events are set in motion. When I teach about Japan's surprise attack on Pearl Harbor, I discuss that the U.S. first had an oil embargo on the island nation as a response to its invasion of China. The 2006 update of Peter Senge's 1990 book *The Fifth Discipline* used terrorism as an example of systems thinking in action. He argued that military retribution in response to a terrorist attack exemplifies a "linear" approach to thinking. It doesn't account for other points of view, including the terrorist's (Senge, 2006, p. 70). When events are drawn together as a loop, one can see that responsive military attacks make the U.S. more threatening to its enemies, thus causing an insurgence of more terrorists (Senge, 2006, p. 70). Linear thinking presents an incomplete reality; systems thinkers view interconnections as causal loops, in which one cause has an effect which then leads into another cause, and so on.

Feedback loops are the most basic element of a system. When I visited New York City's game-based Quest to Learn school in August 2013, I saw feedback loop diagrams posted around in the hallways. One sign read, "Taking the Stairs" and "Healthy Body," with arrows pointing to each phrase. Above the arrows were plus symbols indicating a positive flow. Systems thinkers attempt to break the habit of thinking linearly; life happens in cycles (Senge, 2006). Games, therefore, can be used to serve as a microcosm of real-world systems, in which every action has an effect.

Does it work? Were students at Quest to Learn making the connection from playing games to systems thinking concepts? A study was conducted in 2012 to evaluate students' competency in systems thinking skills. Topics included the interconnectedness of sleep and being tired, as well as causal loops showing the peer pressure competition to wear and collect Silly Bandz (animal-shaped rubber bands) (Shute, Ventura & Torres, 2013). Although the population size was relatively small (one school), the study suggested that students, with teacher facilitation and support, were thinking less linearly and more in causal loops. The findings suggested that after 20 months, "Students who started at Quest to Learn as sixth graders when the school opened in September 2009 significantly improved on their overall systems thinking skills" (Shute, Ventura & Torres, 2013, p. 61).

In the classroom, it can be helpful to break interconnections down into smaller parts. Concept mapping, or mind mapping, can be used to connect parts of a whole. Teachers and students can use poster boards, sticky notes, or interactive whiteboards to examine feedback loops in systems. The idea is to list ideas and then draw lines and loops connecting related ideas. Educational software includes Kidspiration and the browser-based Popplet. Mind Meister offers live, collaborative publishing options. It features an intuitive drag-and-drop interface that works seamlessly across multiple devices. Students can work simultaneously, on iPads or laptops. The result can be seen in real time when projected onto an interactive whiteboard. Many of these applications offer deep educator discounts.

Computer-based systems modeling, such as those found on ISEE System's STELLA Modeler, are loosely based on a bathtub faucet analogy originally described in Peter Senge's *The Fifth Discipline* (1990/2006). Whatever is being measured—from predator/prey relationships to money—flows from the faucet. It is then collected in "stock," pictured in models as a square. Connectors and converters, which are diagrammed to look like plumbing equipment, complete a systems model. Creative Learning Exchange offers educators an easy-to-read document on simulation terminology and tips on implementation. Modeling software helps business leaders to visualize the interrelations between causal loops so they can make better predictions. The overall goal of modeling simulators is to create a learning organization that reflects on past practices and grows together as a community (Senge, 2006).

Before creating models, feedback loops, and causal loop diagrams, have students plot graphs. An example would be plotting weight loss over time on an x-, y-axis. Next, put weight loss over time together to create a causal loop diagram. This will illustrate how multiple feedback loops (e.g., eating less junk food, exercising) interconnect. Exercise may make you energetic (one feedback loop), but also thirsty (on offshoot feedback loop). The goal is for students to move from "describing the 'what' of the system's behavior to the 'why' of its behavior" (Creative Learning Exchange, 2013). Every simulation is based on positive and negative feedback.

The power of teaching systems thinking with games is in its authenticity. Simulations of war can be better illustrated by playing *Rock-Paper-Scissors* than by running through a role-playing military drill. The two-player version of the classic children's game is a system of interlocking rules (e.g., paper covers rock, etc.; everyone "throws" their hand in simultaneously), a goal (one winner per round), and voluntary participation (it is a zero-sum game—one winner, one loser). If you change one part of the system (rock covers paper?), or add in more rules (best out of three rounds), the game's system changes. Therefore, games can be seen as a microcosm of reality.

Playing a game that has systems management as an objective can reinforce the competency. *SimCityEDU: Pollution Challenge!* (2013) tasks players with balancing a virtual city's systems, including school bus stops, pollution, and employment. Lead designer Erin Hoffman explained to me how it works. "When an action is made, there are multiple consequences," she said. "If one piece of the system is modified, it can have surprising or unpredictable effects farther down the line because of the connections between all of the parts of the system." *Reach for the Sun*, created by Filament Games, is another example of a systems thinking game. This award-winning game is played from the point of view of a flowering plant. The objective is to gather soil nutrients, sunlight, and even bees, in order to survive. Each element, including sunlight, pollination, and water, is part of the plant's interconnected system. Master the plant's survival and you have mastered the system. Just about all of Filament's games have a system to engage the player. The system doesn't even have to be that complex. Filament's Dan White told me, "It's not about the complexity of the system, but whether it delivers it with an appropriate amount of fidelity." Coding games and playing games can enforce systems thinking skills, too. The Gates Foundation's Robert Torres wrote his doctoral dissertation on *Gamestar Mechanic* and how students engage with systems. His research is now included on the game-making tool's website.

Game Theory

"Game theory" refers to the mathematical result of when of two or more "rational" people play a game. This book is concerned with game design and its value as an instructional delivery method, not an analysis of combinations and permutations that can result from games. Games are not pure luck, like flipping a coin. Hitting a baseball or throwing rock, paper, or scissors has a human component (people play to win). Because of that, game theory is considered to be more than a branch of mathematics; it's a social science.

In 1928 John von Neumann wrote "Theory of Parlor Games." Von Neumann attempted to link *how* people play games such as *Poker*. As it turned out, parlor games had a lot in common with economic theories such as supply and demand (Chen, Lu & Vekhter, n.d.). To von Neumann, a game was defined as "a conflict situation where one must make a choice knowing that others are making choices, too, and the outcome of the conflict will be determined in some prescribed way by all the choices made" (Poundstone, 1992, p. 6). In 1944 he published the book *Theory of Games and Economic Behavior*. His theory, known as minimax, focused on two-player, zero-sum games such as *Rock-Paper-Scissors*. Zero-sum means that there is one absolute winner and one loser.

John Forbes Nash built on von Neumann's work. Nash eventually won a Nobel prize in economics for his contribution: mixed-strategy Nash equilibria. Unlike von Neumann, Nash's research was about games with multiple players. Nash's troubled life was depicted in the Academy Award–winning film *A Beautiful Mind* (2001), starring Russell Crowe. According to biographer Sylvia Nasar, Nash equilibrium is the moment when each player follows his or her "best strategy assuming that the other players will follow their best strategy" (Nasar, 1998, p. 119).

For the purpose of game-based learning, it can be helpful to review some of the basics of game theory. A zero-sum game is when there is one absolute winner and one loser. The 1982 movie *War Games*, about a computer modeling global thermonuclear war gone awry, is essentially a morality tale of the dangers of zero-sum games. The popular film compared all-out winning (or, equally, completely losing) global thermal nuclear war to the game *Tic-Tac-Toe*. We (or they) attack first, then they (or we) retaliate, both reducing each nation to rubble. Conversely to games such as *Tic-Tac-Toe*, non-zero-sum games, as the name implies, aren't win-lose, but rather win-win. Cooperative games in learning should, of course, be non-zero sum.

In the 1950s the RAND Corporation, a California-based think tank, studied game theory. Nash and von Neumann were hired as consultants to model and analyze Cold War strategies. At RAND, Merrill Flood, Melvin Dresher, and, later, Albert W. Tucker proposed a parable, popularly known as the Prisoners' Dilemma, to illustrate how Cold War military standoffs work. The dilemma, or difficult choice, is described below by Nash biographer Sylvia Nasar. She wrote:

> The police arrest two suspects and question them in two separate rooms. Each one is given the choice of confessing, implicating the other, or keeping silent. The central feature of the game is that no matter what the other suspect does, each (considered alone) would be better off if he confessed. If the other confesses, the suspect in question ought to do the same and thereby avoid an equally harsh penalty for holding

out. If the other remains silent, he can get especially lenient treatment for turning state's witness. Confession is the dominant strategy. The irony is that both prisoners (considered together) would be better off if neither confessed—that is, if they cooperated—but since each is aware of the other's incentive to confess, it is "rational" for both to confess. (Nasar, 1998, p. 118)

The Prisoners' Dilemma led to subsequent research papers that dealt with subjects other than war. Teaching the basics of game theory is good practice because it integrates social studies (economics, causal loops due to scarcity and power) and practical math applications applicable to the business world. People don't just act out, there are always motivating factors; incentives and rewards must be considered. Therefore, one can look at the dilemma as a mathematical game. Mathematicians analyze game outcomes by creating a matrix, already common in math classes such as algebra and statistics. A matrix is a chart of rows and columns where possible outcomes are listed. Another mathematical method for illustrating game theory is to draw decision trees, which have possible answers branching out from the proposed problem.

Nash's observations extended to how auctions work, too. Perhaps you have heard of online auctions that start bidding at extremely low prices, sometimes at a penny. Conventional wisdom would dictate that bidding should start high to ensure a high final price, but when tested, it turns out that auctions that start with very low bids actually tend to end much higher. This is because humans are innately competitive and enjoy a feeding frenzy. This drives up prices—sometimes substantially—on low-bid (or unique-bid) auctions. Because people can't see the previous bids, they consistently assume they were high and therefore drive the price up even higher. William Vickery was credited with this finding. He was posthumously awarded a Nobel prize for his paper on the subject, "Counterspeculation, Auctions, and Competitive Sealed Tenders."

In my 6th-grade social studies class I teach game theory in a simulation lesson with paper clips used as currency. The lesson is from the Council for Economic Education, and it illustrates Mansa Musa's pilgrimage from Mali, through Egypt, on his way to Mecca. First I give each student a small and unequal number of paperclips. Next, I auction off items such as crackers or candy. For round 2, I hand out handfuls of paper clips to every student and run the auction again. The prices skyrocket, illustrating that printing more currency actually devalues money. Like any game, the teachable moment is that purchasing power is dependent on the scarcity of money.

Conclusions and Takeaways

There are several competing definitions of what games are. Interestingly, although most are based in developmental psychology and stem from observing children's games, still it seems frivolous to play in school. Mechanics must match the learning objective to be most effective. When successful, a game's mechanic can become the message, driving home content. Students should also understand game mechanics as a form of literacy, in the same way they are taught to deconstruct novels. Teachers should borrow mechanics and match them with learning objectives. Games are not just interactive; they are systems. Systems can be modeled with games. Mathematicians and economists also use games to analyze human behavior, which is a cross-curricular activity.

Lesson Plan Ideas

Collaborative Brainstorming: Use *Mindmeister* or *Popplet* with students to brainstorm in real-time. Standards depend on the discipline and content area.

Feedback Loop Exit Ticket: Students can diagram simple causal loops in any discipline. Be sure to include plus and minus signs to illustrate positive or negative relationships. Standards depend on the discipline and content area.

Game Kit: Challenges that require little to no technology. Have small groups try each challenge. Standards depend on the discipline and content area—http://beta.gamek.it

Game Theory Dilemma: Have students engage in argumentative writing using dilemmas such as the Prisoners' Dilemma. English language arts classes can write a play or short story describing the situation. Decision trees and mind maps should be used as a pre-writing tool. Social studies can relate it to how cultural and economic interactions play out. Math can attempt to solve the problem using a matrix, as well as a decision tree. Probability outcomes can be analyzed, too. Science can look at the game as a simulation model with predicted results. Standards met include Common Core State Standards for mathematics.

Mansa Musa: Inflation Then and Now: Auction lesson from the Council for Economic Education. Standards met include social studies (economics) and Common Core State Standards for mathematics. This link includes a PowerPoint presentation and a handout to drive home lessons about purchasing power, inflation, and currency devaluation—http://msh.councilforeconed.org/lessons.php?lid=68371

Modeling Hamlet: Use *Forio Simulate* to run systems models to see how Shakespeare's *Hamlet* looks to a mathematician or a scientist. Standards met include Common Core State Standards for English language arts—http://forio.com/simulate/netsim/virtual-hamlet/run

Systems Thinking: How to Create a Digital World: Standards depend on the discipline and content area. Lesson plan from Scholastic—http://www.scholastic.com/browse/lessonplan.jsp?id=1418

Games

Diplomacy, the classic strategy game of consequential actions, playable online—http://www
.playdiplomacy.com

Going, Going, GONE! a game about auctions—http://strongholdgames.com/store/board-games/
going-going-gone

Plague, Inc. is a game in which the player infects the world with a deadly pathogen. It is, in
effect, a systems thinking game—http://www.ndemiccreations.com/en/22-plague-inc

Pox: Save the People from Mary Flanagan's Tiltfactor. The board game that teaches players
about group immunity and vaccinations—http://www.tiltfactor.org/pox

Re-Mission, cancer treatment game—http://www.re-mission.net

What's Your Game Plan, a deck of cards created by Joe Bisz. "Suits" include Lesson, Game,
Mechanic, and Action. It is very useful to help brainstorm about how to bring game
mechanics into teaching—http://joebisz.com/whatsyourgameplan

Resources

Board Game Mechanics—http://www.boardgamegeek.com/browse/boardgamemechanic

"Composition Games for the Classroom," from Joe Bisz, is a presentation about turning lessons
into nondigital games—http://joebisz.com/compositiongames/Composition_Games_for_
the_Classroom.html

Creative Learning Exchange, systems thinking resources for kindergarten through grade 12—
http://clexchange.org

Institute of Play's *Systems Thinking Q Pack* helps integrate systems thinking across the curriculum—
http://www.instituteofplay.org/work/projects/q-design-packs/q-systems-thinking-design-pack

ISEE systems thinking tools—http://www.iseesystems.com

Kidspiration, school-focused mind-mapping tools—http://www.inspiration.com/Kidspiration

Mind Meister, real-time, collaborative mind mapping tool—http://www.mindmeister.com

"The Mystery of *Go*, the Ancient Game that Computers Still Can't Win," an article in *Wired*
about games and game theory—http://www.wired.com/2014/05/the-world-of-computer-go

Popplet is a browser-based and mobile mind-mapping tool. It works great with interactive
whiteboards, too!—http://popplet.com

Prisoners' Dilemma as taught by the Khan Academy—https://www.khanacademy.org/eco-
nomics-finance-domain/microeconomics/nash-equilibrium-tutorial/nash-eq-tutorial/v/
prisoners–dilemma-and-nash-equilibrium

Waters Foundation, featuring systems thinking for schools and free downloads—http://waters
foundation.org

· 3 ·

WHO PLAYS GAMES...AND WHY

One of the most influential papers to affect modern video game design came from Richard Bartle. His Player Type Model, first described in *Hearts, Clubs, Diamonds, Spades: Players Who Suit MUDs* (1996), transformed how games were designed. Bartle's observations still reverberate today—especially in gamification's approach to engagement (adding game elements in spaces that are otherwise not games, such as websites and exercise programs). Bartle graciously granted me an interview, and in it he puts an educational spin on his now famous Player Types Model. Designing games should put the gamers' experience first and foremost. Shouldn't learning design do the same? It is as important to understand the work of Bartle when integrating game-based learning as it is to learn about Howard Gardner when planning to teach students using a variety of intelligence modalities.

Much of the current research I found on game design came from behaviorists and designers, not programmers or computer nerds. Game designers Jane McGonigal and Amy Jo Kim, for example, have Ph.D.s in the field of behavioral psychology. It is common for school districts to have a child psychologist and/or a behaviorist on staff. Most of their days are spent with students who exhibit social or emotional problems. It would be unusual for a school to hire a behaviorist to ensure that the general population is having a happy and fulfilling learning experience.

This chapter compares and contrasts intrinsic and extrinsic motivational factors as they pertain to student engagement. I will also review the field of positive psychology, including the concept of "flow." In the "flow channel," people feel fulfilled because they are so involved in an experience (Csikszentmihalyi, 1990). Applied to games, the flow channel is used to describe the environment where the skill and the difficulty increase just enough to ensure that an experience is neither frustrating nor boring (Lazzaro, 2009, p. 13; McGonigal, 2011, p. 49). This chapter also covers the emotion of fun. If something—even the most serious topic—doesn't have an element of fun, then there is little chance for engagement. Even the most somber of books and movies still put entertainment first. Failure to do so would mean disengaged readers and bored viewers.

Bartle's Player Type Model

Game design has a lot in common with learning design. In a game, systems are created and then set into motion by its core mechanics. The result triggers an emotion in the player. Like education, game design has its models. Bartle's Player Type Model (1996) has had a significant influence on how games are made. The innovation was to create—or design—games for others to play. People play games for different reasons, aside from the rules and objectives. Friends may gather to play cards every week in a setting to chat or gossip. Others may play to win. Bartle's realization was that game designers must keep different personality types in mind. As a teacher, you may recognize components of Howard Gardner's Multiple Intelligence Theory, where people learn visually, kinetically, musically, or simply by listening. Creating games for different player types also has commonalities with differentiated instruction, teaching each learner to his or her strengths.

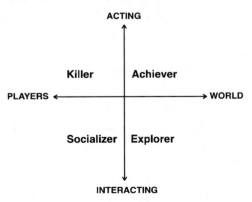

Figure 1. Bartle's Player Type Model.

Bartle, a professor specializing in artificial intelligence and virtual worlds, wrote *Hearts, Clubs, Diamonds, Spades: Players Who Suit MUDs* in the mid-1990s to explain how players interact differently when participating in multi-player environments. ("MUDs are multi-user dungeons, or text-based virtual worlds.) Plotted on an x-, y-axis, Bartle compared player actions, or interactions, of multiplayers in game worlds (Bartle, 1996). The model, also known as Bartle's Player Types, classified four types of players:

- Killers—those who act on, or against, other game players
- Achievers—those who build up their in-game status
- Explorers—those who gather artifacts and look around
- Socializers—those who build friendships. (Bartle, 1996)

I have had some spirited discussions about Player Types with students. In school, lessons can be designed to encourage young explorers to explore. Personally, I prefer games that engage me in exploring, such as the *Tomb Raider* series. In the book *The Multiplayer Classroom* (2012), Lee Sheldon theorized that he was an Explorer Type because he enjoys writing. He researches facts and assembles them into stories, and sometimes into the TV episodes he wrote. Achievers pursue goals (not just extrinsic ones, such as grades). These include class "power-ups" or points from games on a class leaderboard. Socializers enjoy connections made from being with other people. They are the students who want to work together in cooperative groups. Killers obviously shouldn't be as aggressive in a classroom; I find that appropriate outlets for this type are structured debates or the lead roles in skits.

In an article for game business magazine *Gamasutra*, Bartle's Player Type Model was compared to the Myer-Briggs Type Indicator (MBTI) test, commonly used by psychologists to classify personality types. The story focused specifically on David Keirsey's list of four personality "temperaments" (Stewart, 2011). The Keirsey Temperament Sorter (KTS II) test has four domains—Artisans, Guardians, Rationals, and Idealists—which "can be further subdivided, often referred to as Character Types" (Keirsey.com, 2014). Bart Stewart proposed merging Bartle's model with Keirsey's to create a Unified Model (2011). Stewart's proposal tied in theories of "fun" in games (Caillois, 1961/2001; Lazzaro, 2004). A proof of concept ended Stewart's piece, matching current games to fit his construct. For example, Achievers, Explorers, and Socializers all play multiplayer online games such as *World of Warcraft* (Stewart, 2011).

Bartle's model has been widely adopted by designers and is part of virtually every game design course. It seems obvious now that games should be designed for the variety of people that play them. I spoke to Bartle in the March 2014. He is currently a game design and virtual world professor at the University of Essex. Bartle has always been making games. I've noticed this characteristic in several people I interviewed—their minds are constantly designing. Bartle recalled, "When I was a kid I used to make games. I played games the whole time, games are one of those things that you did." Whether it was word games or simply running around, many of his childhood games involved simulation and role play. "I was particularly interested in the world-building thing," Bartle recalled. "The real world sucked. If you were a working-class boy living in a derelict seaside town, there were no prospects of anything because of how you spoke or what your parents did. I really wanted a world where you could be free. That's why I wrote *Ultima* [the classic text-based adventure]. Building imaginary worlds was a way to change the real world. That's why I did it."

I was curious about how Bartle came up with the idea of player types. He explained that at that time, in the mid-1990s, designers were making games that they personally wanted to play. He wanted to show that they should be making games that *everyone* would want to play. Bartle made several analogies in our conversation. "If you're a brewer, you don't necessarily make beer you want to drink," he said. "You make beer for other people to drink. You might not even like beer yourself!" In other words, the designer is someone who should enjoy designing. It is not a prerequisite for someone who makes games to necessarily enjoy playing what he or she creates. What I find fun is not necessarily what a 12-year-old middle school student finds fun to do. It is easy to lose sight of what others may find fun. This is why game designers rely on playtesters.

Bartle continued, "People want to play games for lots of different reasons." If you focus on just one of the Player Types, such as the Achiever type, the designer is doing the game a disservice; only competitive people will play, turning away Socializers or Explorers. The game, therefore, isn't as effective as it could be. "I really expected the paper and the Player Types [Model] to not last very long, maybe 6 months or so," he continued. "I waited for people to come up with a better set. The point I was making was that there are different reasons people play games."

A persistent question on my mind was how to effectively design an educational game. Bartle explained, "Games are designed for purposes. In war games, like the Prussians did (with *Kriegspiel*), it wasn't necessarily fun—but it taught them things." In my classroom I use games as a metaphor for historical conflict. I also use simulations to teach empathy. Bartle suggested starting with subject matter that is interesting to children, "like dinosaurs, pirates, or French musketeers." Next, add the learning objective onto the system. Then, right there on the spot, Bartle designed a game to test people's propensity to xenophobia. He explained:

> You design a game about your company, which is a large company, and it just bought up another company, which is a small company. The small company is closing down offices, and the people from that company come to work in your company. They have different practices and ways of doing things, and there are far fewer of them. Should you take their best parts and practices and adapt them to you, or should you bring them into your existing system which you know works, try to spread them around, keep them in one section?

Bartle's example is a "serious" business game masking what is really being studied: xenophobia. The trick is to make sure that the systems underneath, essentially the game's architecture, are compatible. Learning must be deeply embedded in an educational game. Games, however, cannot teach everything. A flaw in using games to assess behavior pertains to *how* people take on roles, which is formally known as "player agency." Players may be just exploring an aspect of their personality through the game. Stealing cars in *Grand Theft Auto* doesn't turn thousands of people into carjackers. You can't always rely on game data, but if it is well crafted, it can be more reliable than questionnaires and role-playing scenarios. If you want to find out people's attitudes towards immigrants you can just give them a survey, but their answers may be dishonest because people don't want to sound racist.

People learn from games if the game is about something they are interested in; the other facts are just things they pick up that make it easier for them to play. The content both at the surface level and at the gameplay level is why people play. What comes with it is actually what you want to teach. Bartle explained, "That's the vehicle that you attach your educational payload. If you wanted to teach a particular thing, find something where knowing that particular thing will help you, and not knowing it wouldn't hinder you, but it would slow you down a bit. That's how I recommend it from a game designer's point of view." The classic mistake occurs when educators make games and don't know anything about game design. Conversely, the mistake you get from game designers is that they don't know anything about education. This is why edutainment has a poor track record and why "educational" games can make a student cringe. There really isn't a common language—at least, not yet.

Bartle told me that he could name every country in Europe because he plays games. Because of the setting of *Assassin's Creed III*, I have had students who were quite proficient in detailing battles of the American Revolution. "Likewise, I know the geography of the Caribbean because I played so many pirate games," Bartle said. "There are a lot of things you can pick up from just playing—when the actual game involves higher-order problem-solving things, like how to figure out how to do certain things. How to solve (problems); games are very good at that. The trouble is the stuff in the middle. If you want to teach people how to integrate an equation or differentiate an equation there's probably a better way than using games to do that."

Bartle often speaks about how his model is used—and misused. The biggest abuse of Bartle's Player Type Model is when people take all of the types and make content for each one as if each person was an Achiever. Bartle gave me an example of misuses. He said:

> What do Explorers like doing? They like exploring. So, you explore enough, you get a badge. Wait a minute! A badge is something an Achiever wants. Why would you give a badge to an Explorer? They don't want a badge—they want more things to explore. That's for Achievers. Here's another misuse: If you get 15 friends, you get a special pet. Why would someone who wants friends want a special pet? Achievers might want pets. They like collecting pets. Collecting is an Achiever thing. That's where people read the Player Types and create content all for the same Player Type, which is typically just for Achievers. That's one area that I see a lot of.

The Player Type Model was not designed to help web traffic, increase customer satisfaction, or engage students. It was created to improve the experience of players in multi-user virtual worlds. Nonetheless, it is worth knowing about as a starting point in gamifying learning. Bartle gave me an analogy of a novelist who wrote a successful book. Would an author add math problems to a text and ask the reader to track the money spent by a character? The problem is that these add-ons take away from the intended experience of the novel. "People read a story because it's fun," Bartle said.

In a game, there are the core mechanics, such as beating the clock, and player competition. And then there is the aesthetic framework, which can be the game's board or an immersive virtual world. "Games might have a fictional framework. That's what supports what's fun about the game," Bartle continued. "Once you turn it the other way around, having the game support the fictional framework, you're talking about a different beast." Is the setting of *Assassin's Creed: Revelation* the best way to teach about Byzantium? Would you show *Saving Private Ryan* to teach French geography?

Teachers should play games for learning prior to integrating them. Bartle gave me advice on this topic. He said, "Make sure you know what it is you want to teach, and find a game that it isn't about. Because if the students think the game is about what the teacher wants taught, they won't engage with it. Introduce a game about math that has a mechanic of adding and students may become suspicious of how fun it is before they even start. What would be fun is exploring an undersea world and, in order to get over there, I need to get some fuel. You learn math because you need to get fuel and know how long it's going to last. You're not concerned about fuel; you're concerned about submarine exploration." Learning theorists call this a "felt need." For this to occur, use authentic projects connected to real-world situations. Also, keep in mind that if a game is crafted well, then it will be fun. If you don't think it's fun, the student is not going to think it's fun.

Rewards and Motivation

Behavioral sciences date back to the theories of classical and operant conditioning from Ivan Pavlov and B. F. Skinner. Pavlov is often associated with classical conditioning. His famous dogs drooled at the sound of a bell after they learned that a ringing bell was followed by a reward of food. Eventually, Pavlov removed the food and discovered that dogs still salivated just at hearing the bell. Positive and negative reinforcement, in the form of rewards or punishments, is at the heart of Skinner's research. The Skinner Box was a rat-in-a-box contraption with a food lever as a positive reinforcer and an electrical charge as a negative reinforcer. Do people need the promise of food or fear of electrocution in order to learn? Should school be set up like a Skinner Box? Does the quintessential kick in the butt lead to success? Modern research has shown otherwise. While external rewards work in the short term, they do not create satisfied people who enjoy their work.

In the 1990s Alfie Kohn wrote about the trappings of reward systems. *Punished by Rewards: The Trouble with Gold Stars, Incentive Plans, A's, Praise, and Other Bribes* (1999) is one of his more notable books. The proverbial carrot at the end of the stick can often demotivate people. Kohn's criticism was not directed at all reward systems, but those that focus on extrinsic motivation as an incentive. Most of the early behavioral research came from only animal testing (e.g., Pavlov's dogs), not from humans (1997, p. 15). The end result—paychecks, time off, semester grades, student-of-the-month, merit pay, or trophies—may not be enough of a motivator (Kohn, 1997, p. 15). Working toward your vacation days will not make you want to rush into the office; report card grades and summative assessments can have the same (lack of) effect on students. I often make an analogy about cooking: If making dinner or baking cookies is something you find fun to do, then it has an intrinsic reward. That may extend to watching others eat what you cook, another source of satisfaction. If the goal is just to eat, then it is extrinsic. In the long run, extrinsic rewards can discourage performance. Kohn wrote a "framework" describing the trappings of extrinsic reward systems. He wrote:

1. Pay is not a motivator
2. Rewards punish
3. Rewards rupture relationships
4. Rewards ignore reasons
5. Rewards discourage risk-taking
6. Rewards undermine interest. (Kohn, 1997, pp. 18–23)

Intrinsic rewards are the opposite of extrinsic motivators. They are internalized and often represent satisfaction one feels from an accomplishment. These rewards are similar to the self-satisfaction gained from finishing a great book, enjoying a day golfing, the thrill of discovering a secret room in *Tomb Raider,* or defeating a dragon with guild members in *World of Warcraft*. According to Jane McGonigal, intrinsic motivation includes "satisfying work, the experience, or at least the hope, of being successful, social connection, and meaning" (2011, p. 49). These are the reasons that so many people play so many hours of games outside of their school and work days. In front of a computer, players are empowered and feel in control. Amy Jo Kim wrote that video games are *"pleasurable learning engines*—they offer up skills to master, and reward you with greater challenges and opportunities" (Kim, 2012a; emphasis in original). The fun is in the experience of play, not the score. Do you remember how much money you've earned playing *Monopoly*, or the triple word score you got in *Scrabble*? If nothing else, game design can teach teachers how intrinsic satisfaction should come before grades and other extrinsic motivators.

In February 2014, I asked James Sanders, co-founder of the digital badge website ClassBadges, about rewards and motivation. He explained that it might be a "matter of perception." The "artifact"—a badge, a diploma, or a certificate—is just a representation of an achievement. Sanders made the analogy to class attendance and earning gold stars. "If you walk into a class-room and receive a gold star every time you just walked in and found your seat, pretty soon the learning goals aren't going to mean anything," he explained. "Let's say down the hall, you have to turn in your homework 100% complete, 7 days a week, and you have to perform 80% or better on all assessments. Then you earn one gold star. That one star, even though it's the same physical representation as the other class, is more meaningful because of what you put in more work to earn it."

Digital badges should not become the motivational factor; they should simply represent an accomplishment. The idea is to make sure the feeling of achievement comes first, followed by the recognition. Intrinsic emotions depend on whom you want to impress with an accomplishment. This is the social part of gaming and badging. Sanders continued, "Let's say, in order to graduate from high school, you have to earn three science badges from your local community, and there are five museums that offer them. That means a lot because you need to earn all three of them or you are not going to graduate from high school. The importance of it is determined by who is looking at it later."

Pleasant Frustration and the Flow Channel

On its surface, game-based learning may seem to be following a trend of just doing what kids like to do; the proverbial tail wagging the dog. The psychol-ogy of how it works actually runs deeper. Games can focus people into a state of mind called "flow." Psychologist Mihaly Csikszentmihalyi first described the concept. You can see it in the faces of Olympic athletes, Zen Buddhist monks, and, of course, gamers.

Flow represents intrinsic satisfaction. It can best be described as "the way people describe their state of mind when consciousness is harmoniously ordered, and they want to pursue whatever they are doing for its sake" (Csikszentmihalyi, 1990, p. 6). Csikszentmihalyi created a model, known as the "flow channel," to describe the environment where skill and difficulty increase just enough that an experience is neither frustrating nor boring. As shown in the dia-gram reprinted below, he plotted the "flow channel" between the two axes of "Challenge" and "Skills" (Csikszentmihalyi, 1990, p. 74). The flow channel is where people feel fulfilled because they are so involved in an experience.

In the illustration, "A" represents anxiety. The goal of a well-crafted game is to keep the play within the flow channel (McGonigal, 2011, p. 49).

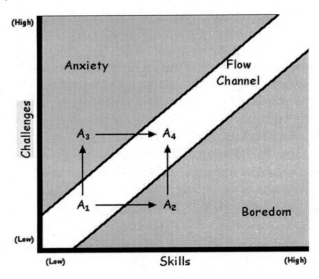

Figure 2. The flow channel. Reprinted from *Flow: The Psychology of Optimal Experience* (p. 74), by M. Csikszentmihalyi, 1990, New York, NY: Harper & Row. Copyright 1990 by Mihaly Csikszentmihalyi. Reprinted with permission.

Flow activities create enjoyment (Csikszentmihalyi, 1990, p. 72). James Gee called this "pleasant frustration," where the challenge is just difficult enough to promote replay and eventual mastery (2005). Csikszentmihalyi considered each set of Caillois's games (discussed in Chapter 2: *agon, alea, ilinx,* and *mimicry*) to be a flow activity (1990, p. 74). Because of a game's design, "participants and spectators achieve an ordered state of mind" (Csikszentmihalyi, 1990, p. 72). *Agon* games are competitive, thereby motivating participants to win challenges. *Alea* games involve randomness, such as the throwing of dice; the feeling of anticipation is the flow. *Ilinx* is thrill-seeking: It is hard to think of anything else while on a rollercoaster. Finally, *mimicry* involves "being in the moment." Karaoke and dance games may be popular because they tap into this part of human behavior. About games, Csikszentmihalyi wrote, "Whether it [a game] involved chance, or any other dimension of experience, [it] had this in common: It provided a sense of discovery, a creative feeling of transporting the person to a new reality" (Csikszentmihalyi, 1990, p. 74).

Like Bartle's Player Types and Kohn's observations, Csikszentmihalyi's work was read by game designers in the 1990s and incorporated into design.

Video games even use adaptive engines to ramp up difficulty. Schools have lagged behind. The flow channel is like the Zone of Proximal Development, psychologist Lev Vygotsky's space where learning scaffolds on previous knowledge. The problem in schools is that the feedback loop is much slower than that which video games provide.

Game challenges do not necessarily need to get more difficult in a linear fashion. Designer Jesse Schell suggested that it is appropriate to level off the anxiety with breaks in the action (2008). Video games let players relax between levels and missions by showing animated sequences to move along the storyline. There may also be time to explore the virtual environment and collect and gather hidden rewards. In fact, it can be considered poor design to just put a player linearly in the flow channel, leveling up difficulty with each mission. The takeaway for teachers is that relief from constant challenge is an acceptable design choice.

Some games are intentionally difficult. QWOP is a browser-based track-and-field game. The computer keyboard letters Q, W, O, and P control the upper and lower legs of a runner. Timing must be precise to break a stride; this nearly impossible challenge is its main appeal. QWOP was featured on July 27, 2011, at an arcade night at New York City's Museum of Modern Art (Chai, 2011). It even made an appearance on TV's *The Office*.

Thatgamecompany's Jenova Chen tested whether a player can self-sustain in the flow channel without a computer automatically scaling up challenges. He designed the game *flOw* for his master's thesis. It lets the player increase or decrease his or her own difficulty of play. The result was an unexpected hit on Sony's PlayStation Network. *flOw* is an aesthetically hypnotic experience, with calming electronic music and visuals that resemble organisms under a microscope. Game mechanics are simple: Move your organism and consume smaller life forms. The more you eat, the bigger you grow. That's it. No score, no badges, no leaderboard. If you grow too big and can't handle the challenges, then you simply reduce in size. The result was strangely addictive. A lesson from Chen was that students might prefer to fine-tune their own learning difficulties. If you watch a child build in *Minecraft* or with LEGO bricks, you will see the same self-regulating behavior.

A fully immersed student is the goal of every teacher. Think of all the activities that consume your students. Those activities may lend themselves to a game-like context because they already are engaging. In my classroom, flow activities usually include opportunities for students to tweak projects they find personally interesting. These include editing in *iMovie*, coding with

Scratch, or building in *Minecraft.* I can tell informally that the class is in a flow state when no one asks to leave to use the bathroom, and I have to ask the class several times to clean up when the bell rings.

Fun as a Key to Engagement

In 2005 Raph Koster published A *Theory of Fun for Game Design,* based on a Game Developer Conference talk. His book, targeted at game designers, reads like a textbook for teachers. Koster discussed Howard Gardner's Multiple Intelligence Theory and how games scaffold skills until mastery level is achieved (2005).

According to Koster, the goal of an activity may be sufficient to make it fun. It's the hope of achieving success that engages players. Once mastery is reached, fun ceases. In other words, "fun is contextual" (Koster, 2005, p. 96). His words ring true for educators just as they do for game designers. Koster wrote, "Fun is primarily about practicing and learning, not about exercising mastery" (2005, p. 96). Fun quickly turns into boredom once a game—or a lesson—is mastered.

The excitement of overcoming an obstacle in a game should entice you to further play. In 2004 Hunicke, LeBlanc, and Zubek wrote a paper that described a taxonomy of fun, "game pleasures." The reference to "pleasure" wasn't a coincidence; it was referring to Maslow's 1943 Hierarchy of Needs Theory, which includes food, shelter and clothing. The act of engaging in a "fun" activity is, after all, what pleasure seekers do. That is why people visit Disney's theme parks, watch 3D movies, and skydive. Pleasures derived from games include:

1. Sensation—Game as sense-pleasure
2. Fantasy—Game as make-believe
3. Narrative—Game as unfolding story
4. Challenge—Game as obstacle course
5. Fellowship—Game as social framework
6. Discovery—Game as uncharted territory
7. Expression—Game as soap box
8. Submission—Game as mindless pastime. (Hunicke, LeBlanc, & Zubek, 2004)

School, certainly, can't be a "mindless pastime." It can, however, be enjoyable on other levels. Discovery learning, popularized by Maria Montessori, can be as fun in school as it is in a game. A well-conceived classroom presentation—where students can discuss and connect a topic to something they are interested in—is "Expression" pleasure. Clearly, you can't put a ferris wheel in your classroom, but you can role play. Games provide spaces for people to socialize with others who share the same interests. Working cooperatively in a problem-based learning activity is also pleasurable—if deployed correctly and if it is designed well.

Part of the allure of gaming is the emotional satisfaction players receive. If the intent is to use a game to deliver learning, then it must be fun. "If the game is not fun," explained Quest to Learn's Shula Ehrlich in a January 2014 interview with me, "it won't achieve what you want it to achieve." There is no special key or magical ingredient, as long as the game mechanic works. Some are intrinsically fun, such as bluffing in the board game *Apples to Apples*. English language arts and social studies games should allow a student to give his or her opinion, followed up with opportunities to judge and persuade others.

For Henry Jenkins, play is not just about fun; it's about engagement. When we spoke, in May 2014, he told me, "As faculty we are engaged in our favorite area of research. We are committed to working long hours with difficult materials. It doesn't mean that it's all fun and games, that it's not challenging and difficult. The goal is to create an environment where engagement drives learning. For engagement to drive learning, you have to have relative freedom with what you're engaged with." Writing this book may not be "fun" in a traditional sense; however, writing is fulfilling to me. I often lose track of time staring at my computer's screen.

Risky Play

Some people theorize that humans are hard-wired for fun. Evolutionary psychologist Peter Gray described "risky play" in his *Freedom to Learn* blog for *Psychology Today*. The post was based on findings from a 2001 study by Norwegian professors Ellen Sandseter and Leif Kennair. Gray and Sandseter and Kennair are among those who believe that humans seek out risky behavior as a survival mechanism. Sandseter and Kennair listed six types of dangerous activities that appeal to most children. Examples of "risky play" included:

1. Great heights
2. Rapid speed
3. Dangerous tools
4. Dangerous elements

5. Rough and tumble play
6. Disappearing/getting lost. (Sandseter & Kennair, 2011)

The above list may explain why children love amusement parks, hiding in clothing racks at department stores, running fast, and climbing trees. The video game series *Assassin's Creed* smartly weaves risky play into its game mechanics—all experienced from the safety of your couch! To "sync" to the map in *Assassin's Creed*, which reveals locations on a map, you must climb a very tall building, then dive off into a conveniently placed haystack. Players also run and chase enemies, hide in bushes, fight (rough and tumble), and use an array of weapons. No wonder Ubisoft keeps publishing sequels! The gameplay is fun and timeless.

Some risky play seems better suited for physical education than math or science classes; however, students can play educational games that involve risk. One ingenious example is *Darfur Is Dying,* the free, flash-based game from 2006. The objective is to forage for water without getting caught. Players take on the role of a refugee. You can choose to be a child, who can run fast but carry very little, or an older character, who moves more slowly but can carry more. You can hide, or attempt to outrun the enemy militia. In May 2014, I spoke to Google's chief game designer, Noah Falstein, about *Darfur Is Dying* and how hiding and chasing deliver its social awareness message. He concurred with Peter Gray and other evolutionary psychologists. Falstein explained:

> Every so often people say, "Why do you make so many violent games? Why can't you just make happy games about people collecting flowers?" People do make games like that. With entertainment in general, there are often life-and-death situations presented. Deciding who to mate, who to date—it is also very Darwinian. We're hardwired to be fascinated by those things and not quite so fascinated by things like picking flowers. I think *Darfur Is Dying* is a brilliant example of a very simple game that puts you into life-and-death situations, which was more like real life. It helped me identify more with people in Darfur than any of the articles I read until that point.

In my world history class, the game's tension provided a compelling experience for my students. They are in the flow channel, focused on getting water without getting caught. The lesson concludes with an exit ticket asking, "Why do you think this game was so hard to play?" Here, students can make the connection about struggling as a refugee in Darfur, because the mechanics are perfectly aligned with the message. Falstein continued, "*Darfur Is Dying* is a great example of a very simple game that doesn't take a lot of graphics or depth of gameplay to give you the sense of how helpless you can feel being hunted down in barren landscapes when all you're trying to do is get water. It's very direct that way." His view is that games give humans an evolutionary advantage. "Play is a safe way for people to prepare for survival in the real world," he concluded.

4 Keys 2 Fun

Nicole Lazzaro, creator of the first motion-controlled iPhone game, *Tilt World*, proposed the "4 Keys to Fun" model. Her firm, XEODesign, used facial data to analyze player emotion (Lazzaro, 2009, p. 9). Teachers can learn from her findings. Researchers hooked up gamers to electrodes to measure eye movement and sweating during play (Lazzaro, 2009, pp. 10–11). This research helped game designers better pinpoint when fun occurs and how the flow channel functions. Game publisher Valve (*Portal, Half-Life 2*) also employs a full-time experimental psychologist to measure physiological responses to gameplay (Takahashi, 2013).

Using facial data to gauge emotional responses isn't new at all—or unique to gaming. Paul Ekman, a psychologist who pioneered the field, created a range of psychometrics to measure emotions (Lazzaro, 2009, pp. 9–10). This is another case of game design applying behavioral research ahead of other disciplines—such as education. Obviously, the goal of a teacher is not to elicit emotions from students... or is it? If boredom is an emotion, then perhaps some schools need to pay more attention to who is learning. You can't force students to love learning. They must associate the act with positive emotions.

XEODesign published a white paper detailing player emotions during play. As a game progresses through the flow channel, the "newbie" player is given more information and increasingly complex tasks until mastery level is reached. Succeeding at the "boss level"—where all in-game skills get applied to a challenge—gives the player the feeling of *fiero*, the Italian word that describes what one feels after overcoming a difficult challenge (Lazzaro, 2009, p. 23). *Fiero*—not the high score—is the ultimate intrinsic reward for accomplishment. It is triggered after defeating the Joker in *Batman: Arkham Asylum* or scoring a home run in baseball. Quest to Learn's 3-week-long boss levels are designed to give students feelings of accomplishment from a great challenge. *Fiero* is the "epic win." (Conversely, games that are too difficult to play may cause players to "rage quit.")

How to get students to experience *fiero* in school is complicated. In many video games it takes several persistent tries—and fails—to win the boss level and give the player glowing pride. The culture of never failing in school can stifle *fiero*, pulling the emotional satisfaction from accomplishment away from the learner. I have witnessed students feeling *fiero* after succeeding in the final mission of *SimCityEDU: Pollution Challenge!* At the end of the game, all of the city's systems required balancing. (This part of the original version of the game was deemed too difficult in the beta test my students tried. The difficulty was eventually scaled back for the game's final release.)

It can be argued that creating *fiero* requires student failure. Failing and quickly recovering fosters grit and persistence. Providing relief from frustration is a game mechanic. It works so well that mobile games have made millions of dollars from selling in-game cheats to enable players to succeed. According to XEODesign, some emotions triggered during play include:

- Fear—Threat of harm, object moving quickly to hit player, sudden fall or loss of support, possibility of pain.
- Surprise—Sudden change. Briefest of all emotions, does not feel good or bad, after interpreting event this emotion merges into fear, relief, etc.
- Disgust—Rejection as food or outside norms. The strongest triggers are body products such as feces, vomit, urine, mucus, saliva, and blood.
- Naches/Kvell (Yiddish)—Pleasure or pride at the accomplishment of a child or mentee.
- Fiero (Italian)—Personal triumph over adversity. The ultimate game emotion. Overcoming difficult obstacles, players raise their arms over their heads. They do not need to experience anger prior to success, but it does require effort.
- Schadenfreude (German)—Gloat over misfortune of a rival. Competitive players enjoy beating each other, especially a long-term rival. Boasts are made about player prowess and ranking.
- Wonder—Overwhelming improbability. Curious items amaze players at their unusualness, unlikelihood, and improbability without breaking out of realm of possibilities. (Lazzaro, 2004)

There are certain "keys" that can unlock the emotions in the above list. People feel different levels of fun during different types of play, depending on the action. Designers, therefore, can customize an experience best suited to unlock certain feelings. Game-based lesson plans should include fun descriptors and goals, similar to how Bloom's Taxonomy of Higher Order Thinking verbs are integrated into learning.

Of course, not all school is fun. Not all websites are fun, either. When I bank online, I don't expect the same experience as playing a video game. I certainly don't want a surprise at the ATM! Nonetheless, more of our lives are becoming gamified. XEODesign research proposed a four-domain model of emotional responses, some of which are appropriate to lesson planning. The 4 Keys 2 Fun are:

- Hard Fun—Challenge, strategy, and problem solving, frequently generates emotions and experiences of frustration, and fiero
- Easy Fun—Intrigue and curiosity generate emotions and experiences of wonder, awe, and mystery
- Altered States—The internal experiences in reaction to the visceral, behavior, cognitive, and social properties
- The People Factor—Players use games as mechanisms for social experiences. (Lazzaro, 2004)

Design is about the experience the person has interacting with something (a lesson plan, a game, an object, a device, etc.). "Serious games" are designed with fun as a starting point. Lesson plans should include some measure of fun, whether it is Hard Fun, Easy Fun, or the People Factor. (Altered States, such as the thrill of skydiving or rollercoasters, is clearly not attainable in a school setting, although it can be in the educational game *Rollercoaster Tycoon*.) Try teasing information to hook students (Easy Fun), then introducing an authentic, problem-based learning task (Hard Fun).

People Fun is clearly social and is a straightforward application of gamification in face-to-face or online learning environments. Lazzaro described People Fun mechanics as "high score boards, profile pages, avatars, gifting, emotes, and chat" (2009, pp. 42–46). Each can be applied to the context of school. High score boards, or leaderboards, can challenge students or teams to improve. Many learning management system applications, including Moodle, Blackboard, and Edmodo, have user profile pages to give students a space to express themselves. Avatars, or digital representations, can range from profiles in social media to animated characters, such as those on Voki, the talking avatar tool. Gifting in social constructs includes "+1" on Google+, liking Facebook posts, or clicking the heart icon on Instagram. Each is a game-like act of kindness. Emotes are common with both students and adults, who often pepper online and text messages with emoticons such as smiley faces. iPads in the classroom can add Emoji as an international language choice. Under settings, choose "Keyboard," then "International," and then click "Emoji."

Remember, if an experience isn't fun, then you have already lost your intended audience.

Conclusions and Takeaways

Game designers have theories and models about players just as teachers have about students. Bartle's Player Type Model is not just a fun discussion point with students, but also a way to gauge teacher-created projects and activities. Bartle warns not to expect his model to be one-size-fits-all; however, if it works, then great!

Many game designers have backgrounds in behavioral psychology. Teachers can integrate intrinsic rewards into lessons to keep students engaged. The flow channel should be the sweet spot for student learning. Another factor for engagement is fun, at least in hooking the student into learning. There are many modalities of fun, including *fiero*, relief from frustration, and social interactions. These theories all support cooperative group learning. In order to achieve some levels of fun, students need to fail and then quickly iterate. Research suggests that this process may build grit and tenacity, a 21st-century "soft" skill.

Lesson Plan Ideas

Bartle Test: I have used multiple intelligence quizzes as an icebreaker activity. How about trying the Bartle Test? This is an icebreaker; no standards apply—http://www.gamerdna.com/quizzes/bartle-test-of-gamer-psychology

Darfur Is Dying: Role-playing, running, and hiding are "fun" mechanics in this very serious game. Ask: Why do you think this game is so hard to play? Students can make the connections about struggling as a refugee in Darfur because the mechanics are perfectly aligned with the message. This can lead in to a discussion of problems in modern African nations. Extending this globally, have students list current problems and try to create difficult mechanics that illustrate the message. Standards met are primarily for social studies—http://www.darfurisdying.com

Games

Jenova Chen's *flOw*, playable for free on a computer browser—http://interactive.usc.edu/projects/cloud/flowing

QWOP, a nearly impossible track and field game—http://www.foddy.net/Athletics.html

Stride and Prejudice is an "endless runner" game set in—and on—text from Jane Austen's classic novel. Risky play without the risk!—https://itunes.apple.com/us/app/stride-prejudice/id727047115?ls=1&mt=8

Tilt World, the first motion-controlled iPhone game, from XEOPlay—http://www.tiltworld.com

Resources

Richard Bartle's *Hearts, Clubs, Diamonds, Spades: Players Who Suit MUDs* (1996)—http://www.mud.co.uk/richard/hcds.htm

Richard Bartle on *Player Type Theory: Uses & Abuses*—http://www.youtube.com/watch?v=ZIzLbE-93nc

4 Keys 2 Fun, a high quality, full-color image; helpful when lesson planning—http://xeodesign.com/assets/images/4k2f.jpg

Flow, the Secret to Happiness, Mihaly Csikszentmihalyi's TED Talk—http://www.ted.com/talks/mihaly_csikszentmihalyi_on_flow

The Future of Work Is Play, Nicole Lazzaro's TEDx Talk—http://www.youtube.com/watch?v=X_3KyV31iqg

The New Era of Positive Psychology, Martin Seligman's TED Talk—http://www.ted.com/talks/martin_seligman_on_the_state_of_psychology

B.F. Skinner discussing his "Teaching Machine"—http://youtu.be/jTH3ob1IRFo

A *Theory of Fun*, by Raph Koster—http://www.theoryoffun.com

XEODesign's research on games and emotions—http://xeodesign.com/whyweplaygames.html

· 4 ·

ITERATIVE DESIGN

Lesson plans evolve over the years. I know mine have! They are constantly revised and iterated. I tweak what worked and what didn't, note how long activities actually took, and account for what was engaging for students to do. (If you are a pre-service teacher, prepare for students to derail your best intentions!) That process—trial, reflection, and revision—is design thinking. Your lesson plans are your design document.

Many learning institutions have learning designers on staff. The Institute of Play, which founded the Quest to Learn school, defined design thinking as a "set of skills, competencies or dispositions relating to the highly iterative collaborative process designers employ when conceiving, planning and producing an object or system" (Institute of Play, 2014). One of James Gee's Learning Principles from games pertains specifically to design. He wrote that games help people to "appreciate design and design principles" (Gee, 2007, p. 221). A game is a designed object to be explored and tested. When I interviewed Gee, in April 2014, I asked him to explain the concept further. He said:

> What we've come to understand is that game designers are designing experiences that kids can have that can lead to learning. But so are teachers. I see teaching as a design act. You're designing good interactivity for learning. [Teachers are] doing something

very similar to game designer. It doesn't mean you have to design a game. Good teachers have always been trying to design good experiences.

Apps and games constantly have updates. The real world isn't a "one-off" project, like a standardized test. Is it fair to judge a student by a score they got on a single assessment designed by someone else? Playtesting and iterating gives designers an opportunity to tweak based on feedback. Shouldn't students be afforded the same, just like in the real world? I asked Gee to elaborate on how design thinking pertains to teaching. He stated:

> Teaching is a design process—if you let them [teachers] be professional. What we've done is deprofessionalize them by writing a script for them, by giving them a test booklet or a game or orders of what to do. Good teachers are designers of on-the-spot learning. Reflect on it, iterate, like game designers. Good teachers are also doing alpha testing and beta testing with their students. They're asking their students: Did that work? What worked? What didn't?

Educational psychology professor Val Shute conducted research about design thinking as a skill set. Shute has also co-published articles on persistence, which is learning from failure. One of her studies, co-published with Rim Razzouk, stated that design thinking involves "an in-depth cognitive processes—which may help our students build their critical thinking skills (e.g., reasoning and analysis)—it also involves personality and dispositional traits such as persistence and creativity" (Razzouk & Shute, 2012, p. 345). I interviewed Shute in February 2014 about the importance of teaching design thinking as a 21st-century competency. She told me, "Engineers are iterative. Architects, too. Failure is a good thing; start anew and iterate to an optimal design. Schools teach that failure is negative. Peer review and teacher feedback is key in iterative process." In other words, the design process can build a student's tenacity and perseverance. It is a competency that can give today's students an upper hand in our global economy.

Games are designed and tested, just like any other product. Perhaps no other medium applies behavioral psychology to the user experience better than game design. In this chapter, several learning game designers share tips about creating meaningful experiences. As part of the feedback loop of learning, students become participatory co-designers. I share reflections from Erin Hoffman and Shula Ehrlich, as well as James Gee. I also include my own experiences integrating iterative design into my middle school social studies classroom.

Paper Prototyping

Tracy Fullerton, director of the University of Southern California's Game Innovation Lab, wrote the textbook *Game Design Workshop,* now in its 3rd edition. Paper prototyping and iterative design is something that The Game Innovation Lab has done for over a decade. Many academic institutions use the methodology to create innovative games. In March 2014 I asked Fullerton how teachers could apply techniques such as paper prototyping and iterative design in the classroom. She pointed out how similar the process was to constructivism, or learning from doing. She said, "It's a version of constructivist education, more focused on systems thinking than just making."

Digital games are sometimes paper prototyped as collectible trading card games. *Pokémon, Magic: The Gathering,* and *Yu-Gi-Oh!* are examples of this. In 2013 Barry Joseph, at the Museum of Natural History in New York City, co-designed dinosaur trading cards with Nick Fortugno. The deck is called *Pterosaurs: The Card Game.* There is also a category of trading card game apps on iTunes. One example of a digital card game is *Calculords,* which features several decks to collect. The strategy game depends on the player's arithmetic skills.

GlassLab's Erin Hoffman explained the design process in creating its first tablet game, *Mars Generation One: Argubot Academy* (2014). We initially spoke about the app in January 2014. It went from trading cards to interactive fiction (covered later in this chapter) to digital. The mechanics of play were worked out first using paper before any money was spent on graphical renderings. The mechanic of argumentation was modeled on *Pokémon* card duels. "For the argument game [*Mars Generation One*], we did a paper prototype," she explained. "We got cards, played *Pokémon* to get the feel for what would work, the phases of battle. We paper prototyped the map exploration."

Because paper-based games seem readily easy to make and modify, I wanted to learn more about the process. In August 2013 I had the opportunity to playtest a nondigital game called *Socratic Smackdown.* It is an "energetic discussion-based humanities game" called *Socratic Smackdown* (Institute of Play, 2014). Teams of four or six students engage in a gamified Socratic discussion. Textual evidence must be made to support claims. The game builds argumentative thinking skills—a Common Core State Standard for English language arts. Mission Lab at the Quest to Learn school designed the game in collaboration with teacher Rebecca Grodner. She even used it for her school's "boss level" (end of trimester challenge) as a method for discussing dystopian novels in small reading groups. The rules were changed, with limits restricting what students could do or say. The remix was dubbed *Socratic Crackdown*, and hosted by Grodner dressed as the *Hunger Games*'s Effie Trinket. I was curious about how Mission Lab designed game-like learning experiences. Katie Salen, founder of the Institute of Play and Quest to Learn, explained the process to me. She said:

> It starts with the learning outcomes, the kinds of actions of "doing." If you see a kid doing something, you say, "Ah! They get this. They understand this concept." Start there. Ask what are the types of situations or actions I could get a kid to do that? Ask what would provide a practice space for ways of doing, ways of thinking. *Socratic Smackdown* came out of that early vision. When we see kids making arguments and debating, we ask what situations can they be put in to arrive at that? That's how you make games and map out the experiences.

I spoke at length with Mission Lab's Shula Ehrlich, co-designer of *Socratic Smackdown*. We spoke in January 2014. Ehrlich first heard about Quest to Learn and Institute of Play while taking classes at Parsons the New School for Design in New York City (Katie Salen taught at Parsons prior to her current position at DePaul University in Chicago). She saw the power of games in engaging students and she wanted to be part of that initiative. After 4 years at the Institute, she became a lead designer. A lot of what she designs is close to project-based learning; some of the designs are more game-like than others.

Quest to Learn uses about 95% paper-based games, although they are moving more towards digital. They do have a *MinecraftEdu* server, and teach digital game design and systems thinking with *Gamestar Mechanic*. Mission Lab is the Institute of Play's design studio situated within its Quest to Learn school. The team is comprised of game and learning designers. They give full-time support to the game-like curriculum. Mission Lab works collaboratively with teachers; each teacher is paired with one learning designer and one game designer. They meet once or twice a week to develop a curriculum and to develop games to be used in the classroom. Most of the original games are nondigital, and often involve cards, dice and/or game boards. Ehrlich told me that they "really like paper-based because teachers and students can modify the games; digital is a black box to most people." Teachers with little to no background knowledge of game design can modify or adapt a nondigital game more easily than a video game. Paper-based games have a low barrier to use, allowing for iteration from year to year.

Mission Lab games offer students different possible scenarios. Ehrlich described the process:

> We call it exploding the game. Stretching out the capacity of the game as a teaching tool. I think it's more powerful than playing a game once. The important thing is what surrounds a game. It's not one discrete thing you play and that's it. A game is situated in a larger learning trajectory. There are lessons before, related activities, and a period of rolling out pieces of the game.

Ehrlich gave me an example of "exploding a game." She described the 7th-grade math game *Absolute Blast*. It is a card game about rockets that teaches the concept of absolute value. In the game, every player has three rockets and needs the highest absolute value to shoot into space. It teaches adding, subtracting, multiplying, and dividing integers, as well as negative and positive numbers. Ehrlich explained:

> To explode it, the teacher rolls out a simplified version: just one rocket instead of three. You only play the cards on your own board, not others. This gets students acclimated to the rules, the basic structure of the gameplay, and math concepts. Then there is more teaching and related activities, and then back to the game, which becomes more complicated. After that the kids reflect until, finally, the full version.

Once a game is exploded, Quest teachers—like other educators—assess student learning. The teacher gives the class a piece of paper with a picture of a frozen game state and asks, "What would you do in this scenario? What would each player do in this scenario? Explain your reasoning." Here the teacher is asking the student to reflect on game strategy as well as underlying skills. Both are higher-order challenges; the game-related question puts the learning in an authentic context. Ehrlich summed it up concisely: "We think of exploding the game as before gameplay, during gameplay, and after gameplay."

After researching paper prototyping, I was inspired to create a student center. After all, student-created games meet many Common Core State Standards—plus, it is a fun activity! I purchased inexpensive plastic drawers and filled them with different game artifacts. The station currently contains several inexpensive items:

- Dry erase spinners
- Dry erase whiteboards
- Plastic poker chips (for game tokens—not gambling)
- Novelty eraser caps (useful as game pieces)

- Different sizes of blank index cards
- Color folders, to be used as game boards
- Hourglasses
- Toy money
- Rulers
- Several sets of dice—and not just 6-sided

Prototyping with Interactive Fiction

Besides paper prototyping—or sometimes, following it—game designers create text-based virtual environments. They serve as kind of a rough draft prior to building immersive, graphic-based virtual worlds. When I initially interviewed Erin Hoffman about creating *SimCityEDU*, I discovered that she had a deep connection to text adventures, also known as interactive fiction. Hoffman, a published fantasy writer, started her career building the text-based, multiplayer *DragonRealms* in 1999. "Interactive fiction is a pet thing of mine," she said. "I've got text-based gaming really deep in my brain." Delivering reading and writing lessons with interactive fiction is an engaging alternative to traditional methods. This section reviews authoring tools that you can use to draw students into content areas.

When Hoffman led her team at GlassLab in prototyping *Mars Generation One: Argubot Academy*, her team playtested a text-based version of the experience (it was code named *Hiro*; the design process is further detailed in Chapter 10). During playtesting, the focus group displayed an unexpectedly high degree of enthusiasm and engagement with the text world. Hoffman recalled:

> What really shocked me was, when we tried this game with about 20 kids in a library, they loved the text-based prototype. It was astonishing. It was so sparse and simple, but the kids had never seen a text-based game before. They actually said, "I never played a game like this; it's completely new." A text-based game immediately causes close reading. I've heard from English language arts teachers that they struggled to get kids to close read. Within minutes of the prototype, their spelling improved—it had to in order to enter in commands. I think there's a lot there.

Interactive fiction situates reading in an authentic learning context; the story becomes the mechanic. Like fan fiction, there is a low barrier to entry. The participatory culture provides feedback and celebrates exemplary work. There is also an active online community of practice, with discussion forums about game design and story ideas. There is also an annual writing competition. Hoffman continued to explain the student playtesters' reactions to interactive fiction. When she introduced the game, she discovered that she had to create a tutorial for the prototype. She said, "The mainstream interactive fiction community presupposes this mass of knowledge, that you've played games all the way back to Zork [a very popular game from the 1990s]. They [the student playtesters] didn't know you had to type 'north' to go north. Once they were taught it, they found it engaging. The spatial stuff, like mapping and cardinal relationships, was challenging."

As adults, it's easy to forget that children didn't share the same life experiences and changes in gamer culture. In the 1990s, wide proliferation of Internet-connected computers brought large numbers of players together in multi-user dungeons (MUDs). This style of game has declined in popularity with the advent of graphic-based virtual environments. Some, such as the massively popular *World of Warcraft,* can have thousands of participants interacting together. Multi-user dungeons have their roots in the paper-based classic *Dungeons & Dragons.* Gary Gygax, a legend in geek lore, created the game in the 1970s. Playing it required a Dungeon Master to run the game by describing the world. The player's character's fate depended on the roll of multisided dice. *Dungeons & Dragons's* core mechanics, Dungeon Master-led adventures and random die rolls, were readily adaptable to become text-based computer games. The first title was Infocom's *Adventure* (1975). Other text-based games followed, including *Zork* (1980) and *Ultima* (1981). Douglas Adams, author of *The Hitchhiker's Guide to the Galaxy* (1984), created a text-based adaptation of his own book. It is still playable online (it is linked at the end of this chapter). Text is still a part of many modern video games. Telltale's *The Walking Dead* (2013) relies on a threaded, multiple-choice, decision-making mechanic to advance in the story.

The interactive fiction player is not reading from the first-person point of view; rather, the reader *is* the protagonist, making choices that have consequences. Furthermore, in a role-playing game, the player makes decisions based on the perspective of someone else. Interactive fiction challenges the writer to apply logic. The genre of interactive fiction is sometimes abbreviated as "IF," which has a double meaning: interactive fiction, and the logic command "if-then." Interactive fiction depends on verb-noun statements from players (e.g., "Open door."). Typically, there is a "command prompt" to type responses. For example:

You can see an apple and a plant here.
>Take apple.
Taken.
>Eat apple.
You eat the crunchy apple.

Interactive fiction applies systems thinking, as the interconnected story unwinds. Storymapping can be employed to study the logic. An effective idea is to have the student draw a physical map of a story's location while reading. The text-heavy narrative is a natural fit to teach writing. This approach is an example of Gee's Text Principle, where texts are not simply read, but "understood in terms of embodied experiences" (2007, p. 106).

Richard Bartle's Player Type Model (described in Chapter 3) was specifically intended for multiplayer games in this genre. In Bartle's game design course he puts 30 students together in one room and has them play a text adventure together. His students are doing something else besides play; they are learning how to spell, create commands, read, and visualize locations, all things they wouldn't ordinarily do. They are thinking and they are learning. Bartle noted, "It's not something people play every week, but it's a tool in your toolbox."

Authoring Tools

Threaded stories can be easily created using Microsoft's Word or PowerPoint, as well as Apple's Pages or Keynote. At the bottom of each page or slide, insert multiple-choice questions that hyperlink to jump to other pages (or slides) in the story/presentation. There are also many websites, including AuthorStream, Slideshare, and FlipSnack, that host uploads of presentations (sometimes the document needs to be saved as a PDF, depending on the web application).

There are several options for building interactive fiction online. iStory is a web and mobile application for writing and sharing threaded stories. The storylines are closed-ended, similar to multiple-choice tests. It has a lot in common with the *Choose Your Own Adventure* book series, in which the reader's choices continued at specified page numbers later in the book. Each choice can continue the story or end it. The authoring tool in iStory is called StoryForge. Users can pick from the following templates: Choose Your Own Adventure, Text Adventure Game, Short Story, Poetry, or Other. After adding a text narrative, click "Choices" and choose which page opens next.

When complete, click "Play" and submit for review. Twine is a similar tool to use to tell nonlinear stories. It is available as a free download and features a vibrant community, as well as a story database. Twine is free, open source, and an excellent tool to teach reading and writing.

Upon completion of writing interactive fiction, class periods can be spent playtesting peer games. Reflection, feedback, and a practical application of systems thinking all come together in creating a text-based world. All disciplines can participate, too. A math puzzle or a student-created word problem could be used as an obstacle. A student can use interactive fiction to map out famous locations, too. The adventure can take place in a novel the class is reading or in a historical time period.

More advanced users may opt for Text Adventures, a U.K.-based authoring tool. The website is free and anyone can legally download and modify it, if desired. Pictures, embedded video, and sounds can be added to make it more robust. Players can explore rooms, collect artifacts (think: Bartle's Explorer Player Type), and interact with nonplayable characters (NPCs). Typing in commands, such as "NW" for "northwest," moves the player around the game world. A downloadable version is available for schools with limited Internet connectivity.

Hoffman used Inform7, a free, downloadable authoring tool, to proto-type *Mars Generation One*. Inform7 has an "all natural language interface" that includes visual story maps. Hoffman told me that the resulting code "was like reading a strange book—but it is readable!" There are several featured research reports and white papers posted on its home page to champion the efficacy of interactive fiction as a new media skill.

Chronicles of the Time Society: Independence

Interviewing Hoffman led to a side project venture for us. We decided we could take my students back in time to the signing of the Declaration of Independence. We both saw the clear educational connection to reading, writing, typing, spelling, and geography. Hoffman initially set up a wiki for us to work asynchronously (she lives in California; I am in New Jersey). We also spoke via Skype every Thursday afternoon. Our interactive fiction game was called *Chronicles of the Time Society: Independence*. Below is our text adven-ture's original narrative frame:

> You are a member of the elite Time Society, a secret international organization that protects the timestream of the universe. In your time it is 2253, but you have been given a mission

to travel back to the summer of 1776 and ensure that the Declaration of Independence is successfully signed. One of the signers has fallen ill, and you must take his place in history. Good luck, Inspector!

There were several considerations we discussed. For example, when in the year would I be teaching about the Declaration of Independence? How long would the whole experience be? It could run for multiple days or a single class. Our initial conversations pertained to the major insights I wanted students to come away with, and possibly any key figures I'd want them to encounter. Another issue was the setback penalties for losing the game, also known as "fail states." An example in a board game is falling down the chute in *Chutes and Ladders.* Feedback from making wrong choices can reinforce what the players need to do the next time they play. In an email to me, Hoffman explained the complications of building a threaded history game. She even bounced ideas off of Michael John, her colleague at GlassLab. Hoffman wrote:

> There are tons and tons of dependencies that all had to come together in order to make the Revolution happen. So we [Michael John and Hoffman] netted on this expression of "history is fragile," which can be experienced through game mechanics. But what that would mean is designing lots of different failure states and then messaging what happened as a result of that failure state. Then in each of these cases, we would actually cause them to lose the game and get bounced back to the Time Society (where they could try again). There, they'd experience the alternate history that happened as a result of this not happening. It's a way in which narrative could be especially powerful because we could convey in just a couple of paragraphs a whole alternate world that emphasizes how rare our particular history is.

Engaging with a text-based game can easily seem more like work than play. Therefore, *Chronicles of the Time Society: Independence* was playtested with my students. Playtesting allowed Hoffman and me to not to lose sight of the conceptual takeaway. For example, we noticed students spending a considerable amount of time exploring colonial Boston. The learning objective was to convey the frustration and helplessness colonists felt from being taxed by King George, not a geography lesson. My students concluded each round of play by anonymously answering questions on a Google Form. Below is the text of the survey used to assess the early iterations of the game:

> *Thank you so much for helping us playtest this game! Your comments will be extremely helpful in making the game better. It's still very early, so we know there are a lot of things we can improve. Please don't hold back in your criticism!*

- *What grade are you in?*
- *Who do you think this game is for?*
- *What age group? 5th, 6th, 7th, 8th grade? Other?*
- *If you kept playing, what do you think would happen next?*
- *How would you describe this game to a friend?*
- *How would you describe this game to a teacher?*
- *If your teacher considered playing this game in class, how would you describe it?*
- *What did you want to do that you couldn't do?*
- *What do you think you learned?*
- *What do you think video games could teach in school?*
- *What kinds of games do you play in school?*
- *If you played another level, what level would be most exciting to you: Independence Hall (Philadelphia, where the Declaration was signed), George Washington at Mount Vernon, or John Adams in Boston?*

In the end, we decided to create separate missions. In the Time Society head-quarters, players choose canisters. The first world, described in this section, was the "Chase Canister." A future economic mission is planned. It is intended to give students the feeling of frustration from being taxed without having government representation. In June 2014 Hoffman submitted the game to IndieCade, a festival for independently published games.

The next section details how to bring students into the design process. I would recommend adding playtest questions such as the ones above, in addition to formative assessments such as exit tickets. This creates a feedback loop of "what works" and brings students further into the learning conversation.

Playtesting

I have found that my students take an increased ownership in an activity if they are testing it out. They also are more active, looking for bugs and glitches while problem solving within the game's system. Regardless of a project's success, student interest piqued. They knew that their feedback, gathered by online surveys, would have a real effect on the game's final outcome. Erin Hoffman explained, "Kids feel like they become collaborators because they know it [playtesting] is important. They get more highly engaged in the learning if they're invested."

Every developer I interviewed detailed the many rounds of playtesting their games underwent, as well as the sorts of questions to ask. (Other products are tested, too. Websites are usertested. Consumer goods are tested with focus groups. Movies are screentested.) The Institute of Play published a free, downloadable *Q Design Packs for Games and Learning Design* that includes playtesting forms for the classroom. Students reflect on whether the game was fun and challenging, and remark on the clarity of the rules (Institute of Play, 2014).

Playtests should focus not on the game, but on the game experience (Schell, 2008). A game is a system that can have unintended consequences. Perhaps a section of a game is too easy or difficult. Directions may be convoluted and confusing. Even worse, the student may learn something from a game that has nothing to do with the learning objective. For example, playing *Bingo* with students may review vocabulary, but it is disconnected and not authentic (for vocabulary building, I prefer crossword puzzles).

When my students playtested *SimCityEDU* and *Chronicles of the Time Society: Independence*, it was difficult to watch them get confused during play and not help. If I did assist, I would ruin the chance of the game working as a stand-alone product. Hoffman told me that she has witnessed newer game designers get so wrapped up in their games that they fail to see how someone couldn't play them in a certain way, the "right way." It is optimal for testers to have no product knowledge. It can be difficult to observe a child struggling to understand a function and resist intervening. The designer must remember that once published, the user will be on his or her own playing the game. It must be as intuitive and natural as possible, especially right away. There is a seconds-long window that exists between trying something and quitting. "I've noticed that there is a tendency to draw too many conclusions on the basis of a single playtest, and also to overweight confusion in playtesting," Hoffman explained. "You learn eventually what to pay attention to. It's an intuitive skill you build up over time. You have to ask questions like: 'What did you think just happened? What did you expect to happen? How is this making you feel? What does this remind you of?' Those kinds of questions can be more effective than: 'Is this confusing? Does this make sense?'"

Jesse Schell wrote that game mechanic and design questions should be avoided in favor of assessing the overall experience, such as what made the game fun (2008, p. 401). Other questions include: If the game has physical pieces to manipulate, are they age-appropriate? Who should be playing this game? There was a case in my class when students were playing an online social studies simulation game and soon enough, it was discovered that the game had an interactive that could be randomly clicked until the correct answer was revealed. The core mechanic should have been a puzzle, but became an exercise in trial and error. This impasse became a teachable moment as students critiqued the game.

Mobile learning apps have unique playtesting challenges compared to nondigital classroom games. In January 2014 I spoke to Rex Ishibashi, CEO of Originator, developer of preschool titles *Endless Reader* and *Mr. Potato Head Create & Play*. The company tests informally about twice a week, then more formally about every three weeks. Because the parent is with the child during play—perhaps helping the child—Originator apps actually serve dual customers. Therefore, it tests children with parents present. Ishibashi explained, "If the music is delightful for the child but annoying and grating to the adult, we have to change it." Originator must be able to present an experience that is fun for a preschooler and doesn't make the parent feel guilty about using it to entertain the child. A child most likely would not ask for a learning app unless it was fun.

Teachers—and students—at Quest to Learn are trained in game design. It all starts when a new game is prototyped. Mission Lab designers meet with teachers once or twice a week (depending on the teacher's level of experience) and plan ahead the upcoming curriculum with game-like activities. Teachers begin by identifying the skills and content that students struggle with. In that initial meeting, the curriculum committee brainstorms a learning goal. The game designer next reviews mechanics to meet that goal. Then he or she creates, or ideates, game ideas. Designers then paper prototype and playtest together, as a team. At this stage, the game may be still pretty rough. The designer and the teacher will meet again for more feedback. Shula Ehrlich shared with me some of Mission Lab's playtest questions: "Was it fun? Was it getting at the learning goals? Did it feel right? Was anything off?" The game designer then takes the feedback and works on a prototype. Following that revision, it is played again, this time with the curriculum team. Finally, they test with four students from the teacher's class.

Ehrlich explained the value of student focus groups. New students, in 6th grade, start by taking a class called "Sports for the Mind." It is a game design class that integrates digital arts and photography. "Students give amazing feedback because they've been playing, designing, and modding [modifying] games for a long time," she said. Students complete playtest reflection forms that ask: "What did you think of the game? How would you change it? What is clear? What doesn't work?" From there, designers almost always change things. Success is measured by asking what the teacher thought, as well as if students were having fun and grasping the concepts, skills, and content.

Project-based learning activities may not always turn out to be completely student-centered. Playtesting can turn learning from a top-down, teacher-led model into a true conversational act. My students know I will ask for feedback about what was clear, how fun the experience was, or where they would make changes. It is essential to have a complete feedback loop for the co-design relationship to function.

Students as Co-Designers

As I put together notes for this book, I started to reminisce about board games from my youth. My first inclination was to create paper-based games to teach my students about history. Sure, playing games is engaging and student-centered, but what about having the learners design, playtest, and iterate their own creations?

I designed a game-based learning unit called *Revolutionary War Games,* about America's independence. The unit was taught during the spring of 2014. In it I tried to apply only "fun" game mechanics, such as role-play, guessing, and arguing. The narrative shell put the student in the role of a game designer trying to win the exclusive rights to create content for an Independence Day festival. I set up four stations—or "quests"—around the classroom and divided the class into equal groups.

The first three quests were fairly straightforward to complete. One station used *Minecraft: Pocket Edition* on iPad. The task was to build a Revolutionary War fort, take a screenshot, and export it to the Pages word processing app. The final step was to create a paragraph-long description. Some students were experienced in *Minecraft,* while others had been purposely avoiding it (games, like clothes, fall in and out of fashion). More proficient players helped out newer users. The second station was a remix of *HedBanz.* The game, which is sold in most toy stores, comes with plastic headbands that affix illustrated cards. Sitting in a circle, players ask questions and guess who or what is depicted on the cards on their own heads. Students researched war heroes collaboratively, drew pictures on blank index cards, and played the remix as a group. The third quest, the badge design station, took the least amount of time to complete. Using a simple website, students created achievement awards for Revolutionary War figures, as if they were designing a video game. Captions had to integrate the cause-and-effect loops required to win the badge. Students were quite creative in their badge design. One soldier was awarded the "#braveman" badge for his heroism on the battlefield. The badge art depicted *The Wizard of Oz*'s Cowardly Lion—after he was awarded his regalia!

The longest and most involved station to complete was the board game maker station. I advised students to split into two groups at that station. They could modify the directions and the rubric, which simply scored student-created artifacts (e.g., game board, chance cards). A game board wasn't necessary if they decided to remix a card-based game. The point was to encourage creative play through freedom. Students were directed to brainstorm their favorite mechanics in games they like. Once they created their list, they then parsed the content. Upon completion, they playtested the other group's game and completed the playtest form (from the Institute of Play's *Q Games & Learning Design Pack*). Finally, students iterated their design before turning it in.

While the project looked good on paper, the playtest questions I asked exposed many flaws. Each station had its own issues. First was timing: Badges took about 2 days to finish, while the board game took about 5. The *HedBanz* remix station's research took up more class time than I anticipated. A flipped learning approach—with research being done from home—may have worked better. Also, *Minecraft* took some students longer to learn than others. I could have "seeded" environments to create the same starting landscape (*Minecraft* randomly generates how worlds look, which can take time to customize, depending on the fort). There was a behavioral issue, too. One student "joined" other virtual worlds and set buildings on fire. I had to enforce a "no griefing" rule, gamer-speak for shaming losers; it's the digital version of bad sportsmanship.

In April 2014 I explained the activity to James Gee. I was worried the bumps in the road would affect student learning (almost all students tested well and enjoyed the activities). I was relieved to hear him agree with my game-inspired—rather than game-based—approach. "You're doing it right because you're putting the things into a larger system of multiple activities and multiple modalities and then it becomes a learning system," Gee remarked. "You're not just putting a digital game in there." He was referencing his Multimodal Principle, in which "meaning and knowledge are built up through various modalities (images, texts, symbols, interactions, abstract design, sound, etc.)—not just words (Gee, 2007, p. 224). Teaching with games requires an enormous amount of teacher-led reflection to facilitate students in making connections. Gee elaborated why students should be in the learning conversation. He said:

> You should be testing with your students. You're incorporating them as consumers or players and you're treating your audience with respect. Students increase their ownership, just like how people beg to be beta testers in new games. They get ownership, which means they are co-designing with you. Game designers need alpha and beta

testers. Game designers, unlike teachers, aren't isolated and alone. They design and iterate together all the time. They do postmortems. They have conferences where they compare designs. Imagine a game developer conference where teachers are treated as designers. We're never going to get there until society treats teachers more as professionals, with more respect.

After the *Revolutionary War Games* project concluded, I gathered student feedback to ascertain what students found was fun to do. Should stations be merged or eliminated in the next iteration? What I didn't do was expect my students to pass from section to section seamlessly. By showing students that each activity is a work in progress and that feedback matters, I created a culture of co-design. Teaching is a design science, and learning is a conversation.

Postmortems

Playtesting, paper prototyping, and postmortems can enable students to understand the interconnected relationships of parts of a system. Game-based learning can be used to give students a deeper understanding of content. Putting a student in front of an educational video game does not accomplish this. True learning with games involves a thorough analysis of how games teach (Gee, 2007). This can include how to make games, which puts design and systems thinking into practice.

A postmortem occurs after a creative project concludes. It is common with designers and in film. Literally meaning "after death," a postmortem gives creators a chance to discuss what worked and where they came up short. Pixar co-founder and president Edwin Catmull shared the company's design process in *Creativity, Inc.* (2014). Design and technology intersect at Pixar, where computer-animated favorites such as *Toy Story* and *Finding Nemo* come to life (Steve Jobs was the CEO of both Pixar and Apple, both companies known for design). Upon completion of each project the team conducts a postmortem. Catmull and co-author Wallace listed five reasons why this is fundamental to the creative process:

1. Consolidate what's been learned
2. Teach others who weren't there
3. Don't let resentments fester
4. Use the schedule to force reflection
5. Pay it forward. (2014, pp. 216–217)

Similarly, designer Shula Ehrlich described the postreflection process at Quest to Learn, where they judge a game's success based on its purpose. Games at Quest have different purposes: to introduce concepts, to offer spaces for practice, and to assess learning. This is different from many schools where games are used primarily for test reviews. Ehrlich will observe a class, distribute playtest reflection forms, and then analyze the data from pre- and post-test assessments. An important postmortem question is, How easy was the game to roll out? If it takes 45 minutes to explain, it's too complex. Students must be able to grasp the game quickly. Time can't be wasted reviewing complicated rules. For Ehrlich, "The big three questions are: How fun was it? Did it reach the learning goals? Was it easy to roll out in the classroom?"

Postmortems go beyond teacher reflection. Because design is a conversation—and the students are among the co-designers—it is only appropriate to end projects with one. After I finished the *Revolutionary War Games* project, I noticed that one station took less time to complete than the others. Should I eliminate it next year, or consolidate it? Does easier work give students relief from frustration in a project? My anecdotal evidence is nowhere as strong as what I learn from asking my student beta testers.

Idea Forums for Teachers

When I attended the Games for Change Festival, I saw a true idea forum—it is not a conference one attends to simply check off one's list of required professional development hours. There were inspirational talks, but there were also brainstorming sessions and panel discussion. Developers and academics exchanged business cards and everyone seemed to want to advance the art of game design.

There are an increasing number of alternatives to traditional teacher conferences. One is Edcamp, where there are no prearranged speakers or sessions. Teachers simply get together and share ideas. According to its website, its "(un)conferences" are participatory and "strive to bring teachers together to talk about the things that matter most to them: their interests, passions, and questions" (The Edcamp Foundation, 2014). Edcamps are free and promote an exchange of ideas.

Ideas are exchanged on social media, too. One collaborative space of note is EdTechBridge. I first heard about this initiative after I visited with BrainPOP. One of BrainPOP's researchers, Katya Hott, teamed up in the venture with Steve Isaacs, a video game design teacher. Isaacs, who lives near me, met with me in July 2014 to explain more. He said, "The purpose is to bridge the cultural divide between educators, developers and entrepreneurs." The partnership began at SWSXedu (South by Southwest Education, the annual conference in Austin, Texas). Hott was running a problem-solving session in which the participants worked together to find a solution. The problem in this case was the lack of a common language between developers and educators. The result was a weekly Twitter chat (search: #edtechbridge) that takes place every Wednesday evening. The Twitter community has enabled relationships to begin and partnerships to evolve. Teachers can also connect with a website, edtechbridge.blogspot.com, and its Google+ community. Isaacs told me that they want to bring more stakeholders into the fold. At the GLS Conference, Cameron White, associate director of co.lab, suggested to Isaacs that researchers should be added to EdTechBridge (more on co.lab in Chapter 13). The future may open up to give students a voice, too.

Conclusions and Takeaways

Video games are paper prototyped or built into text-based worlds prior to final release. Teachers should look to use early versions of games, or make their own. Paper games are easier to modify. Students should design games, too. Teaching one another and peer reviewing becomes more engaging when someone is playing your designed object. Plus, it is a Common Core State Standard and a 21st-century skill—of course, you only get one shot to take a standardized test!

Learning is an iterative process. Students should be your co-designers, completing the feedback loop of learning. Student interest may be piqued further knowing that a lesson, game, or project is being playtested and that their opinions count. Be sure to use playtest forms with students and have them beta test each other's projects. It is okay to ask students if a lesson felt more like work than play. You may be surprised with some of the responses. The student is the target player/learner; effective student-centered learning should be a conversation. Have a postmortem with students—not just other staff members.

Lesson Plan Ideas

Absolute Blast: Mission Lab's absolute-value math game for grades 6 through 8. Common Core State Standards for mathematics apply—http://www.instituteofplay.org/work/projects/print-play-games-2/absolute-blast

Board Game Challenge: Small groups create or remix board games. Students should playtest with another group, and then iterate (redo) to make it better (more fun, more interesting, more fair). Instruct the class to first brainstorm the mechanics of their favorite games (e.g., bluffing, arguing, guessing). Ask: Which match up with the topic of your game? Next, the students design the game board or cards and write simple directions that make it perfectly clear how to play. Give students the freedom to mod the rubric or directions. For example, a card-based game doesn't require a board. After projects are graded, each team has a postmortem and completes a feedback handout. Standards vary depending on the content delivered.

Community Talks: Quest to Learn hosted a TEDx Talk event—so can your students! The Institute of Play's Mission Pack, created for wellness education, can fit other curriculum standards—http://www.instituteofplay.org/work/projects/mission-pack-tedx-questschool. Clips of Quest to Learn presentations serve as effective exemplars—http://www.ted.com/tedx/events/7172. Or try Ignite talks, which are 5 minutes in length and restricted to 20 PowerPoint slides—http://igniteshow.com. Standards met include Common Core State Standards for English language arts.

Phylo: The biodiversity trading card game. The website includes free printable rules and cards. Standards met include Next Generation Science Standards—http://phylogame.org

Socratic Smackdown: Mission Lab's nondigital game to teach argumentation. I play this game about every other week. Have students study competitively the night before play to level up the challenge. Standards met include Common Core State Standards for English language arts, which are listed in the printable version of the game—http://www.instituteofplay.org/work/projects/print-play-games-2/socratic-smackdown

Twine in the Classroom: Students take a short story or historical event and write a threaded story. This lesson will get students deeply involved with the content. Twine is a free, downloadable platform to tell "nonlinear" stories. The learning curve is simpler than with other interactive fiction tools. The result resembles a *Choose Your Own Adventure* book. As part of the iterative design process, students should work in dyads or triads and then playtest and peer review classmates' twines. Standards met include Common Core State Standards for English language arts—http://twinery.org

Games

Calculords, a tablet-based collectible card game to teach arithmetic—http://www.calculords.com

Coming Out Simulator, interactive fiction, semiautobiographical game about a "coming out" experience—http://ncase.itch.io/coming-out-simulator-2014

A *Dark Room,* a free text-based game about resource management—http://adarkroom.doublespeakgames.com

Device 6, interactive fiction with maps and pictures—https://itunes.apple.com/us/app/device-6/id680366065?mt=8

Educational Text Adventure Games—http://textadventures.co.uk/games/tag/educational

HedBanz, the commercial nondigital game that is easily modifiable—http://www.hedbanz.com

The Hitchhiker's Guide to the Galaxy, playable interactive fiction co-written by Douglas Adams, author of the original book—http://www.douglasadams.com/creations/infocomjava.html

How to Play *Pokémon*, rules that are easily adaptable to any paper-based game—http://howto play-pokemon.com/howtoplay-pokemon-page04

Time Society Chronicles: Independence!—http://timesocietygame.com

The Walking Dead, an episodic game that features a threaded storyline. It's a helpful reference point for contextualizing interactive fiction to students who are unfamiliar with the genre (though content is not "school appropriate")—http://www.telltalegames.com/walkingdead

Resources

Adventure Development & Runner Interactive Fiction Toolkit (ADRIFT), authoring tool to build interactive fiction—http://www.adrift.co

Choice Games, play text adventures or write your own, using ChoiceScript—http://www.choiceofgames.com

Choose Your Own Adventure book series—http://www.cyoa.com

Design Thinking for Educators Toolkit, a free download that includes tips on how students can brainstorm and iterate on ideas—http://www.designthinkingforeducators.com

Edcamp, the free (un)conference for teachers—http://edcamp.org

EdSurge, educational technology news, including games, and its Tech for Schools Summits—https://www.edsurge.com

EdTechBridge, from teacher Steve Isaacs and BrainPOP's Katya Hott. Chats on Twitter—https://twitter.com/hashtag/edtechbridge, and on their blog—http://edtechbridge.blogspot.com

Educator's Guide to Copyright—http://www.copyrightfoundation.org/files/userfiles/file/Educators Guide.pdf

FlipSnack, to upload and host interactive PowerPoints—http://www.flipsnack.com

Games As, Institute of Play's exercises to get educators to imagine use of games in the classroom. Katie Salen recommended this as a starting point for teachers—http://www.instituteofplay.org/work/projects/games-as-guide

The Game Crafter, a website to create prototypes of board, card, and dice games. Templates are available to create booklets, game pieces, boards, tiles, shades, and more—https://www.thegamecrafter.com

GameKit, from Institute of Play, featured challenges and ideas to create and mod paper-based games—http://beta.gamek.it

Go: A Kidd's Guide to Graphic Design (2013), by Chip Kidd, illustrates design concepts. It was created for school-aged children—http://chipkidd.com

Inform7, interactive fiction free authoring tool that uses "natural language."

Inklewriter is one of the easiest to use threaded storytelling tools. It works in a computer's browser and features an education portal. Inklewriter won 2013's Best Website for

Teaching and Learning from the American Association of School Librarians—http://www.inklestudios.com/inklewriter/education

Interactive Fiction Writing Competition—http://www.ifcomp.org

iStory, to build threaded stories—http://istoryweb.appspot.com

The Key to Success? Grit, Angela Lee Duckworth's TED Talk on grit, tenacity, and perseverance—http://www.ted.com/talks/angela_lee_duckworth_the_key_to_success_grit

Mars Generation One: Argubot Academy was first built using Inform7—http://inform7.com

Multiplayer Online Battle Arena (MOBA) games are team-based. They can be adapted as argumentation games, such as *Socratic Smackdown*—http://en.wikipedia.org/wiki/Multiplayer_online_battle_arena

Paper prototyping tips from a game designer—http://www.gamasutra.com/view/feature/130814/the_siren_song_of_the_paper_.php?print=1

"A Practical Guide to Game Writing," explained by Darby Devitt, lead writer for *Assassin's Creed: Revelations*—http://www.gamasutra.com/view/feature/134542/a_practical_guide_to_game_writing.php?print=1

Promoting Grit, Tenacity, and Perseverance: Critical Factors for Success in the 21st Century, Department of Education Office of Educational Technology Report—http://pgbovine.net/OET-Draft-Grit-Report-2-17-13.pdf

Q Design Packs, from the Institute of Play. Free resources, or "packs," for teachers and schools interested in adopting games and learning—http://www.instituteofplay.org/work/projects/q-design-packs

Quest Learning in Action from Institute of Play video series, video for each of the Seven Game-Like Principles—http://vimeo.com/channels/qla

Quest to Learn Curriculum Exemplar, featuring postmortem reflection questions—http://www.instituteofplay.org/wp-content/uploads/2013/09/IOP_QDesignPack_Curriculum_Exemplar_1.1.pdf

Quest to Learn: Developing the School for Digital Kids—http://dmlcentral.net/sites/dmlcentral/files/resource_files/Quest_to_LearnMacfoundReport.pdf

Text Adventures, interactive fiction authoring tool—http://textadventures.co.uk

TinkerEd, from Teacher Suzy. It connects educational technology start-ups with teachers—http://tinkered.co

Vassal, to play board games online—http://www.vassalengine.org

· 5 ·

PLAY-BASED LEARNING

This chapter reviews the educational and psychological history of play and games. I consulted several experts on play, including Bernie DeKoven, author of *The Well-Designed Game* (1978). He was an early influencer of the play movement. DeKoven's book was quoted often in one of the most comprehensive game design textbooks, Katie Salen and Eric Zimmerman's *Rules of Play* (2003). He shared with me his insights on how freedom promotes play. This is especially useful in a constructivist classroom. Being free to play explains the enduring popularity of LEGO and *Minecraft* (DeKoven has consulted for LEGO). I also interviewed Claire Greene and Wendy Smolen, co-founders of the Sandbox Summit, an annual toy, game, and learning conference, and Rex Ishibashi, CEO of Originator, developer of mobile games and digital toys such as *Endless Alphabet* and *Mr. Potato Head Create & Play*. Finally, I talked with TeacherGaming's co-founder, Santeri Koivisto. TeacherGaming distributes the "official" educational modification of the world's most popular sandbox, *Minecraft*.

Learning by Playing

Playing in school can often be considered to be ancillary—a sidetrack to "serious" learning. According to the extensive research and writings from Maria

Montessori, Jean Piaget, and Lev Vygotsky, play is integral to a child's development. Play occurs within the context of a game (Salen & Zimmerman, 2003). In other words, you play a game; however, not all play has the structure of a game (Salen & Zimmerman, 2003). The Cooney Center's Jessica Millstone pointed out similarities to me. We spoke in January 2014. "There are many parallels to the theory of game play and game design to Vygotsky and John Dewey and experience-based learning," she said. "Middle school and high school teachers sometimes feel that there is no room for play in upper-level classrooms. There is a benefit of play for learning."

Montessori's *The Secret of Childhood* (1936) emphasized discovery-based learning. The joy one feels from discovering something happens to be a popular game mechanic. Players of *Tomb Raider* feel a deep satisfaction in working out a puzzle and advancing a piece of the story. Kurt Squire is a former Montessori teacher and a current games and learning professor. He wrote that Montessori schools are "a model of what a game-based learning system should look like" (2011, p. 49). This could explain why there are so many Montessori-style apps and games on touch-screen tablets.

Swiss psychologist Jean Piaget's constructivism, or "learning by doing," is very much a part of modern-day project-based learning. It is the opposite of teacher-led instruction, replacing the "sage on the stage" with the "guide on the side." Many of his theories stemmed from observing children playing marbles together (Piaget, 1962). To Piaget, games represented a method to assimilate information and to learn cultural norms (1962). Games such as tag and hide and seek are passed down generationally. Piaget classified different types of games: *practice games* and *symbolic games*. Practice games have no structured rules. These include imitating others and make-believe. Animals engage in this type of play. When a dog fetches a toy rather than retrieving a duck, the act is practice for a real-world situation. Symbolic games occur when children pretend an object is something else, such as using a banana as a telephone. A third classification, *games with rules*, was included alongside symbolic games (Piaget, 1962, pp. 110–112). Game-based learning is typically a structured game with rules.

Leveling up in a game—where challenges are progressively increased—has commonalities with moving through Vygotsky's Zone of Proximal Development. This is where new knowledge is built, or scaffolded, onto what is already known. Scaffolding builds to mastery. In a video game, a player starts at level 1 and moves up to a "boss level"—where all skills and knowledge are tested. In my practice, I use the Zone of Proximal Development in technology workshops. People new to using audio editing are relieved when I compare it to editing tools used in Microsoft Word. Effective learning games use this philosophy; mastering the game represents content or skill mastery. This is an example of James Gee's Learning Principle of "Achievement," in which "there are intrinsic rewards from the beginning, customized to each learner's level, effort, and growing mastery and signaling the learner's ongoing achievement" (2007, p. 223).

Vygotsky stated that games are a natural method to prepare children for adult life. He wrote, "Games are the natural form of work in children, a form of activity which is inherent to the child, as preparation for his life in the future" (Vygotsky, 1997, p. 93). In Vygotskian terms, children's play is a subset of games. The purpose is to create a system to self-regulate behaviors. Self-regulation is when children observe one another to learn what is socially acceptable to do. It bears similarities to communities of practice, in which new learners assimilate information from more experienced members (Lave & Wenger, 1991). There are many preschools that put Vygotsky's theories directly into practice. Tools of the Mind teachers—including my wife—use make-believe practice play to teach ("Tools of the Mind Curriculum," 2014).

In the 2014 book *Free to Play*, evolutionary psychologist Peter Gray wrote that humans are hard-wired to play. It is so ingrained in our genetic code that limiting play can be detrimental to development (Gray, 2014a). Furthermore, rough play can serve to build grit and help with the social skill of self-regulation (Gray, 2014a). Gray embraces free play over structured gameplay. Free play describes the situation when "children learn to make their own decisions, solve their own problems, create and abide by rules, and get along with others as equals rather than as obedient or rebellious subordinates" (Gray, 2014a, p. 18). Playing tag on the playground is more desirable than an organized dodgeball game in gym class.

Gray also described how children of similar ages play more competitively than do those of more mixed ages. Scaffolded knowledge of the world is passed from older to younger children. A playground with a mix of ages leads to mentors and more cooperative play (Gray, 2014a). Formal learning (e.g., schools) is set up with children progressing based on birth year, not developmental ability. Informal learning, from online forums to hands-on Maker Spaces, has a culture of mixed-age apprenticeships.

I asked Bernie DeKoven about where "fun" fits in play-based activities. We spoke in April 2014. He stated that it is a mistake to try to bring in or add fun to a discipline. He said, "Find the people who have fun in the discipline, find what's fun for them in that discipline, and then share that with the kids." He had students invent new rules for elementary school science. He explained, "Kids had fun playing with measurements, I felt the kids were really catching fire." It wasn't the task of measuring things that was fun; rather, students began to internalize what drives scientific theory out of their own sense of play. He began to let students create new mathematical symbols. Parents 45 years ago didn't understand his vision. "The problem was, it didn't prepare the kids to take tests in 5th and 6th grade," DeKoven recalled. "Parents were really worried that their kids wouldn't be prepared to pass the state test. I tried to give something long-term, like a love for the discipline."

To DeKoven, the philosophy of play is simple: Give people enough freedom, and they will play. He recommended exemplars from museum-based education. For example, San Francisco's Exploratorium is a museum that has many interactive exhibits. DeKoven explained, "There are thousands of things for kids to do, read a little bit, and try things. Kids just go around pushing buttons to see what it does." DeKoven also recommended another museum, this one across the continent in New York City. He suggested reviewing the work of Barry Joseph, the associate director for Digital Learning and Youth Initiatives at the American Museum of Natural History. (Joseph has a highly resourceful blog with an amusing name, Moosha Moosha Mooshme, linked at the end of this chapter.) Joseph leads many hands-on activities and he has even co-designed a trading card with Nick Fortugno, *Pterosaurs, The Card Game*. It is a dinosaur card game that includes an "augmented reality" iPad app. Point the tablet's camera at a trading card and the dinosaurs on the cards spring to life!

The Adventure Playground movement is another play-based learning experience cited by DeKoven. Adventure Playgrounds first emerged out of the World War II London rubble. DeKoven explained, "Kids had no place to play, so they played in rubble of the war, building things, playing with water, dirt, mud, getting messy and creative." Nowadays, Adventure Playgrounds are popping up all over the world. At the Berkeley, California, location, DeKoven observed children painting, hiding, and making little clubhouses. There was also a zipline and firepits. "Children were protective with each other," he said. "There was so much learning going on. Things they tried didn't come from an external direction. If they wanted to paint, or nail a piece of wood on a vertical surface, they learned from each other how to do that."

Play-based learning has a Montessori-like feel to it. Children discover from play. "Adults have forgotten about the importance of play in their own lives," DeKoven said. "That's why I focus on adults. You don't have to teach kids how to play. Every time I work with kids and adults, it's fundamental to not make it more fun; start where it is fun. Freedom is an absolute necessity for the play to be meaningful and for the learning to be something the kids could truly internalize." This echoes James Gee's Discovery Principle: Learning occurs when "overt telling is kept to a well-thought-out minimum, allowing opportunity for the learner to experiment and make discoveries" (Gee, 2007, p. 226).

Is it realistic to have a strictly play-based classroom, devoid of structure? Can one effectively teach in a setting that is even more constructivist than a Piagetian or Montessorian classroom? In April 2014 James Gee expressed to me the struggle between free play and teacher-directed instruction, using "liberal" to describe the free play argument and "conservative" for structured learning. Like most things in life, strive for moderation. There must be a balance for learning to realistically occur. Gee explained:

> The liberals are interested in projects. They say, "Let's just turn them loose, and be in a rich environment, and back off with the teaching." That doesn't work. Good project-based learning still requires a teacher to mentor you to know what to pay attention to, to give you information when you need it—just in time and on-demand [Gee's Explicit Information On-Demand and Just In Time Principle], to constrain the experience so it doesn't get out of hand and you know what to pay attention to. Sometimes these labels by liberals mean to turn the kids loose, that they don't like instruction. Then conservatives say, "All you should have is instruction." But good learning is instruction of all different types: mentoring, telling, and just in time and on-demand modeling.

I spoke to digital media expert Henry Jenkins about play and learning. We spoke in May 2014. He felt that play, in many ways, is more useful for thinking about education than games. Jenkins echoed Gray's research (and others I interviewed, including Google's Noah Falstein). He said, "People in a hunting society play with bows and arrows; people in an information society play with information." Jenkins referenced Bruno Bettelheim, author of "The Importance of Play," an influential paper from 1987 (linked at the end of this chapter). To Bettelheim (as well as DeKoven and Gray), play is about a free engagement with the materials around you. Jenkins continued:

> Bettelheim tells us that play involves a certain degree of anxiety because it's about forcing us to conform to the expectations of systems we're playing in. Play is more open-ended, often more innovative, giving us freedom to define the activity on its

own terms. A playful approach to education is one that gives us permission to play, focuses on the context of play as much as the product it encourages us to be. It is more open-ended and encourages us in the way we bring these activities into the classroom. We learn through play. We need that freedom to be unstructured.

The issue, of course, is that school tends to see play as a disruption. Jenkins concluded, "Games are rule-driven and play is not. It is much easier to bring games into the classroom, into an institution, than play. We tend to view play as the disruption of the class clown, rather than the innovation of the really creative, probing student. I think we have to value that before we bring play into schools."

Digital Toys

In 1994 game designer Will Wright was interviewed by *Wired* magazine about an upcoming project he called "Doll House." Wright had trepidations about his game because it wasn't really a game at all. Playing with dolls, after all, is not like playing *Twister* or *Monopoly*. Wright had trepidations. He told interviewer Kevin Kelly, "I have in mind a game I want to call 'Doll House.' It gives grown-ups some tools to design what is basically a dollhouse. But a dollhouse for adults may not be very marketable" (Kelly, 1994). The digital dolls in Wright's Doll House were eventually released under a different name: *The Sims*. The name refers to "simulation," as in a simulated version of real life. In April 2014 I spoke to James Gee about what should be learned from playing with digital toys such as *The Sims*. He said:

> It's not just about game mechanics. It's about asking, "Are there good forms of interaction for learning and engagement?" Games are part of that. Often, what you end up producing is a hybrid. It's not a pure game, but it's good interactivity. The best-selling game in history is *The Sims*; people say it is not a game. Who gives a damn? It's good interactivity. We're producing interactivity that's engaging and relates to real learning. Whether or not the thing is a pure game, whether everything in it is a game, is quite irrelevant.

What Gee is saying is to focus not on toys and game environments, but on learning goals. Piaget used children playing with dolls as an example of symbolic play; dolls come to life based on the imagination of a child. He wrote, "When the child changes one object into another, or ascribes to her doll actions analogous to her own, symbolic imagination becomes the instrument for the game, and is no longer the content, the content in this case being the group of persons or happenings represented by the symbol" (Piaget, 1962, p. 119). Wright's toy—or game—was successful because it tapped into a psychological need for symbolic play. It has also spawned an entire genre of toy-like or "god" games, where the player controls a fishbowl-like world. *The Sims* has sold millions of copies and has moved from computers to iPhone app to casual Facebook game.

Henry Jenkins shared an anecdote with me about a time when he interviewed *The Sims* creator. (I interviewed Jenkins in May 2014.) Will Wright told Jenkins that teachers wanted to "fit" *The Sims* into the disciplines they taught in school. For example, characters and avatars that vote could teach civics. Wright told Jenkins that what's valuable about *The Sims* is that the learning environment is undisciplined. The world is open-ended and, out of that, a variety of different types of learning takes place. He continued, "Playful—or game-based—learning focuses on passion-led, engagement-based learning where children pursue things that are important to them, develop skills and research, learning how to master knowledge. But that's not tied to a specific set of curricular standards that is tested at the end of the process." Play and games do not always neatly fit within the regimen of standards-based curriculum. "In some ways it works better for kids to work outside, to engage in games outside the classroom, then bring them back to bear on the things they are learning in school so young people can form their own connections back to school-based curriculum," Jenkins concluded.

Tablet Toys

My 3-year-old son loves the iPad. (I know I am not alone among parents!) He especially loves Toca Boca's preschool apps. *Toca Cars* is a virtual toy car set; *Toca House* features colorful characters performing household chores. Toca Boca developed several digital toys on tablets for children aged 2 through 8, designed for use *outside* of school. Toca Boca's CEO and co-founder Björn Jeffery told GamesandLearning.org (the Cooney Center's news portal) that the company is creating a brand. A search for "Toca" in Apple's App Store reveals how the company's offerings stand out among the many apps. The support website, directed at parents, distinguished itself as a digital toy—not a game. According to its support page:

> Toys don't have rules. Toys can be played with in any way and only your imagination sets those boundaries. In that sense, toys are more open-ended and can be played with

in many different ways. Digital toys are the same, but even more versatile as you fit so many of them in one device. Games, however, have specific rules, a "right or wrong" way of playing, and often an emphasis on winning and losing. This is not necessarily a bad thing, but it *is* different. (Toca Boca, 2014)

The above statement shows how Toca Boca is attempting to draw a line between toys and games. Children *use* toys to make games. Toca Boca's focus is on engagement, not curriculum. It also attempts to brand itself with world-wide appeal. The characters mumble in gibberish, eliminating language barriers. As with other media, such as books and educational television, parents should play a Toca Boca app with their children, and then ask questions to facilitate real-world connections.

In an effort to learn more about digital toys and games, I contacted Rex Ishibashi, CEO of Originator (maker of *Endless Alphabet, Endless Reader,* and *Mr. Potato Head Create & Play* mobile apps). We spoke in January 2104. *Endless Alphabet* was an App Store "Editor's Choice." The company, based in Silicon Valley, is made up of five core team members originally from Callaway Digital Arts, formerly based in New York City. Callaway was a start-up funded by venture capitalist firm Kleiner, Perkins, Caufield & Byers. It originally focused on e-books with interactive elements to enrich the story experience. According to Ishibashi, Callaway's founder believed that e-book pages should be read sequentially, in order, for a cover-to-cover experience. Children, however, navigated quickly to the table of contents to find their favorite interactions within the e-books and "played" just those pages. It wasn't the story that was compelling on those pages; rather, it was the interactions. Ishibashi told me about *Another Monster at the End of this Book,* a Sesame Workshop title. He explained that Callaway gathered data on page views. Children were navigating directly to the section where Grover was setting up a wall of blocks. They would play the blocks page for minutes on end. This realization led to *Endless Alphabet's* nonlinear interface.

Children's interactive books and mobile games are often played in short time spans. According to Ishibashi, about 60 to 65% of all of the interactions on its apps occurred on an iPad; about 35% were on an iPhone. A parent may hand over an iPhone to a child to play for just a few minutes. These devices can be "digital nannies." About half of Originator's interactions happened while a family was away from home or in a car. Ishibashi said, "We started orienting our games really around shorter experiences that can be enjoyed in five minutes, but can be expanded to 10, 15, 30 minutes."

Endless Alphabet features a carousel of letters. Although the team at Originator aren't Montessori-trained, the drag-and-drop puzzle interface bears many similarities to the teaching style. Pick a letter and a word appears, then gets scrambled when a silly monster runs through it. Completed puzzles trigger a fun animation as a reward. Endless puzzles have no "kill screen" (where the player loses), no points are aggregated, and levels aren't saved. Ishibashi told me that education is deeply rooted in *Endless Alphabet*, but ultimately there has to be a "fun factor," otherwise the child will lose interest.

Originator's team is passionate about delivering a high-quality experience. Each of the five company members has children, but they make no claim to being expert educators. Ishibashi explained, "We're teaching preschoolers, trying to make the lessons that we feel are important to a 2- or 3-year-old. A lot of apps out there really pander to kids, simply doing what is already done. Part of what we're doing is using the interactivity and focusing the experience on short session times where they are learning something in a way the classroom can't accomplish."

My son enjoys dressing up Originator's virtual *Mr. Potato Head* more than the physical version of Hasbro's classic plastic toy. Originator was given full creative license to develop it. "Potato truly comes to life in fantastical variations not limited by the challenges of plastic manufacturing, retail, and the physical box," Ishibashi explained. The character can be dressed and then animated. The app was intended to be marketing support for the physical toy. Ishibashi amusedly recalled how a Hasbro executive said that he could see a day when the plastic toy becomes the marketing support for the app.

The Sandbox Summit

Each year there is a toy, game, and learning conference known as the Sandbox Summit. I interviewed its co-founders, Wendy Smolen and Claire Greene, in April 2014. The Summit is "an idea forum," a sort of sandbox. Smolen and Greene said its mission is to be at the crossroads of play, education, and technology.

The Summit sprang from a need. Smolen and Greene had been meeting every year at various toy fairs and comparing notes. Around 2007, they both began to notice how many new toys seemed to come with a microchip. Their mutual concerns were: What are we teaching? What's happening to play? Are digital toys creating a generation of children merely adept at pushing buttons? Are we raising children to become standardized test takers? Smolen told me that they decided to collectively work together to help guide manufacturers and designers.

Toys are now found in unintended places. Telephones and computers, formerly tools for adults, have become playthings. "Kids are playing and learning in different platforms that we never imagined," Smolen explained. "Our mission is to make sure they still learn 21st-century skills: thinking, solving problems, interacting socially, and physical skills." Greene then continued, "We rolled our eyes at toys with electronic components. Why infuse toys and games with this? Just because there is a sound or a light didn't mean it was teaching anything. Push 'A-B-C' or '1–2-3' and then ring a bell has no cause and effect, like the centuries before of traditional toys and games."

The Sandbox Summit keeps the conversation about play, learning, and technology. In other words, children shouldn't just consume electronics; rather, they should be producing and learning. The market has improved; it now includes the aforementioned Toca Boca and Originator apps, as well as kid-based coding tools such as *Daisy the Dinosaur*. "We promote this industry from a transmedia point of view," Smolen continued. "Research is an important component. Teachers want to know: Does this work? Does gamification help disenfranchised earners? We help percolate these ideas. Technology is here; let's harness its power for good." Greene suggested, "Look for child-directed learning, not an app that talks the whole time. You want the child to figure out the learning, have the child make the discovery. The more they discover, the more they learn." The notion of discovery crossed over to the Summit's 2014 theme: It's okay to fail. Greene concluded, "We need to give our kids an opportunity to fail, to figure out how to redo it and try again. This builds resiliency and empowers them to succeed."

Sandbox Games

The best way to teach something is not always with a structured game, but by using the tool set that a sandbox provides. At the 2012 Games for Change Festival, Valve announced Steam for School's Teach with Portals. It features lesson plans for *Portal 2* (2011) and other titles such as *Universe Sandbox* (2011). *Portal 2* is one of the most successful video games of all time. It is a test of practical physics, spatial learning, and problem solving. The game is essentially a first-person shooter, except that the "gun" isn't really a weapon. The player shoots holes in a futuristic room, creating "portals" to other locations in this room. The game is highly challenging, and a great example of flow in gaming. The "Puzzle Tool" is essentially a level editor where users can assemble Rube Goldberg–style challenges. *Portal 2* was not intended to be an educational tool; nonetheless, its applications for teaching are far-reaching.

There are several other physics sandboxes readily accessible for classroom implementation. *Algodoo* is a physics canvas available as a free computer download. The drag-and-drop interface lets users create objects with texture and characteristics. After the model is created on the playspace, click "Play" to enable gravity. Using *Algodoo*, students can play with velocity, drag, and other concepts from physics in a fun, simulated setting. Scenes can be shared online in the *Algobox*. It is used as a project space for many schools, including Quest to Learn. Similar to *Algodoo*, *Newton's Playground* is a virtual lab for students to engage in Gee's Probing Learning Principle of trial-and-error scientific experimentation.

Open-world sandbox games give the player a choice of engaging in story-based missions, exploring the virtual world, or creating and building content. Players in games such as *Assassin's Creed* and *Grand Theft Auto* follow a map to specified locations in order to trigger missions. Between missions, players can engage in mini-games, such as virtual card and board games, or mini-missions. Mini-games are not essential to moving the storyline forward, but can power-up the player as in-game currency accrues. This type of virtual world seeks to give the player the illusion of freedom.

Perhaps the biggest sandbox to play in is *Minecraft*. Markus "Notch" Persson, a Swedish computer programmer, originally developed it in 2009. (On September 15, 2014, Persson announced that Mojang was purchased by Microsoft and that he was leaving the company.) *Minecraft* boasts hundreds of millions of active users that either destroy (mine) or build (craft) a blocky, virtual world. It was an independent release by Persson's company, Mojang (a nonsensical Swedish word). Over time, the game crossed platforms to console and mobile. Rather than iterating the *Minecraft* game with nonstop sequels as most game publishers have (with, e.g., *Grand Theft Auto V*, *Assassin's Creed IV: Black Flag*), Mojang pushes out content updates to the growing world. *Minecraft* is well known for the ability its players have to modify (or "mod") the experience. It can be argued that modding *is* the game. Persson's game is also a platform to create content, as Facebook is for social games designers.

In March 2014 I asked game design professor Richard Bartle to explain *Minecraft*'s popularity. Bartle's text-based games existed to give people an alternate universe to explore; *Minecraft* empowers users by giving everyone a canvas on which to build their own virtual world. He compared it to the timeless success of LEGO. He said, "It's the great construction set, and you can build what you like in the sandbox mode." Bartle elaborated:

As for what you use *Minecraft* for [in education]—the question is, what are the learning outcomes, which tend to be expressed in much blander terms. Are your students more creative than when they went in? The teaching profession acts as a brake on that type of thing. Personally, I like that, because when people play, they explore not just what they are playing with, but also their own play processes. I like *Minecraft*, but it's not something that addresses curricula in all places because curricula are made for other media.

To keep the experience student-centered, the teacher should not create everything in *Minecraft*. It is up to the teacher to assign activities in a sandbox. Don't fall into the trap of creating an elaborate world in a sandbox for students to explore. It is always more desirable to have the student take the role of designer.

MinecraftEdu

TeacherGaming is a partnership between Finnish teacher Santeri Koivisto and New York City teacher Joel Levin. It distributes the authorized educational modifications of *Minecraft* and *Kerbal*. I interviewed Koivisto via Skype in February 2014 (he lives in Finland). He told me how he began using the off-the-shelf version of *Minecraft* in his classroom and observed how students experimented by trial and error when building in "Creative Mode." His inspiration also came from playing it personally; other teachers saw what he was doing—as did the students—and wanted to emulate his success. It was then that he realized something was there, because teachers wanted it too.

TeacherGaming offers a classroom and school discount on *Minecraft*, which is customized for student use. The safe-for-school version is called *MinecraftEdu*. (I experimented with the iPad version, *Minecraft: Pocket Edition*, and ran into issues when outsiders joined some of the students' worlds.) Along with private servers, TeacherGaming features lesson plans on the website's wiki. Mojang, creator of *Minecraft*, isn't directly involved with TeacherGaming's distribution. "Mojang wants to concentrate on making fun and entertaining games," Koivisto explained, "Education is solely on us."

In April 2011 Koivisto and representatives from Mojang happened to be at the same local science fair. While there, Koivisto asked the Mojang team if he could be the exclusive Finnish distributor of *Minecraft* for schools. Around the same time, over in New York City, teacher Joel Levin published a blog post about his use of *Minecraft* in the classroom. Koivisto replied to Levin by video, which led eventually to a Skype chat. They decided to form a joint venture, though it was another 8 months before Koivisto and Levin met face-to-face. E-Line Media next entered the picture. Koivisto explained that TeacherGaming needed a group to collaborate with that was "action first," complementing its "solutions-oriented" philosophy.

Koivisto met with *Minecraft* creator Marcus "Notch" Persson. They had a deep conversation about how to keep licenses secure in schools. Persson then said, "If we trust that most of our players won't pirate the game, why shouldn't we trust the schools?" Persson was clearly very supportive of integrating *Minecraft* into schools. (Mojang's other sanctioned mod is for U.N.-Habitat, in which developing nations model architectural plans.) TeacherGaming's newest partner, Squad (developer of the rocket kit simulator *Kerbal Space*), has been equally enthusiastic about the branding and distribution of its game in schools.

According to Koivisto, *MinecraftEdu* is not as successful in Finland as one might think (*Minecraft* is an export of Sweden, a neighboring Scandinavian country). "Teachers like me, 1 out of 50 maybe, have the skills and interest to use games in general—or even Google Docs," Koivisto explained. The core of TeacherGaming's business model is to support teachers who have not yet reached the "sweet spot of technology integration." Koivisto spends a lot of time visiting schools that use *MinecraftEdu* as a teacher/trainer; he visits classes and stays in the background, letting the teachers work.

I asked Koivisto about how he suggests differentiating students of mixed ability. While some students are highly proficient in *Minecraft*, others may have little to no experience. He said that he encourages students to help one another by matching experienced students/players with novices. Playing together allows for face-to-face peer support. The multiplayer server is in the same physical class room, which gives students the choice to communicate by voice or by text typing. A student's being able to teach the content indicates transfer of knowledge. "This is a great way for teachers who want their teaching to be more interactive, more conversational," Koivisto explained. "Rather that asking what mathematics would you want to learn, ask what kind of math would you want to learn using *Minecraft*." The virtual setting makes learning authentic.

Playing open-ended games in school sounds fun and looks like constructivist learning, but what about the assessment piece? Koivisto agreed that this presents a quandary. At the time of my interview TeacherGaming was working to bring qualitative data and quantitative data out of the game by watching kids play as time lapses. The game is really an extension to teaching and learning. Unlike multiple-choice questions that have absolute right answers, games are open-ended. For group presentations, Koivisto has had students share their creations in *Minecraft*. In his opinion, "We should use games 3 to 5 hours a week to connect things and broaden the experience." The challenge for TeacherGaming is that game developers create for the single, private user. Bringing an off-the-shelf game into school use requires openness in licensing. That can be a tremendous hurdle.

The School as a Sandbox: PlayMaker School

Los Angeles's PlayMaker School is the school as a sandbox. GameDesk, founded by Lucien Vattel, is the school's parent organization. Its model can be replicated using resources on the school's website. It shares many professionally written lesson plans on its Educade portal. Examples of game-based ideas include lessons on using *Angry Birds* to teach physics as well as nondigital activities. PlayMaker was launched in 2012 as a school within the New Roads School. As of this writing, PlayMaker had been launched for the 6th-grade curriculum. Vattel and Joseph Wise are co-directors and collaborate on ideals.

I interviewed Joseph Wise, the school's co-director, in January 2014. Wise has been in education for about 41 years. To Wise, students are potential content creators, not consumers. He worked at the New Roads School and then started the Center for Effective Learning. The Center's goal was to take current university research and find ways of implementation. Some schools are piloted as working research projects. The challenge for Wise was to get theory and best practices out of the ivory tower and into the classroom.

Wise wanted to switch the direction of learning and assessment. "In traditional classrooms you see a lot of procedure, the teacher does content talking," he said. "We need to get the students doing what the teachers are doing. You are an expert at yourself. Allow kids to ask questions as experts." In other words, follow the constructivist model of Piaget: Learn by doing.

The school doesn't have a game designer on staff. Wise's view is that educational games work well as content carriers, but not at carrying a lot of theory. For example, playing the nation-building game *Civilization* integrates world history information; the gameplay—turn-based strategy—is not how or why people made decisions. Civilizations were built by greed, power, altruism, or other ideologies more abstract than what games can deliver. Wise favors sandboxes, "open ecosystems of learning." This type of open approach crosses disciplines; open play has more than one right answer. He said, "We like to ask, 'Give us three ways such and such might happen.'" For example,

PlayMaker has a small lab and a game space that projects virtual balls on the floor. There is a vertical projector and infrared cameras to see where everyone is located. Wise then asks students: "What are the rules?" He explained, "They first create rules in which their team wins right away. Then we discuss and reflect. Games need achievable challenges, which is tied to learning. We believe learning takes place in the conversation."

Play is constant at the PlayMaker School. Games provide a context to provide meaning to the content. For a vocabulary building, students get cards to play. If they use words (correctly) at any time, they win a badge. In another activity, students were paired and were given a paper with a grid. It was colored in with pictures of school buses, the moon, and monsters. They had to communicate the picture to their partner without showing the actual picture. Wise explained, "Within 20 minutes they came up with Cartesian coordinates. The need led to the idea. Next they played *Battleship* using their new coordinate system."

PlayMaker uses a toolkit called Lens of Culture to teach world history (e.g., Mesopotamia, Greece, Egypt). The Egyptian-themed Quest of the Pharaohs unit is an example of PlayMaker's sandbox approach. The unit teaches about ancient Egypt and brings together multiple content areas. Students create the rules and then extract the content. Wise explained, "A 21st-century skill is to take something that is implicit and extract something explicit." In this activity, students are tasked with creating rules for commerce, so there is the need to understand commerce at a deeper level. Wise told me how last year's class came up with a council of gods, using sacrifices for the proposals. One group, situated near the desert, wrote a well-written proposal for camels; however, a neighboring council wanted the camels, too. A proposal to go to war was put forward. In the end, students chose to not go to war, due to the great degree of risk. Later in the Egypt game, the class had to determine the mass and weight of an obelisk. Using a tourist photo with bicyclers in it, the students estimated the height of the bicycles and then estimated the scale of the obelisk. They used the class's 3D printer to print the obelisk, and figured water displacement to determine the volume. As in real life, problems arose. In this case, scaling wasn't quite right, so they printed four 3D obelisks, and then plotted the results. The unit integrated discovery and inquiry learning.

In another lesson, students pretended to crash land on a planet. "They wore buckets on their heads and then attempted to find resources and complete tasks, like figuring out circumference of planets," Wise recalled. The teachers wanted students to adapt the Lens of Culture toolkit for their planet. As a result, math, science, English language arts, social studies all integrate.

Content at PlayMaker is sometimes delivered through live-action role-playing (LARPing). Seekers Unlimited provides guidance on the programs. According to its website, "When students enact a role and immerse themselves into an ongoing narrative, they experience a level of agency uncommon to more traditional, top-down methods of instruction" (What Is Edu-LARP?, n.d.). Wise explained, "We are trying to be different. We don't teach 21st-century skills. We find situations where students have to use those skills." At PlayMaker, the student becomes part of the game experience.

PlayMaker remodeled three rooms to create a Maker Space, an Adventure Room/Lab, and the Dream Lab. The Maker Space has power cords, a 3D printer, a pegboard to hang tools, and a *Minecraft* server. They have even scanned images from the real world and ported it into *Minecraft*. Using an Xbox Kinect as a 3D scanner, they began to make a chess set featuring the student's actual heads. "Everyone is an expert at something," Wise proudly concluded.

Conclusions and Takeaways

A degree of freedom must exist for play to thrive. Humans are evolutionarily hard-wired to seek "risky play." Play happens in structured games. Free play can be sustained digitally in the classroom by using digital sandboxes and open-ended toys. Game mechanics can also be simulated. Because of its open-ended nature, it can be difficult to assess play. Be sure to keep the learning objective focused and apparent to the student, and loosen up the reigns on the path the child takes to achieve it.

Lesson Plan Ideas

Educade: Hundreds of free lesson plans from GameDesk, the parent company of the PlayMaker School. There are lessons for *Newton's Playground, Algodoo, Portal, MinecraftEdu,* and live action role-play (LARP). It is an invaluable resource for game-inspired lessons. Standards are listed and vary, depending on discipline and content—http://www.educade.org

Everyone's a Critic: A free, downloadable game from the Institute of Play. It was part of its collaboration with the Museum of Modern Art in New York City. This activity works well outside of museums, including in student displays. Standards vary, depending on discipline and content—http://www.moma.org/pdfs/docs/learn/moma_everyones-a-critic.pdf

MinecraftEdu: Lesson plans are for health, math, science, social studies, and technology. Standards are available for each discipline and content area—http://services.minecraft edu.com/worlds

Teach with Portals: Lesson plans for the Rube Goldberg–inspired game *Portal 2* and its free level editor. Next Generation Science Standards apply, especially pertaining to physics—http://www.teachwithportals.com

Games

Algodoo, downloadable for free, it is a fun physics sandbox—http://www.algodoo.com

Kerbal Space Program—play the free demo, then check out *KerbalEdu* (on TeacherGaming's website)—https://kerbalspaceprogram.com

Newton's Playground, a physics platform using stealth assessments—http://www.empirical-games.org/projects.html

Originator apps from the developer of *Endless Alphabet, Endless Reader, BeBop Box, Mr. Potato Head Create & Play* and *Mrs. Potato Head Create & Play*—http://originatorkids.com

Pterosaurs, the Card Game, a card-based dinosaur game from the American Museum of Natural History's Barry Joseph and game designer Nick Fortugno—http://shop.amnh.org/a701/pterosaurs-the-card-game.html

Toca Boca digital toys and games for young learners—http://tocaboca.com/games

Universe Sandbox puts the universe at your fingertips. You can manipulate planets, black holes, and star systems, play pool in zero gravity, or see what happens if the moon is moved closer to the earth—http://universesandbox.com

Resources

Adventure Playground, in Berkeley, California—http://www.ci.berkeley.ca.us/adventureplayground

Bruno Bettelheim's "The Importance of Play"—http://www.theatlantic.com/magazine/archive/1987/03/the-importance-of-play/305129

DeepFUN, Bernie DeKoven's website, featuring several games and activities—http://www.deepfun.com

EduLARPing (live action role play) from Seekers Unlimited—http://seekersunlimited.com/about-us/what-is-edu-larp

Exploratorium, a hands-on science museum in San Francisco, featuring an interactive website and apps—http://www.exploratorium.edu

Peter Gray's *Freedom to Play* blog, from *Psychology Today*—http://www.psychologytoday.com/blog/freedom-learn

Moosha Moosha Mooshme, Barry Joseph's American Museum of Natural History blog—http://www.mooshme.org

New Media Consortium Horizon Report on Museums—http://www.nmc.org/publications/2013-horizon-report-museum

Sandbox Summit—http://sandboxsummit.org

· 6 ·

LEARNING IN COOPERATIVE MODE

Each year my 7th-grade students collaborate to create a "Virtual Student Constitution" on a wiki (a wiki is an online document that more than one person can edit). The idea for the project came from an article in the *Guardian* titled "Mob Rule: Iceland Crowdsources Its Next Constitution," which described how Iceland, in the process of recovering from a collapse of its banks and government, decided to use social media to get citizens to share their ideas for a new constitution.

My students are each given a laptop or an iPad and "meet" online (rather than face-to-face) in cooperative groups. Their task of is to rewrite the school's student handbook—their "constitution." The Edmodo social network was the virtual meeting place. Although it has the look and feel of Facebook, it's private and secure. Edmodo has a feature called "Small Groups" in which side chats can occur. Students can have fun personalizing their pages with avatars; teachers can award digital badges on profile pages.

The classes are given five student handbooks from middle schools around the state. Each group edits a portion of the wiki, which includes both text and talking avatars made using Voki. There is one wiki for each of my four 7th-grade class sections. There can be several hundred edits over a 5-day period. The "game" began as students competed to control editing the wiki page—only one person can edit at a time. The mechanics of play are: arguing, collaborating, and voting, all on content of interest to students—their handbook. Following the project, students vote via interactive remote whether to ratify their Virtual Student Constitution wiki. After the vote, we compare the U.S. Constitution to Iceland's crowdsourced constitution.

Earlier in the school year, my students collaborated on an e-book that was eventually published and distributed in Apple's iBookstore. Each student worked with a partner to research information, gather copyright-friendly pictures, and create glossary terms about one of the 13 original American colonies. They used a variety of text and online sources for information. Students were taught about how Creative Commons and copyright law worked. A small group of students volunteered extra time during their lunch to create the overall concept. It was decided that historical fiction would be the best vehicle to grab and hold the reader's attention. A few students also created original artwork for the lead characters—in this case, three magical, time-traveling unicorns. I scanned their drawings and added them to the "Gallery" widget. Once the book was completed, we submitted it for review to Apple. Our book is still available in the iBookstore.

What I constructed, using small groups and interest-driven learning, was essentially a multiplayer game. For example, the Constitution project used the mechanics of social collaboration (People Fun), frustration and relief (from wiki edits), and voting. When I interviewed media scholar Henry Jenkins in May 2014, he pointed out how simulations lead to deeper connections to content. He used the decades-old Model U.N. program as an example; it is an experience that has always been game-based. Jenkins said:

> It's a role-playing game where you simulate the activity of the United Nations. You just don't begin by playing; you do research, you read the U.N. charter, and you read up on the culture. You prepare to play the game. Coming out the other side, the best teachers have students report back to the school on what happened in the game. It becomes a springboard for writing and speaking activities. A very small part of the Model U.N. experience is the game. The other activities pull back into school's regimes. The game inspires young people to learn more deeply. That's really a better model for thinking about how games and play relate to each other.

Learning cooperatively was popularized over 30 years ago, thanks to educators such as Spencer Kagan. His Kagan Structures include Jigsaw groupings and Round Robin discussions. This chapter compares project-based, problem-based, and inquiry-based learning to game-based learning. The truth is, each of these is not all that different from the others. The great news is that if you are familiar with any of the aforementioned techniques, then you are not too far from game-based learning. Be inspired by how games teach. For this chapter I share my students' experience with the *Historia* civilization-building beta test. I also spoke with *Multiplayer Classroom* author Lee Sheldon, as well as Jim Bower, creator of *Whyville*, the first browser-based virtual world for learning. (I met Sheldon at the Games in Education Symposium in August 2014. This was almost 5 months after my interview with him. He laughed and was amused when I told him that I put his interview in the chapter pertaining to cooperative learning. My decision was based on his effectiveness at teaching small groups in a large class.)

Cooperative Learning

Mathematicians and game theoreticians know cooperative games as non-zero-sum games. Cooperative games are when "players can make enforceable agreements with other players" (Nasar, 1998, p. 96). No winner is required. Fundraising walks and crowdfunding websites are examples of cooperative games (Kim, 2012b; Kim, 2014e). They are win-win (as opposed to win-lose, like *Rock-Paper-Scissors*). No one really trains to win the Susan G. Komen Breast Cancer Walk the way they would the Boston Marathon (Kim, 2012b; Kim, 2014e). Most people run in most races simply to participate.

One of my favorite cooperative social studies games is iCivics's *Separation of Powers/What's for Lunch?* It is a nondigital simulation about how a bill becomes a law. Students are divided into groups and play five rounds in which they create the school lunch menu. The simulation puts students in the roles of Lead Chef, Menu Writer, and Nutrition Inspectors. Each round is led with prompts and a timer on our interactive whiteboard. The lesson plan is actually a cooperative game in which there is no winner or loser. After the final round, I debrief to see who can connect the dots to how the U.S. government is structured: The Lead Chef is the Executive Branch, the Menu Writer is the Legislative Branch, and the Nutrition Inspectors are the Judicial Branch. Some students seem confused as to why they were planning lunch in social studies. After I debrief, they realize why, and the learning "sticks." The activity's mechanic is role-playing with some degree of frustration. Delivering content in a fun, relatable, and interactive manner—and then switching in the content—is an engaging way to learn.

Kagan Structures

Spencer Kagan is an expert on cooperative learning. Since the 1980s, he has published several books on the topic. Kagan Structures encourage student engagement. My personal favorite grouping is the Jigsaw, in which members switch out and rotate around the physical classroom. In a Jigsaw, "students are assigned a subpart of a classroom topic to learn and subsequently teach to others via reciprocal teaching" (Gee, 2007, p. 204). For example, in a group of three, one can be the note taker, another can be the researcher, and the third would be the photographer, in charge of curating digital imagery. Kagan's books and websites state that there are about 200 different combinations. Four common groupings include:

- Rally Robin—In pairs, students alternate generating brief oral responses
- Timed Pair-Share—In pairs, students share with a partner for a predetermined time while the partner listens. Then partners switch roles
- Round Robin—In teams, students take turns responding orally
- Rally Coach—Partners take turns, one solving a problem while the other coaches, then partners switch roles. (Clowes, 2011)

Some groupings are better for certain activities. For example, Timed Pair-Share works well for anticipatory sets, or warm-up activities. The Round Robin arrangement is appropriate to discuss findings in inquiry lessons, while the Rally Coach ensures each member gets a turn to lead. Kagan has a magic number for optimal group size: four. Kagan favors teams of four because they "maximize and equalize active participation compared to any other number" (1998). The second best size is a pair (Kagan, 1998). The idea is to keep groups smaller and manageable, as well as even in number to promote equity. It can be helpful to have student desks arranged in a way that promotes cooperative learning.

Small groups are also desirable in the business world. Amazon founder Jeff Bezos nicknamed this dynamic the "two-pizza rule," where any team is small enough that two pizzas would be a large enough lunch order (Brandt, 2011). Building teams with players/students of varying abilities is a useful career skill. Business teams are often the same size as guild communities. Multiplayer game guilds "can be made up of any number of players, depending on the common goals and play style that guild members decide upon" (Sheldon, 2012, p. 30). The next section reviews several anecdotes about how guilds and multiplayer learning work effectively together.

Lee Sheldon

One of the most effective examples of a game-like learning environment is Lee Sheldon's Multiplayer Classroom approach. We spoke in March 2014. In 2012 he published *The Multiplayer Classroom: Designing Coursework as a Game*. Sheldon's book reviewed the iterations his syllabus took in his game design course. His grading policy moved from percentages to Experience Points (XP), as in multiplayer video games. The higher a student scores, the more he or she advances, or "levels up." Unlike many professors, Sheldon doesn't deduct points for students who don't come to class; instead, he awards points for coming. "It's a positive," he told me. "I get almost perfect attendance. Colleagues think I'm crazy." His syllabus also includes "expansion packs," similar to purchasable downloadable content (DLC) such as extra maps.

Sheldon started his career as a television writer and producer. He wrote for *Star Trek: The Next Generation*, *Charlie's Angels*, and the long-running daytime soap opera *Edge of Night*. In 1994 he left television and began writing games. Eight years ago Sheldon entered the academic world, first at Indiana University; currently he is at Rensselaer Polytechnic Institute in upstate New York, where he is an associate professor and co-director of the Games and Simulation Arts and Sciences program. He teaches courses in writing for games, game design, and level design.

I interviewed Sheldon about his experiences. He pointed out to me that the trend of game-based learning isn't all that new. "Humans have been using storytelling and gameplay to teach for over a millennia," he said. "First and 2nd-grade kids play games. In 3rd or 4th grade something happens and education gets 'serious'—multiple-choice questions and lecturing. We lost the ability to play and now we're fighting hard to get it back."

Sheldon's students are grouped in guilds. This arrangement was inspired by massively multiplayer online games. Grouping students can promote an intrinsic love of learning. Sheldon gave me an example of how this works. Sometimes he will add extra credit questions on exams that benefit an entire guild, rather than just the students who answer correctly. He explained, "If one person answers that question, everyone gets credit for it. It's not enough [credit] to change a slacker's grade from an F to a C. They try because they get peer acclamation for that. It's an intrinsic reward." This is an important lesson about what games can teach. It is an example of XEODesign's "fun" emotion of *naches*, or *kvell* (Yiddish for "pleasure or pride at the accomplishment of a child or mentee") (Lazzaro, 2004). There is a deep satisfaction felt when helping friends.

When students meet in Sheldon's physical classroom, they work in "zones." This arrangement is similar to stations or centers in kindergarten through grade-12 settings. Teachers sometimes arrange student desks to accommodate certain projects. Like all teaching, setting up a learning space is a personal preference. When organizing a class as a playspace, be cognizant of what works best for the student. I use conventional rows because most of my activities wind up taking place away from the desks and in stations around the room. Some of my colleagues configure their rooms differently, with desks paired together, or in a large circle. The classroom space is, in essence, the magic circle where play happens. Combining Kagan's preferred grouping with Sheldon's guild configurations suggests arranging desks in clusters of four.

I was curious to hear examples of how Sheldon teaches his college courses with a game-like narrative. Writing is so ingrained in his methodology that his classes are "episodes." Similarly, he refers to students as "players," sometimes using the words interchangeably. To Sheldon, narratives should not rely on cut scenes and conversation trees. He said, "I'm interested in environmental and nonlinear storytelling." When creating storylines for games and projects, don't assume it is the same as when writing for other media. This is an important tip in designing game-like (or problem-based and project-based, for that matter) activities. The game's narrative provides a frame for Sheldon to keep his students engaged.

Collateral Learning

There exists a balance between pedagogy and entertainment. Starting with curriculum creates boring experiences. On the other hand, focusing too much on engagement can leave little room for education. Sheldon has a name for this sweet spot: "collateral learning." According to Sheldon, "Collateral learning means that students learn in spite of themselves. They don't even know that they're learning." Movies and books teach collaterally. You may watch the World War II drama *Saving Private Ryan* and be moved emotionally by the story. In the process, you learn what happened when the Americans led the D-Day invasion on Normandy Beach. Teaching with narrative games is the same. The focus isn't merely on the act of learning; rather, there is a felt need to acquire the knowledge in order to progress in the story. Learning can be incidental if the learner is situated in an authentic setting (Lave & Wenger, 1991).

Sheldon's journey with collateral learning began at Indiana University. (His journey is detailed in the *Multiplayer Classroom*.) It began with a project sponsored by a grant from Robert Wood Johnson. The goal was to see the importance of student fitness and health simply from playing a game. "We didn't teach them anything, no food pyramids," he recalled. "I came up with a mystery of a professor that disappears, and then wild things happen. It ends with the character being whisked away by a flying saucer." The activity had students solving puzzles and solving a mystery by running around the campus. Body-mass index (BMI) tests showed that participants became healthier and fitter. "They got across the campus in less time than shuttle bus by walking; the collateral learning was sleeping in more and walking," Sheldon said. The smartphone game *Zombies, Run!* has a similar mechanic. Boasting a community of over 500,000, this fitness game puts players on missions collecting items while "outrunning" hordes of zombies. The app uses GPS and audio cues to motivate runners.

Sheldon next told me about "The Lost Manuscript," a class in which students had to learn Mandarin Chinese in order to find the lost manuscript of a famous Chinese novel. Cultural exchange was part of the fiction, creating an immersive, game-based experience. The first few "episodes" (or classes) were in a lecture-style classroom. Then, for one of the classes, Sheldon had a woman burst onto the scene to engage in a heated argument with the learning designer. The dispute was in Mandarin, and took place just outside the room. Next, the learning designer (or as Sheldon told me, "a teacher playing the character of a learning designer") came back in and introduced herself to the students. Student interest about the conflict was piqued. They wanted to understand the disagreement. Sheldon next detailed further episodes of "The Lost Manuscript." He said:

> The class was supposed to go to Beijing (in the game-set classroom), following another group of students. The teacher informed the class that something went wrong with the first group and this class won't be going in 3 months—but in 2 weeks! Knowing it was a game accelerated their learning. For the next class, we moved chairs around like an airport, used an Xbox Kinect (sensor), and partition screens to create an information kiosk. The 1-hour, 50-minute-long class required students to clear customs, change currency, find their hotel at the kiosk, call the hotel, arrange transportation, and read signs in Chinese around the room, like "Restrooms," "Planes This Way," and "Transportation." They were originally told that someone would meet them and guide them. When they arrived at the airport/classroom there was only a crumpled-up piece of paper saying, "Welcome Rensselaer Students"—with no sign from who would help them. Helping themselves, they got through it all in 30 minutes, by collaborating.

What Sheldon created was a live-action video game. He brought in volunteers who spoke Mandarin Chinese to play customs agents, as well as other people in the airport. In video game parlance, they are called nonplayable characters, or NPCs. Sheldon explained, "There was emergent gameplay going on. They solved all the puzzles I gave them, and they wanted to continue. That's what narrative brings: the desire to want to know what comes next. I just don't create scenarios, but ongoing narratives."

The final exam was a police investigation about where to find the lost manuscript. Sheldon used social media to have actors send tweets and messages to students. He said, "In the beginning, students were in four study groups of three each. There were four characters tweeting all of them. As the class went along, one person tweeted one group saying, 'Don't trust this other person. The manuscript is worth a lot of money; they are not going to preserve it, they're going to sell it.' Another one said, 'Don't trust that one.'" Sheldon used the narrative to split the loyalties of the students and the characters in the story. Students studied outside of class because the learning was meaningful—and fun. They weren't listening to lectures. Each class leveled up in challenge as in a video game.

Of course, hiring actors to engage with kindergarten through grade-12 students presents logistical and ethical challenges. A middle or high school teacher can, however, deliver a blended learning experience on an educational, social platform such as Edmodo, Schoology, or Moodle. Sheldon explained to me how his online course for Excelsior College included two extra student accounts controlled by the instructor and teacher's assistant. "They are the hint system in the game, driving discussion if it lags," he said. "Then they become part of narrative." The false student can also serve as a "docent," providing help, guidance, and assistance. A middle or high school teacher could tell students that the extra accounts are guest students from neighboring districts.

Sheldon is currently working on a project proposal for the National Science Foundation. It is for teachers of engineering and science. The game's narrative is about "an extended Irish family who emigrated to a new land, only the new land is Mars. It's a family drama—*Downton Abbey* in outer space." Titled *These Far Hills*, the objective is to get a biosphere up and running for others to follow. By learning concepts from engineering and science, the student/players can move through the story. The lead character is a middle-aged woman with many children. Her father is her mentor. The story begins when the first child is born on Mars (the Mars setting calls to mind *Mars Generation One: Argubot Academy*, GlassLab's argumentation tablet game). Sheldon explained where collateral learning comes in. He said:

You need to keep up with engineering necessary to keep up the biosphere. The father is getting stern with her, and then you learn he is dying and he won't live to see his dream. The father-child dynamic allows me to create a lot of emotion, which helps them to learn. The song "I'll Miss the Rain in Dublin," written by a guy in Saratoga, inspired the last scene. At the end, they make it rain inside the biosphere and then they see their father's grave outside on the red soil of Mars. Emotion draws the student into the learning.

Unlike a narrative in a typical problem-based learning unit, Sheldon's scenarios are ongoing (of course, college classes do not meet everyday). He explained, "You prepare your syllabus and lesson plan, which is a design document. The narrative builds from class to class, with cliffhangers, so they [the students] want to come back." Sheldon teases out upcoming classes, or episodes, using social media. Games and stories are how humans remember things—not by memorizing lists of disconnected facts. The trick is creating a compelling enough storyline.

Building Civilizations Together with *Historia*

In May 2014 my 6th-grade students began playtesting a civilization-building game. We were one of 25 classes chosen to partake in the roll out. The game, *Historia*, is a true multiplayer experience. It is based on a paper-based activity that I describe later in this section. The digital version is a cooperative game that uses the computers as a station and the teacher as the "Game Master." In other words, students work together face-to-face and use technology to aggregate their progress. This is an effective model to use computers for game-based learning without sacrificing the dynamics of face-to-face interactions.

The *Historia* story begins a few years ago when two 6th-grade social studies teachers, Rick Brennan and Jason Darnell, gamified their world history textbook using worksheets. Similar to the video game *Civilization*, each unit, called an "Epoch," presented students with a "Dilemma." The Dilemma was similar to a problem presented in a problem-based unit. Brennan and Darnell sought to digitize the game. They formed the Histrionix Learning Company and partnered with E-Line Media, the company that distributes *MinecraftEdu* and produces *Gamestar Mechanic* with the Institute of Play.

I initially spoke to Kate Reilly, product manager for *Historia*, in January 2014. We spoke about the process of selecting and marketing teacher-created games. She also visited my classroom to help me roll out the playtest. Reilly explained how E-Line Media receives several in-bound requests a day from people who have a game—many of whom are teachers. E-Line is looking to move beyond just playing a game. Its objective is to engage, empower, and motivate students to continue learning. "We're looking for a big idea," Reilly said. "When Rich and Jason came along with *Historia* it became clear that their world history game infused curricula. [It was] really much more than helping kids learn world history content. It was really about building leadership skills, building a passion for inquiry, critical thinking, getting kids to think about problems through the filter of opportunity and risk, and build strategy skills in that way." The gameplay can transcend the content and can be applied anywhere. Reilly envisions future *Historias*. "The battle for innovation between Thomas Edison and Nicholas Tesla could be a *Science Historia*," she predicted.

In *Historia*, students team up as a fictitious country. It begins with Mesopotamia and runs until modern times. "Pillars" measure the strength of the civilization. Each student is responsible for one Pillar. For example, the student who is the Minister of Economics is responsible for the Economy Pillar. In the paper-based, classroom version, Brennan and Darnell used worksheets for students to track their civilization's growth. Each handout had a graphic of an actual pillar, where advancements were detailed. The Science and Technology Pillar starts with the plow and ends with the Internet.

As one can imagine, the paper version got complicated. Aside from the high amount of photocopying involved, there was a lot of time spent tracking Pillars, money, resources, and strategies. There was authentic math taking place, but it was low-order, simple arithmetic. E-Line Media's digital version does all of the bookkeeping for the player. Reilly explained, "Purchasing advancements will feel more like buying something from Amazon. Click what you want and the money is deducted." In partnership with E-Line, Getty Images and the Smithsonian Institute provided the primary source imagery in the computer version. Reilly continued, "We want to have the focus on the historical images, not something cartoony, and we want to make the information beautiful and exciting to kids."

The beta test of the digital version featured a "Tech Tree," where advancements branched out. The Tech Tree resembled other video game advancement systems that used skill branches. It closely resembled the Skill Tree in Ubisoft's *Watch Dogs* (2014), in which players choose upgrades to their character's tactical skills or driving abilities. *Historia*'s Tech Tree was the most engaging element in the version my students tried. Teams strengthened their civilizations by purchasing advancements on Pillars. The simulation gives an authentic learning experience of economics for all Pillars because points— called Culture Points (CP)—were scarce.

Over the course of the game, students encounter cultural barriers. Some of the planned barriers will include innovations, battles, dilemmas (e.g., how to build pyramids, kinds of workers to use), and great floods. To advance in the game, students conduct research to figure out what will happen and then develop a preparation strategy to face whatever will come next. (The beta test relied on our class textbook and Internet resources.) The team's dynamic changes as the civilizations change. Teams can be organized as a democracy, monarchy, or a dictatorship. Students learn government from being in a government. Of course, dealing with other people on a team who have their own ideas brings conflict. Reilly stated, "Students come to the table with a persuasive argument, just like a cabinet minister would to advise the president on a course of action. Then you have to make a case for your strategy, debate it out, then the entire class sees how you did."

The full release of *Historia* is planned to include content in its package (similar to how *Civilization* added a "Civilopedia" filled with facts to help players succeed). The target age is middle school. Reilly was confident that *Historia* will be successful because, like *Gamestar Mechanic*, "it was created by teachers and iterated with students before it even saw the light of a publishing day."

Citizens of *Whyville*

Whyville was one of the first browser-based virtual environments. It remains popular to this day. Children continue to meet in *Whyville* to create and play together. Participants, known as "citizens," earn virtual currency, called "clams." The platform is free, and it is a safe space for younger students to play.

I spoke with *Whyville*'s founder, computational neurobiologist Jim Bower, in February 2014. He has been involved for many years in building computer models to figure out how brains work. He sees games as just one piece of the educational puzzle. He explained, "The core [idea] that kids love *World of Warcraft* or *Assassin's Creed* and therefore we can make it educational and 'win' is not true. It is much more complicated than that. Any teacher knows that." Bower prefers student-created environments instead of games designed to deliver content. He used the equal sign as an example of a concept that can be taught with a game. He explained:

> They're [students] introduced to it in kindergarten or pre-K. Kids think the equal sign means the answer comes next. They don't understand that it is an expression of balance. They think of it the way computer scientists think of it: an output. But in math, it's a balance between left and right. Can you get all the way through math and not realize what an equal sign is? Sure. But can you build a higher understanding of math? No. Can you standardize test them? Sure, as long as the answer is on the right!

Bower wanted a "motif" to teach the mathematical concept of equality. "It should be obvious to a 3-year-old, but complex enough to be interesting to a college student," he stated. Researchers found it in a mobile, the decoration that hangs from ceilings and baby cribs. A mobile must be balanced—or equal—to hang properly. He explained, "With mobiles, you can go from addition, subtraction, multiplication, division, all the way up to systems of equations." The equal sign is the game mechanic of balance; the tablet game *Dragon Box* is a perfect example of using balance to teach algebra.

Publishers sometimes design games by looking at a textbook, or other traditional material, and asking, "Can we make a game about that?" This is Bower's issue with most learning games. He said, "They take what's wrong with textbooks and replicate it in a game—which is simply ridiculous." In *Whyville* there are 150 to 200 different types of game-like activities, including ones that children invented themselves. *Whyville* also works with the Educational Development Center to get to the pedagogical structure that supports learning, not just content and skills (such as the concept of equality as balance, rather than the skill of arithmetic). *Whyville* focuses on building structures. This is the artifact that Bower finds missing in content-driven games. "Games are one form of play, but not the only form," he concluded.

Bower's connection from computational neurobiology to learning and education was brought together by simulation technology. His story began with a faculty position at the California Institute of Technology (Caltech) in 1984. He built a general-purpose simulation system for building models of the brain, called Genesis. It was designed to do research for graduate-level training. Because the entire field of neurobiology is theoretical, models and theory were important to understanding how things work. At Caltech he used his position to get involved in education, particularly "to explore simulation-based learning as a basis for young children to play with the dynamics of science." The challenge was to get science into schools, and then figure out how to get computers to engage students.

At this time, Bower founded the Caltech Precollege Science Initiative (CAPSI). He told me how, over the course of 17 years, CAPSI spent "about $25 million to figure out how to get hands-on, inquiry-based, constructivist, kids-based science into public schools." He next began working with his friend, Alan Kay, an inventor of the original Apple Macintosh interface (Kay worked at the famed Xerox PARC project, where the graphical user interface (GUI) desktop was first developed). They talked about simulations for children and education. Working with Apple, they built the first virtual world for learning, in 1985. They installed it in the Los Angeles County library system. It was so successful that the librarians insisted it be taken out. Bower said, "The librarians complained that the Macs were blocking the card catalogue!"

In 1998 his Caltech program had seemingly run its course. In California there was a struggle between textbooks and hands-on science kits. Bower decided to end the project and to launch the company Numedeon. The following year, Numedeon started *Whyville* as an informal, broad-based educational site. It still has a fairly large number of registered users. Bower said that the number of registered users exceeded 7 million, nowhere near competitors such as Disney's *Club Penguin*. "We don't really care," Bower told me. "We're really figuring out how to work with real teachers, grow with students, bring best community practice to 5th-grade classrooms, and make things holistic rather than one by one. It's very critical to the gamification business, how you replace an entire curriculum, not one piece."

Conclusions and Takeaways

Cooperative learning is basically a game. There is no need to reinvent years of proven research and practice. Like a game, projects should focus on the storyline and mechanics first. The learning will follow, and students will pick up knowledge collaterally. You can integrate technology without sacrificing the valuable time of students working together face-to-face.

Lesson Plan Ideas

Lost at Sea: I begin each school year using team-building activities to model cooperative learning. In this survivalist lesson, individual students first rank items from a shipwreck by importance. The second step puts the student in a group to defend his or her position. Is fishing line a more valuable item than a shaving mirror? The activity lends itself to inquiry-based learning common in history and science classrooms. This is an effective ice-breaker; however, standards may not apply—http://dsa.csupomona.edu/osl/studentmanual/files/Lost_At_Sea_327.pdf

Persuasive Commercials: The task is to educate and persuade others. Students will be able to do this by making a commercial. All projects will be created using either iMovie, Windows Movie Maker, or Animoto, a web-based application. Students in other class periods/sections should view the commercials and vote to see which was the most convincing. The class will be divided into teams, one per commercial. Social studies standards apply, as do Common Core State Standards for English language arts, pertaining to argumentation, apply.

Separation of Powers: What's for Lunch? iCivics's paper-based, cooperative game about how laws are written. Standards are posted on iCivics, along with the entire lesson—https://icivics-icivicsinc.netdna-ssl.com/sites/default/files/Separation%20of%20Powers_3.pdf

Student Constitution: Your students have been nominated to attend the Virtual Constitutional Convention. They will help draft (write) a new Student Handbook. The Virtual Constitutional Convention will meet face-to-face in class, as well as online via Edmodo, or Today's Meet. Edmodo features virtual small groups, which I have found to be easy to manage. The class will be divided into groups. Topics should be common in all handbooks (e.g., dress code, electronic use policy). Each group will be responsible for drafting a topic from the Student Handbook. A 2/3 (66.7%) vote is required to ratify the final Student Constitution. Voting will take place in class. Social studies standards apply, as do Common Core State Standards for English language arts, especially those that pertain to argumentation. Each person in a group has a role and will be graded individually. Student roles include:

1. The Researcher—Responsible for reading different schools' student handbooks in the state, as well as your school's
2. The Writer—Responsible for the wording of the assigned topic
3. The Devil's Advocate—Responsible for coming up with scenarios that "punch holes" in the group's wording

Virtual Field Trip iBook Project: Class-created interactive book to be submitted as a free iPad download in Apple's iBookstore. Using iBooks Author (a free Mac app), the teacher can compile each group's work into separate chapters (one per team). Creative Commons–licensed images of, for example, famous buildings, statues, or artifacts, can be included as an interactive gallery. Common Core State Standards for English language arts apply.

The Whyville Times: After young learners play in *Whyville*, have them read and summarize articles in the virtual community's online newspaper. Topics include Creative Writing and Entertainment. Common Core State Standards for English language arts apply—http://j.whyville.net/smmk/whytimes/index

Games

Forbidden Island, a cooperative board game set on a treasure-filled island—http://www
.gamewright.com/gamewright/index.php?section=games&page=game&show=245

Historia, a civilization-building game—http://playhistoria.com

National Model United Nations, the long-running simulation—http://www.nmun.org

Pandemic, a cooperative board game (also playable via iPad app) in which the goal is for every
player to win—http://zmangames.com/product-details.php?id=1246

Play Brave, social and emotional learning in a massive multiplayer online game—http://www
.playbrave.org

Settlers of Catan is the classic board game of resource management and negotiations—http://
www.catan.com

Story Cubes are sets of dice affixed with images, rather than numbers. The idea is to tell a story
based on the dice the player rolls—http://www.storycubes.com

Ticket to Ride is a board game set in the early 1900s. The goal is to create train lines between
cities. It is an authentic way to teach geography and an excellent example of "collateral
learning"—http://www.daysofwonder.com/tickettoride

Whyville, a vibrant virtual community for elementary students—http://www.whyville.net

Zombies, Run!, a running game that puts players on missions collecting items and outrunning
hordes of zombies—all while actually running!—https://www.zombiesrungame.com

Resources

Buck Institute of Education, resources for project-based learning—http://bie.org

Challenge-Based Learning—https://www.challengebasedlearning.org

The Corns Visit the 13 Colonies, my students' e-book in iTunes (free)—https://itun.es/i6gP67k

Innovative board game companies: Calliope Games—http://www.calliopegames.com, Days of
Wonder—http://www.daysofwonder.com, GameWright—http://www.gamewright.com,
ThinkFun—http://www.thinkfun.com, and Z-Man Games—http://zmangames.com

Kagan Online, resources for cooperative structures—http://www.kaganonline.com/index.php

Montclair University School of Business (NJ) GloBus Strategy Simulator, a game-based
method to teach about global business strategies—http://business.montclair.edu/file/2125

Multiplayer Classroom, Lee Sheldon's blog—http://gamingtheclassroom.wordpress.com

Online Stopwatch, works great on an interactive whiteboard—http://www.online-stopwatch.com

"Project-Based Learning Explained," a short explanatory video—http://www.commoncraft
.com/project-based-learning-explained-custom-video-project-bie

Tabletop is a YouTube show hosted by Wil Wheaton. It features him and his famous friends
playing board games—http://geekandsundry.com/shows/tabletop

· 7 ·

GAMIFICATION AND QUEST-BASED LEARNING

Gamification can turn a nongame activity into a game. Shopping is one example. People often return to stores not for products, but for experiences. I could drink coffee almost anywhere, yet I often frequent Starbucks. When I enter a store, I am greeted with the smell of freshly ground coffee and hipster music. The machines behind the counter are positioned to enable the baristas to face the customers. I can pay for my drink using the Starbucks app on my iPhone: All I have to do is shake the phone at the register. In exchange for purchasing coffee, I am awarded stars. The hope is that I "level up" from "green stars" to "gold stars." The app includes other free rewards every week, such as a song from iTunes or a free game. There is even the fun mechanic of shaking my phone to pay. The store is filled with positive aesthetics, and I am moved along with a reward system (stars). Clearly there is more at work here than just a cup of coffee.

According to a Pew Internet & American Life Project report, gamification is "interactive online design that plays on people's competitive instincts and often incorporates the use of rewards to drive action—these include virtual rewards such as points, payments, badges, discounts, and free gifts; and status indicators such as friend counts, re-tweets, leader boards, achievement data, progress bars, and the ability to level up" (Anderson & Rainie, 2012).

Designers often mix in game-like elements in unexpected places to create meaningful interactions. Visitors to websites may find progress bars encouraging completion of online profiles and badges to reward behaviors. All of social media can be considered a game; the score is based on shares, views, and "liked" activities. Gamification is a nascent field, especially in education.

Games and learning scholar James Gee told me about two types of gamification, and each is in competition with the other. We spoke in April 2014. He said, "Gamification is just extrinsic motivation. Or gamification is a way to try to motivate people by quest-based learning in the ways games are highly motivating. There really are two trends going on out there and battling each other, both of them popular. Unfortunately, our schools are mired in test prep." More often than not, gamification is seen as a reward system.

This chapter reviews how to implement gamification techniques that keep learning intrinsically engaging. I also analyze the quest-based approach, in which the teacher creates a journey for the student. Using a quest model as a support for gamification can make school more game-like and less like a chore. I review some common gamification techniques that work fine as stand-alone activities, such as having students create digital avatars. Other mechanics represent parts of games. Don't expect to add dice to a lesson, call it a game, and expect students' interest to be piqued. Gamification must be integrated into learning. One example is Amy Jo Kim's Social Action Matrix, which appropriated Bartle's Player Type Model to the social web. Kim has written extensively about the rise of cooperative games (e.g., *Draw Something*, *Words with Friends*) as being non-zero-sum—everyone wins!

Gamification Mechanics

To a game designer, almost anything can be viewed as a game. Whether it is a well-designed game is another story. In March 2014 I asked Carnegie Mellon's Jesse Schell about viewing school as a game. "The school system is set up as a game," he said. "Everything you do, you get scores. There's a leaderboard. We give out bumper stickers to parents that say, 'My Kid is an Honor Roll Student.' It is a game, just a badly designed game." School has notoriously slow feedback loops (from teacher to student and then back to teacher). It can be the opposite of James Gee's Explicit Information On-Demand and Just In Time Principle, in which "the learner is given explicit information both on demand and just in time, when the learner needs it or just at the point where the information can best be understood and used in practice" (2007, p. 226). Aside from issues with feedback, school can also be inequitable. The rich—who may hire tutors and discuss schoolwork at the dinner table—get richer.

Because gamification can strip out the parts of a whole system, taking pieces here and there from this list will not instantly turn your lesson plans into a game. It's not a pantry of ingredients. The elements detailed in this section should be used to deepen the journey or acknowledge "mile markers." I would not simply add a leaderboard; however, if it was done in the spirit of fun, it can be engaging. Keep in mind that adding rewards or feedback mechanisms will not make a boring activity into something fun; use gamification mechanics *with* games and projects.

Leaderboards

Leaderboards, like badges, can encourage student iteration. Noticing the high score in a game, or your own score, triggers competition in many people (Bartle's Achiever type). Of course, not everyone is competitive; don't expect to engage every child with a leaderboard. Essentially a public scoreboard, when misused, the leaderboard can discourage children from trying (that's why grades aren't publicly posted). Instead, try using a leaderboard for nongraded game tallies. I regularly use a leaderboard for Quest to Learn's *Socratic Smackdown*, its nondigital argumentation game. I modeled mine after Rebecca Grodner's, the game's co-designer. Grodner is an 8th-grade English language arts teacher at Quest. Individual scores are viewable on dry-erase boards. They are also tallied as part of a team score. The result became a cooperative—not competitive—game.

None of the *Socratic Smackdown* scores were used for grading purposes. It is important to emphasize to students that game scores are not grades. I explain the rationale to students to drive the point home. Using in-game assessments can stifle creativity in game-based solutions. Authentic assessments work well in sandbox projects, such as building in *Minecraft*.

My advice is to create teams of equal ability. In *Socratic Smackdown*, stronger arguers can coach those who require more refinement and practice. Having a lower batting average on a champion team still makes everyone a winner! Figure 2 shows the leaderboard for one of the teams, I modeled on Grodner's example.

Team 1: Student	9/5/14	9/19/14	10/3/14	10/17/14	Total
John					
Sam					
Alexandra					
Allison					
Total					

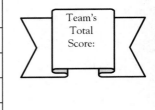

Figure 1. Team-Centered Leaderboard.

Anecdotally, I have noticed that as a result of my posting a leaderboard, some students redo work so that they could improve their standing. I paired up boys and girls in my 6th-grade social studies classes to play *SimCityEDU: Pollution Challenge!* (Previously, they playtested it individually.) Student teams looked for the leaderboard in the game's dashboard. Rather than trying to better their personal bests, the teams became more competitive.

In February 2014 I asked educational psychologist and researcher Val Shute about putting names on leaderboards. Does it motivate students to replay? She said, "There are different mechanics, one of which is competition. As it turns out, boys are more incentivized than girls, who like collaboration as an incentive. It depends on your target audience. Do not say, 'in all cases'—for girls, as a generalization—it may be a turn-off. It depends on who is competing against whom." It's better to compete with your own personal best.

Badges

A classroom-based badge system can also serve as a scoring mechanism, as well as an artifact of achievement. Essentially a digital version of a Boy Scout or Girl Scout badge system, it can promote a feedback loop of social participation. The core mechanic of social engagement is when people enjoy "shared activities" (Kim, 2012b; Kim, 2014d). Requirements to earn badges include social skills, such as sharing, expressing, and collaborating (Kim, 2012b; Kim, 2014d). Aside from social dynamics, people play games together because it is fun. Fun can be categorized depending on the desired outcome (Lazzaro, 2009). Multiplayer games are engaging because the interactions stimulate

People Fun (Lazzaro, 2009, pp. 40–46). People Fun mechanics includes the "social experiences of competition, teamwork, as well as opportunity for social bonding and personal recognition that comes from playing with others" (Lazzaro, 2004). Badges should trigger People Fun by acknowledging the connections from working together.

Badge issuance is an embedded assessment—an incremental check for understanding. Embedded assessments are built into educational activities and serve as part of the feedback loop of learning. This is not new to teaching, or mutually exclusive to game-based learning; many teachers already post mini-due dates and deadlines before a project is due. Formalizing embedded assessments adds feedback to students and teachers, thus creating an iterative design loop. The result should be better student work (known as "deliverables" in the business world). Digital badges are discussed further in Chapter 8. The first badge should be easy to earn, and is intended simply to spur motivation. All participating students should be able to win this badge at the beginning of their learning journey.

Modding

Did you ever change a recipe? Perhaps you added a no-calorie sweetener instead of sugar? Maybe blueberries in a muffin mix instead of chocolate chips? That is called modding (short for modifying). It is my favorite gamification mechanic. Modding a game bends the rules and changes the system. Think about board games you played that came with a timer. Did you always use it? People have their own house versions of *Monopoly* and *Scrabble*. Part of the charm—and success—of *Minecraft* is that modding is part of the game experience. In fact, *Minecraft* is a mod of another game, *Infiniminer* (video game modding is covered more extensively in Chapter 11). Learning should *matter* to the student. Therefore, students should be given an opportunity to customize their own learning.

It takes confidence in lesson planning to let students mod projects, directions, and even the rubric. When it's done correctly, students may show an increased ownership in their own learning. Remember what Bernie DeKoven said about freedom and play in Chapter 4? If not, it bears repeating: "Freedom is an absolute necessity for the play to be meaningful and for the learning to be something the kids could truly internalize." As long as the student is meeting the learning objectives, why not give them freedom to pursue their interests in activities?

Avatars

I give students freedom to choose silly avatars in learning networks such as Edmodo. An avatar is "an online representation of a participant in a game or social network" (Sheldon, 2012, p. 30). Nintendo's Mii is an example of a game avatar. Xbox and PlayStation have similar tool sets to let players customize their online selves. Students can create even sillier avatars using Voki, which doubles as a presentation tool. Voki Classroom is available, and features lesson plans and activities using its avatars. Their digital self can read whatever is typed in a text box. While not games, avatar creators give children the ability to have fun, which can make learning memorable.

In-Game Economies

Many games feature "in-game economies." In the *Assassin's Creed* series, opponents can be looted and pick-pocketed. Money can be found by unlocking hidden treasure chests. Currency can then be used to improve buildings, purchase outfits for the avatar, and buy maps. The science fiction-themed *Mass Effect 3* awards currency known as Paragon Points. These points are earned by "being a positive, kind, and friendly player, during conversations and stories" ("*Mass Effect 3* Wiki," 2014). Paragons can be used to upgrade weapons, health, and armor. *Historia* (detailed in Chapter 6) uses Culture Points to advance student civilizations. An "in-class economy" can reward students who progress in a meaningful way while also integrating math and financial literacy lessons.

Game Geography

Games often use maps. Some, such as *Risk!*, attempt to be geographically accurate. Others are more abstract; Atlantic City's streets are not in a perfect square, as in *Monopoly*. *Battleship* plays on a grid, while *Settlers of Catan* takes place in regions. *Dungeon and Dragons*, which bears similarities to *Lord of the Rings*, has a fantasy geography that develops as the game is played. Open-world video games are virtual worlds that players are encouraged to explore. *L.A. Noire* faithfully recreates almost all of Los Angeles during the late 1940s. Other games riff on historical accuracy, such as *Red Dead Redemption*, a fictionalized version of the American West and its borderlands with Mexico. Games with downloadable add-ons sometimes include maps. The war simulation game *Call of Duty: Black Ops* featured several maps where multiplayer "capture the flag" tournaments took place.

Isn't it easier to understand a map after you've driven somewhere? In order to progress in the game, a practical, hands-on knowledge of geography develops. Mapping of game worlds is important to know because it *matters* to students who play these games. The *Assassin's Creed III* release in 2012 made my job teaching the American Revolution infinitely easier. My students knew exactly what the battlefield of Concord looked like because they experienced it virtually. The game puts its protagonist, Connor, at the foot of the famous bridge where British Redcoats were fought. (Connor is half-English and half-Native American and sometimes speaks in a Mohawk dialect; his real name in the game is Ratonhnhaké:ton.)

Teaching the "five themes" of geography (location, place, human-environment interaction, movement, and region) to children who barely venture out of town can be an arduous task. It can be too abstract for children to remember places they have never visited. I have trouble doing that myself. When I go away on vacation, the travel books I buy always make better sense when I read them after the trip has ended. To that end, consider creating simple board games with dice or spinners and small game pieces to have students "experience" traveling in the place you are teaching. Another option is a virtual field trip using Google Earth. Remember, engaging learners in virtual worlds is learning by simulation, which is learning by doing. This helps the knowledge "stick."

Easter Eggs

Near a computer? Go to Google's Image Search and type "Atari breakout" in the box. The search results will become a fully playable version of the 1980s Atari video game *Breakout*. What you just uncovered (thanks to my hint!) is an Easter egg. In an affinity group (online spaces of mutual interest), members share game "cheats." Cheats are not condoning cheating; rather, they can encourage the sharing of knowledge. They can help to uncover hidden challenges, known as "Easter eggs." (The game *Super Mario Bros.* was among the first to feature Easter eggs.)

Easter eggs provide "transgressive discovery: by bending the rules of the game in just the right way, the players get to see or experience something that more lawful players would not" (Salen & Zimmerman, 2003, p. 279). Warren Robinett is credited with subversively hiding the first Easter egg in the Atari

2600 game *Adventure*. He recalled the story in an essay featured in the book *The Game Design Reader* (2006). He wrote, "In this deviously hidden secret room, I affixed my signature, in flashing lights, 'Created by Warren Robinett.' I did this in the tradition of artists, down through the centuries, identifying themselves as authors of their own works" (Robinett, 2006, pp. 712–713).

Easter eggs empower the student to test the boundaries of the learning system. Uncovered Easter eggs can also be acknowledged with digital badges. For example, as part of a podcasting project I do, I award a "Magical Mystery Badge" once the student deciphers a backwards recording. The student must figure out on their own how to use the tools available to decipher the recording. A hint, written in reverse, is part of the badge's description. Another way to hide Easter eggs is by using QR codes. QR codes are like bar codes that are read with a mobile device and take the user directly to a website or a picture. Easter eggs are common in movies, too. Disney's *Frozen* (2013) included characters from *Tangled* (2010). Try leaving some hidden surprises for your students to find in their learning journey!

Gamification as a Tool... not an Add-on

Gamification is not without its share of critics, especially among the many game designers I interviewed. For a game to function, the interlocking elements of an achievable goal, rules, voluntary participation, and feedback must all be present (McGonigal, 2011, p. 21). Separating out the feedback system, like awarding gold stars for handing in homework, doesn't mean you've created a game. This is why I recommend using the above mechanics in concert with projects. It should also be noted that gamification is becoming ubiquitous in the corporate world; Samsung awards badges internally to motivate its employees. In the growing wearable fitness sector, the Nike+ iPhone app awards achievements to users. FitBit motivates the same way, with badges and social sharing.

In January 2014 Filament Games's Dan White told me that all games include elements of gamification; however, they "don't trick players into learning." He feels that education should already be intrinsically motivating. "There is a time and place for 'light gamification,' but I wouldn't lean too heavily with creating structures and systems that have students progressing because of extrinsic motivation," he said. Richard Bartle (a speaker at the 2012 Gamification Summit) called the movement a bandwagon. We spoke in March 2014. Not mincing words, he said, "the technical term for it is cheap psychological tricks." He then elaborated how gamification can be misappropriated. He said:

> If you design a game, you want [people] to play it because it's fun—not because you've written a Skinner Box and you're forcing them to play your game because you're using cheap psychological tricks. It means your game is not fun and you have to have another method. If you are a game designer, you want people to play because they like your game—not because you tricked them by giving them rewards. Imagine a machine, like a car, and it all has to work together. You say let's take the wheels off of this car and attach it to this plank of wood and call it "car-ification" and now you can ride around in this plank of wood. Kids would like that, but that's not car-ification, it's just playing with wood.

Bartle is stating that gamification should not be tacked on to learning. It needs to be integrated into an environment, whether it's a game or a classroom. Don't add badges to a rubric and call the activity a game. Instead, use the achievements to tell a student's story of learning. When I spoke to Val Shute in February 2014, she concurred. She said, "Games are a system with core elements, like ongoing feedback and adaptive challenges. Learners have control of the environment with clear rules and goals. This inter-operational system is a well-defined game."

The critics of gamification describe the misuses. I often read the same thing about educational technology in general. You can't throw in iPads and SMART Boards into a classroom and expect students to succeed. Educational technology is a tool to extend learning and empower students. Similarly, gamification, when properly implemented with a narrative shell, can be effective. To work best, a teacher requires professional development training on games and learning. In January 2014 the Cooney Center's Jessica Millstone explained to me, "Gamification is a kind of a dirty word in our field, when it's not really games, but an add-on or a layer." Millstone cited *Historia* and the PlayMaker School as effective examples of gamification because of the deep and experiential learning involved. Both are holistic and involve role-playing. Quest to Learn doesn't consider its methodology to be "gamified"; rather, the learning principles are called "game-like" because not all of its lessons are full games.

In open-ended "sandboxes" such as *Minecraft* (and, for that matter, LEGO), the intrinsic satisfaction comes from building in the game environment. (*Minecraft* is on the Xbox Achievement badging system.) TeacherGaming (*MinecraftEdu* and *KerbalEdu*) co-founder Santeri Koivisto explained where he sees gamification in open-world games. "We should learn because learning makes us better humans, more technological, more skillful," he said. "Why should we want to get points? Schools and kids don't need that in a sandbox. The joy of finding new things, manipulating the world, is good in itself." Game communities come with their own intrinsic rewards. For example, when *KerbalEdu* is used to teach advanced physics, a student may share his or her project with the game community. The community provides feedback and rewards.

There is promise for gamification in education. I spoke to Games + Learning + Society Center's Kurt Squire in January 2014. He said, "The devil's in the details on implementation." Schools already have structures and systems in place and may not necessarily need gamification. Shifting ownership to the student empowers the student, personalizing the learning. "Gamification can be good or poor, like games themselves," he said. "There is a commoditization of it, like applying it to anything." Jesse Schell had a problem with the word itself—but not the intent. (He is not alone; several respondents in the Pew Research Center's Future of Gamification survey also disliked the term.) We spoke in March 2014. To Schell, gamifying may simply imply more interactive participation from users. It shouldn't come as a surprise that people would want to design products to be as compelling as some games. "Games have good qualities, games have good feedback, games are very engaging, games make people satisfied about their progress, games make people feel good about themselves. I want people to feel those things," Schell concluded.

For gamification in schools to really work, it takes more than points and badges. Gamification mechanics are parts of a whole, just like educational technology. It should be used as a teaching tool, not the focal point of learning. When I teach presentation skills, I don't focus on PowerPoint transitions; rather, I use slideshows as a tool for teaching and learning.

Quest-Based Learning

As Ralph Waldo Emerson famously wrote, "Life is a journey, not a destination." Real engagement comes from the journey. In a game, it is called a "Quest" or a "Mission." In a book or a movie it's the character's arc. We watch or read how the main character grows as a result of events in a story. Similar to video games, Quest schools—such as Quest to Learn in New York City and ChicagoQuest—use a narrative to frame game-based units.

In the summer of 2013 I had the opportunity to observe new teacher professional development training at Quest to Learn, a public school co-founded, designed, and developed by the Institute of Play. The school opened in 2009 initially for just the 6th grade, and has since extended through the 9th grade. It teaches the same Common Core State Standards as a typical school, and it participates in state standardized testing. The difference is in its approach. Quest has an "approach to pedagogy that connects game design and systems thinking across a standards-based curriculum" (Rufo-Tepper, Salen, Shapiro, Torres, & Wolozin, 2011, p. 49). Seven "Principles of Game-like Learning" guide the school:

1. *Everyone is a participant*—A shared culture and practice exists where everyone contributes, which may mean that different students contribute different types of expertise.
2. *Challenge is constant*—A "need to know" challenges students to solve a problem whose resources have been placed just out of reach.
3. *Learning happens by doing*—Learning is active and experiential. Students learn by proposing, testing, playing with, and validating theories about the world.
4. *Feedback is immediate and ongoing*—Students receive ongoing feedback on their progress against learning and assessment goals.
5. *Failure is reframed as iteration*—Opportunities exist for students and teachers to learn through failure. All learning experiences should embrace a process of testing and iteration.
6. *Everything is interconnected*—Students can share their work, skill, and knowledge with others across networks, groups, and communities.
7. *It kind of feels like play*—Learning experiences are engaging, learner-centered, and organized to support inquiry and creativity. (Institute of Play, 2014)

Some of Quest to Learn's principles—design thinking, systems thinking (interconnectedness), playful learning, and constructivism (learn by doing)— have been already mentioned in this book. The teacher's role at Quest is to put the student on a mission. In February 2014 I asked Katie Salen, founder of Quest to Learn, about how she went from co-writing the influential game design book *Rules of Play* to launching a game-based school. Salen was also a design professor at Parsons The New School for Design in New York City (she currently teaches at DePaul University in Chicago). Salen said:

> I think games can teach us so much about how to design other things. I actually wrote the book [*Rules of Play*] to help people understand how games work so they can apply those principles to design things that weren't games. Quest to Learn was a by-product

of that thinking. It didn't faze me that the choice of what we could design was a school and not a game. Writing *Rules of Play* was an exercise to help people literally understand how games work. Doing that set up the whole theoretical foundation for what became Quest to Learn. It's not a one-to-one mapping, but that book was all about systems. At Quest, that was one of the founding ideas. If you really want to make a change, you have to think at a systemic level. You cannot just design a game, or a piece of curriculum, or just work with teachers; you have to think of the design of the entire system, which was, in this case, an entire school. That's the connection.

Quest to Learn is quest-driven (hence the name). The curriculum puts students on 10-week problem-solving "missions." Quests take place within missions, lasting a day or two. The missions are similar to those found in video games because they include opportunities to "level up" until the final level. Leveling up in challenge is similar to Vygotsky's Zone of Proximal Development in which new knowledge is scaffolded on what learners already know. More skills are learned until mastery is achieved. It is the flow channel at work, and it translates well into school settings.

At Quest to Learn, the boss-level week is when students "bring all of their skills to bear throughout a design process: brainstorming, prototyping, testing, iterating, and finally, publicly sharing their solutions with family, friends and classmates" (Parker, 2013). All of the gained skills and knowledge are applied to overcome a final challenging task. Activities include building a Rube Goldberg machine, video creations, and robotics, and developing ideas to end the systemic problem of bullying (Parker, 2013). The boss level asks students to "work together to make something that they do not yet know how to make" ("Boss Level at Quest to Learn," n.d.). The notion of a culminating activity in a project is not quite the same. Boss levels ask students to apply what they have learned. During boss-level weeks, Quest to Learn actually adjusts the school schedule and even the physical classroom layouts. The result is a noisy and excited classroom filled with active learners. When I reach a boss level in a video game, *I expect to fail.* If the challenge is too easy, I assume that the rest of the game will be that way. Sometimes it can take dozens of tries to win a match. If the goal is to increase tenacity and persistence, try adding boss levels to your culminating activities.

My school district implemented problem-based learning to deliver instruction. Problem-based learning has its roots in medical school training. Students are given an authentic narrative and a problem to cooperatively solve. After observing teacher training at the Quest to Learn school, I started to think about how to turn my problem-based learning units into game-based missions. I asked Salen to explain the difference between the two approaches. She said:

> The philosophy has a total overlap. Games are spaces of inquiry, spaces of problem solving. Games have a couple of particular affordances to them, like you know when a game is over. That notion of an end point is really important. The notion is a stylization of behavior or mechanic that gets repeated over and over again—it affords choice to the player. Students feel like they're driving the space. You can constrain the problem space enough so you can anticipate types of choices a player might make. Those are really specific things to games. The way they handle challenges, the way they provide feedback. The philosophy of learning is the same—it's problem-based, it's inquiry-based. The wrapper in which that is situated just looks different.

When creating a storyline to accompany a problem-based unit or mission, the narrative comes first, setting up an authentic challenge to solve. Video games with strong narrative storylines, such as *Assassin's Creed* or *Bioshock*, also begin with gameplay and action, delaying the storyline details until the player is hooked in. If a game had no narrative, then the player would just be pressing buttons on a controller. This differs from young adult novels, where the action typically begins on page 1.

Quest learning designer Shula Ehrlich described how games are framed within a storyline. We spoke in January 2014. At Quest, a mission is a curriculum unit housed in a larger framework, with a game-like narrative. The mechanic involves a student solving a problem. A teacher can add a narrative frame around projects with a mission/quest structure. Quest's 6th- and 7th-grade missions tend to be more "fantastical and narrative heavy. Context gets more real world in higher grades." An example is the 6th-grade cell biology science mission, *The Way Things Work*. Introduced in the second trimester, the goal is to help Dr. Smallz, a doctor who has shrunk himself and journeyed into a human body to cure a disease. Smallz has lost his memory and knowledge and now can't get out. As students learn about body systems, the doctor begins to send hints, such as, "I see long red strings, where am I?" Quests build knowledge and skills with smaller challenges to get to a larger, overarching goal. Ehrlich concluded, "It is, in some ways, problem-based, but in a game-like framework."

In April 2014 I asked James Gee how a game-based learning curriculum compared to other approaches. He said:

> Whether we call it project-based or problem-based or inquiry-based is completely meaningless. The question is, "Is it any good?" They're all the same. Focus on kids

doing, and not just knowing. One of the best ways to know is to do. When you do something, you have to solve a problem, you have to recruit facts, so you do get fact-based learning. You also get the ability to solve a problem. If you just teach facts, the person may get them retained, but the person doesn't know how to solve problems. I don't give a damn what we call it. I want to know what it looks like when it's good. I would suggest for people to look at good examples of learning, where kids are solving problems and are sometimes doing it collaboratively and are using multiple tools to do it. The principles that we know work well for learning and teaching are substantiated from games. They're also substantiated in many other things that are working. Give me an example of what's good. Give me an example of how it works. Give me an example of why it works.

If a student is authentically challenged, then learning will take place. If it is effective, then knowledge should transfer and stay with the learner (Lave & Wenger, 1991). Simulation can help with the retention of new knowledge, almost as much as experiencing something for real. The simulation can be delivered in a project or a game.

The Player Journey

Creating a journey for that student can help him or her stay on the path to mastery learning. In March 2014 I asked Jesse Schell about the player's (or student's) journey. "Stories serve to connect the dots," he said. "Journeys are about storytelling and your journey as a learner. What you are able to accomplish is contextual." In short, humans remember better with stories. Games put the player in the role of the story's protagonist, thus codifying the experience. In games, the player takes "agency" of a character.

To social game designer Amy Jo Kim, the journey must be meaningful. When one plays a game, there is the intrinsic satisfaction from completing and mastering missions. She created the Player's Journey Framework to describe the experience. Kim posted a description on her blog. She wrote:

- Onboarding—the initial *Newbie* experience that teaches the ropes and sets expectations for what's to come
- Habit-building—the triggers, activity loops and feedback systems that turn *Newbies* into *Regulars*
- Mastery—the "elder game" that opens up to *Enthusiasts* who've mastered the system and want to go deeper. (Kim, 2014d)

Kim's Player Journey can show student growth. This model is also similar to the Zone of Proximal Development. Children learn formally, in school, and informally, in situated spaces (e.g., from family members, instructional YouTube videos). In both settings, they set out to master skills and content. They also mature in the process. In that context, Kim's journey is not just a game, but also a space to develop. Keep the journey meaningful so the learning matters.

Social Engagement

When I first saw Bartle's Player Type Model (described in Chapter 3), I immediately thought of how this would help me differentiate instruction. I could tailor activities for competitive students and those who are high achievers. The reality was more sobering than I expected. After all, Bartle created his model for multi-user dungeons, not my classroom. My school isn't located in Middle Earth or Narnia. And I can't add Killers to my lesson plans (it implies competition—try explaining that to an administrator!).

Bartle told me that his model appears in all sorts of unintended places. We spoke in March 2014. Gamification is just the latest use of Bartle's Player Types. "For gamification, they look at my Player Types Model because they know it works for games," he said. "But they're not writing games. What they really want is a screwdriver, but no one's invented a screwdriver yet, so they use my hammer, which I suppose is better than trying to turn it with their teeth."

Richard Bartle spoke highly of a modification of his model: Amy Jo Kim's Social Action Matrix. He told me, "If you're going to adapt a model, that's how you do it, instead of wholesale apply it. She looked around for different things, and that's what shined best for her." Kim updated the Player Type Model to better align with social interactions. She replaced the "Killer" type with "Express"—a much more friendly descriptor. Completing her axes, "Compete" took the place of "Achiever," "Explore" replaced "Explorer," and "Collaborate" replaced "Cooperate" (Kim, 2012b).

Games—like learning objectives—are designed with verbs. Kim extended her matrix by adding Social Engagement Verbs. These included: "build, design, customize, challenge, curate, and share" (Kim, 2012b). Social Engagement Verbs are reminiscent of Bloom's Taxonomy of Higher-Order Thinking Verbs ("Identify" is a lower-order, or skill and drill, verb; "Compare" or "Create" are higher-order). Of course, no model is perfect. Like Bartle, Kim recommends modifying her version to fit a product (in this case content, skills, or, better yet, a love of the learning process) or an intended audience (students). Below is Kim's Social Action Matrix:

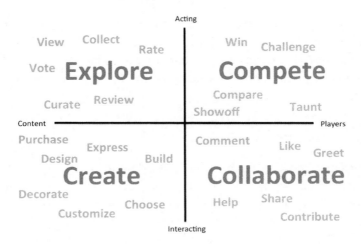

Figure 2. Social Action Matrix. Image courtesy of Amy Jo Kim, Ph.D. Reprinted from Social Engagement: Who's playing? How do they like to engage?, by A. J. Kim, 2012. Reprinted with permission.

Do all of Kim's descriptors sound familiar? Don't I already do this by having students engage cooperatively? The answer, of course, is: Yes! Social engagement works best in non-zero-sum games. As previously mentioned in this book, this style of gameplay is cooperative. Gamify activities to focus the design better on each learner. Keep in mind that the above matrix is intended for social gaming and website design.

Offering choice is always a smart idea to boost the social engagement in projects. Explorers would enjoy peer feedback and collecting images from Google. Helping one another iterate on work is a positive and social experience. Competitors may like the idea of class museums that put culminating projects on display. Displaying side-by-side work is a win-win competition. Collaborative work should already take place in a student-centered classroom. There are many Internet tools, from wikis to Google Drive, enabling students to work together. Lastly, Creators involve the creation of a project deliverable. Incorporating social meaning to a student's learning environment personalizes the journey or quest.

Conclusions and Takeaways

Gamification is a trend in business and e-commerce that has entered the educational world. Some mechanics may work in the short term, while others tend to be extrinsic. Stories and quests are a better approach for school set-tings. Quest to Learn's Game-Like Learning is effective and should be inte-grated in a game-based setting. Kim's Social Matrix has similarities to Bloom's Taxonomy of Higher Order Learning; each is an action verb (games are writ-ten with verbs). Kim's matrix is about what people—including students—want to do to be socially engaged.

Lesson Plan Ideas

Caterpillar Game: Math board game created by Alicia Iannucci (Quest to Learn)—http://www .edutopia.org/blog/caterpillar-game-real-world-math-alicia-iannucci

Galactic Mappers: Paper-based geography game for 6th grade with embedded assessments, from C. Ross Flatt from Quest to Learn. Social studies standards apply—http://www.edu topia.org/made-with-play-game-based-learning-assessment-video

Game Map Cartography: Adapt a geography assignment to an authentic task of creating a game world map. Task the students to create a game-like map; include locations for fast-travel and a key that features play to trade goods and Easter eggs. Mapping locations is useful for spatial thinkers. English language arts teachers can map out worlds in fictional lit-erature (e.g., the districts that make up Panem in the *Hunger Games* books, Neverland, Middle Earth). The map should contain mathematical properties such as a grid and scale. Natural science standards can include the physical features in the map. Social studies and Common Core English language arts standards apply.

Institute of Play Mission Pack: Dr. Smallz (The Way Things Work) science unit—http://www .instituteofplay.org/work/projects/quest-curriculum/mission-pack-dr-smallz

Institute of Play Mission Pack: I Spy Greece, world history curriculum—http://www.instituteof play.org/work/projects/quest-curriculum/mission-pack-i-spy-greece

Institute of Play Mission Pack: Shark Tank, math and financial literacy presented in an authen-tic game-like structure—http://www.instituteofplay.org/work/projects/quest-curriculum/ mission-pack-shark-tank

Institute of Play Mission Pack: Self on a Stand, English language arts unit—http://www.institute ofplay.org/work/projects/quest-curriculum/mission-pack-self-on-the-stand

Puzzle Challenge: One of the more straightforward methods for gamifying teaching is to throw in puzzle challenges. Many games have puzzles (e.g., *Portal, Tomb Raider*). Puzzles can be seen as practice for solving problems gradually. Make sure the mechanic fits the content, such as a letter puzzle in an English language arts game. Or try a science riddle about chem-istry. Standards depend on discipline and content area.

Scavenger Hunts: Classrooms and museums have begun to use mobile devices for scavenger hunt games. QR ("quick response") codes are the simplest to create. QR codes are essentially square-shaped bar codes that can be scanned with a mobile device camera. The code, read by a QR reader app, scans and launches a website or image. QR codes can be gener-ated for free from any number of websites. The image can be saved and then pasted on a document. Some teachers copy small QR codes on worksheets to bring students directly to web content. An even more interactive idea is augmented reality (AR). Teachers and students can embed in everyday objects hidden images that can be viewed only with a tablet's camera. Aurasma is an AR app to launch an "aura," which can be a simple digital animation, audio, or picture. Blogger Erin Klein used Aurasma to dazzle parents during back-to-school night—http://www.scholastic.com/teachers/top-teaching/2013/09/bring-magic-your-open-house-augmented-reality. Standards depend on discipline and content area.

Talking Avatars: While not a game, creating talking avatars embodies something more powerful: play. Using free websites such as Voki or Blabberize, have students create real or fantasy likenesses. Both tools work well for students to present work. Standards depend on discipline and content area.

Games

Google's Atari *Breakout* Easter egg—http://goo.gl/PnBNw4
Institute of Play's downloadable game-like lessons and units (quests and missions)—http://www.sharemylesson.com/mypublicprofile.aspx?uc=3752684

Resources

Aurasma augmented reality app—http://www.aurasma.com
Blabberize, make talking avatars using digital images—http://blabberize.com
Easter egg directory—http://www.eeggs.com
Edmodo, the school-based social network to deliver quest-based instruction—https://www.edmodo.com
Gamification.co, resources and an annual conference on gamification—http://www.gamification.co
Just Press Play, gamification at Rochester Institute of Technology—https://play.rit.edu
Pixar's Easter eggs—https://www.youtube.com/watch?v=jzWxue95WdU
Prezi presentations about quest-based learning and gamification, from Chris Haskell, clinical assistant professor of educational technology at Boise State University—http://prezi.com/user/haskell
QR Code Generator—https://www.the-qrcode-generator.com
3D GameLab, gamified K–12 learning management system (LMS), that uses a quest-based approach—http://3dgamelab.com
Voki Classroom, to have students create talking avatars—http://www.voki.com

· 8 ·

PERSONALIZED LEARNING

Not all learning is formal—much of it occurs outside the classroom. I have traditional degrees and certificates from university trainings and workshops. I have also enrolled in massive open online courses and watched instructional videos on YouTube. If I take a professional development workshop on Teq's online platform, I am awarded a badge that can be exported to the cloud, via Mozilla's Open Badges initiative. This system of informal learning is more personalized to better suit my individualized needs. It is my personalized learning environment!

The current educational model has its roots in both the Industrial Revolution and the medieval university system. Many reformers are rethinking the model of student-earned, teacher-assigned letter grades and social promotion based on birth year. *Whyville's* Jim Bower didn't mince words. "It's ridiculous to have 32 kids in your classroom grouped by age," he said. "It's the dumbest—and easiest—way to group. There's no reason why that needs to be that way." ClassBadges's co-founder James Sanders concurred. "I would love to see the gradual elimination of the idea of grade levels. That we group students based on when they were born and have them progress at the same time is ridiculous," he stated.

Newer models of personalized learning are delivered in a gamified system. Difficulty automatically adjusts, based on student ability. It is essentially differentiated instruction facilitated by a computer's adaptive algorithm. The reward is frequently a micro-credential: a digital badge. In January 2014 I asked the Cooney Center's Jessica Millstone about personalized learning. She said:

> All of [the Cooney Center's] research shows that games are one of the best ways to have a personalized learning environment in class, because games are self-paced. You can do it on your own. It rewards failure. You have to try until you get it right. You have to play to get the knowledge out of it. The Cooney Center is an advocate of personalized learning and adaptive learning because games can seamlessly scale back the content it delivers, if needed. Our surveys show that teachers that use games can level the classroom, from special education to gifted. Games help to self-pace the acquisition of knowledge. Then the teacher can lead the reflection.

GlassLab designer Erin Hoffman had a similar opinion. We initially spoke in January 2014. She told me, "We hope *SimCityEDU* and *Mars Generation One: Argubot Academy* help the teacher create pockets of personalized experiences and then provide a context for students to have a collaborative group discussion where everybody is learning a lot more. Personalized experience creates engagement and relevance." Using personalized learning tools in formal settings still requires teacher facilitation. In some cases, as we shall see, this system works better with older students and adult learners. Designer Shula Ehrlich, from Mission Lab, the Institute of Play's nondigital lab, took another stance. We spoke in January 2014. "Adaptive and personalized learning takes away from students collaborating, even working with others at different levels," she said. Learning becomes too isolated and can stifle cooperative and collaborative work in a face-to-face classroom. "The ultimate personalized learning environment is always a really good teacher," Hoffman concluded.

In this chapter, I review digital badges in the context of personalized learning. Badges are a reward system, like those from the Boy and Girl Scouts, as well as those in video games (incidentally, both the Boy Scouts and the Girl Scouts have a Game Design Badge). The Mozilla Foundation is currently attempting to make an "open" system of badges. Basically a free platform, its Open Badges Initiative promises to clarify how people move through their careers. Better yet, employers can offer badge requirements, thus making the path to a career more transparent. I interviewed Mozilla's Emily Goligoski about Open Badges, as well as its new design toolkit, BadgeKit. I spoke to Mozilla's Chloe Varelidi, designer of the Discovery project, about badges for students in elementary, middle, and high school. Goligoski and Varelidi spoke to me in March 2014.

This chapter also features an in-depth conversation with ClassBadges's James Sanders and Youtopia's Simeone Schnapper. Both freely share their vision and experiences with digital badges. Applications for badging Common Core skills are also suggested. Computer-based personalized learning requires technology to increase difficulty to continually challenge the learner. David Liu, the COO of Knewton, an adaptive platform for learning, shares his insights, too. It is important to understand when to intervene with a student who is learning on a computer application.

Digital Badges and Learning Pathways

Engaging a student intrinsically in the learning process, rather than with extrinsic motivators—such as grades—is the goal of every teacher. Awarding badges for academic accomplishments is a method to gamify the education. Video games use a digital badge system to acknowledge player achievements. Microsoft's Xbox offers "Achievements," while Sony's PlayStation awards "Trophies." Achievements and Trophies can also be shared online. Sharing accomplishments extends the personal game experience to social spaces.

Communities of practice enable sharing in educational endeavors (Lave & Wenger, 1991). The idea of open badges is to combine all recognitions together to enable adult learners to tell a narrative, like a visual résumé. Emily Goligoski is a Mozilla Foundation researcher. She explained, "Portability and interoperability is important in a badge infrastructure. There are plenty of badge sites, but badges are limited to that particular community of practice." In other words, learning communities need the ability to view and share one another's achievements. Goligoski is currently working on Mozilla's nascent BadgeKit project, a set of tools to enable anyone to create badges.

A badge system has three interconnected participants: "the issuer, the earner, and the displayer" (Mozilla Foundation and Peer 2 Peer University, 2012). In the classroom, as opposed to a video game, the teacher is the issuer and the student is the earner. Many website tools are available for teachers to create virtual classrooms, complete with predesigned badge artwork. It is not necessary for a student to accumulate badges in a linear fashion. He or she may—or may not—decide to earn badges in any sequence, even after an activity has ended. Logging onto Khan Academy's Learning Dashboard is helpful example of how this works. On Khan, you will see an integrated badge system geared for self-paced learning at the middle and high school levels.

Badges in game-based learning have evolved to include recognition for participation and/or mastering content or a skill. In a video game, the computer has a clear algorithm that determines when a goal is met and a badge is granted. Chloe Varelidi, who currently runs the Mozilla Open Badge Discovery project, told me that she is excited about the development of peer-to-peer issuances. She said, "Badges are not just top down, reinforcing current systems, but peers in a learning cohort." Her background is in game design, and she has worked for Quest to Learn. Groups can test each other's culminating activity, give feedback, iterate, and then award badges. Recognition from a peer can be more meaningful to some students than the grade from the teacher.

Why Badge?

Game designer Jesse Schell believes that badges are only meaningful "if there is a social framework where it matters and people actually care." We spoke in March 2014. He also expressed concerns about open systems. They have the potential of growing so vast that no one cares. In other words, if everyone has a badge from somewhere, it could devalue the entire system in the same way money drops in value as more is printed. He did point out opportunities where badging works best. He recalled an anecdote from his youth. Schell said:

> When I was about 13 or 14, I took on juggling as a hobby. I didn't know anybody doing it—[I learned] from books, kind of figuring it out for myself. Around 1986 a book came out called the *Complete Juggler* by a guy named Dave Finnigan. It was the most comprehensive book on how to do tricks. What was fascinating was that it had a badge part to it. At the end of each chapter there were literally badges. If you could do these 15 tricks so many times in a row and fill out this form, get a witness to sign it, mail it to us with $3, we'll mail you this enamel pin that says you completed this. I found it immensely motivating. When I look back on what worked, the notion that someone said what it meant to be good at something was a nice structure.

For Schell, there was a meaningful challenge put forth, and he cared about the outcome. Students have to want to earn. Furthermore, Schell doesn't necessarily see extrinsic motivation as a negative. External motivational factors could be a support structure, like a trellis on a building where vines grow. "If you have too much trellis, nothing can grow," he explained. "There needs to be balance and context. A badge system needs a clear statement: These are the things you have to do to constitute success or adequacy in this field and these are the steps in order to get there. The badge part of it, I think, is secondary."

There is a debate about whether badges can serve as both an educational assessment tool and an intrinsic motivator. Digital learning expert Henry Jenkins voiced criticism about the use of badges to gamify informal learning. Jenkins wrote, "Informal learning works because it is informal" (2012). The overuse of badges bears the risk of the system becoming an extrinsic motivator that can actually stifle the free exchange of ideas (Jenkins, 2012). Similar to Jenkins, Mitch Resnick (from the MIT Media Lab, developer of the kid-friendly coding app *Scratch*) voiced concerns on the HASTAC website (HASTAC is a partner organization in the Mozilla Open Badges project). Another critique of badge systems is that certain personalities—essentially, Bartle's Achievers—will take on a collection-like mentality. Resnick worried "that students will focus on accumulating badges rather than making connections with the ideas and material associated with the badges—the same way that students too often focus on grades in a class rather than the material in the class, or the points in an educational game rather than the ideas in the game" (2012). Resnick's colleague at Digital Media Learning Central, Cathy Davidson, wrote that badge systems that work most effectively are the ones that "best recognize competencies, skills, training, collaborative abilities, character, personal contribution, participatory energy, leadership and motivational skills, and other so-called 'hard' and 'soft' individual and cooperative talents" (Davidson, 2012).

Mozilla's BadgeKit includes a design tool to enable issuers to limit availability, to make badges rare or difficult to earn. This would result in a career pathway that is unique to the earner. Emily Goligoski described the pathway as a person's professional anecdote. In fact, the feared "collection frenzy" has yet to come to fruition. Chloe Varelidi stated, "By design, Open Badges avoids the traditional notion of badges collections." We build projects to discover, make badges, and build like a puzzle. Like it or not, badges are an increasing presence in education, including in learning management systems and online grade books.

Badges and Common Core Skills

One of the main goals of the Common Core State Standards is to prepare students for "college- and career-ready performance." According to CoreStandards.org, "English language arts and math were the subjects chosen for the Common Core State Standards because they are areas upon which students build skill sets which are used in other subjects." Badges can acknowledge the mastery learning that has occurred "along the way." Badge accumulation can occur in a nonlinear fashion; some students may earn different badges than others.

Embedded assessments can be built into an overall learning experience. A teacher can award Common Core badges during a unit, rather than at the end. In this respect, badges can support differentiated learning. For instance, a student may earn a badge, at any time, for meeting CCSS.ELA-Literacy. SL.7.4: "Present claims and findings, emphasizing salient points in a focused, coherent manner with pertinent descriptions, facts, details, and examples; use appropriate eye contact, adequate volume, and clear pronunciation."

The Common Core guides only English language arts and math teaching. Other disciplines, such as science and social studies, should "anchor," or support, the Standards. In social studies, a student can earn a badge for meeting CCSS.ELA-Literacy.RH.6–8.9, when he or she can "analyze the relationship between a primary and secondary source on the same topic." Similarly, science teachers can recognize students who meet CCSS.ELA-Literacy.RST.9–10.10 by reading and comprehending "science/technical texts in the grades 9–10 text complexity band independently and proficiently."

In order to maximize student engagement, a teacher can add Easter egg hidden challenges. Easter eggs empower the student to test the boundaries of the learning system. A student may solve a secret riddle in a lesson, and, in the process, meet CCSS.Math.Content.HSS-MD.B.5a: "Find the expected payoff for a game of chance."

Youtopia

There are many options for online badge systems, including Youtopia, which I first became aware of by virtue of being a part of the Discovery Educator Network. It is used by Discovery Education to conduct professional development with feedback and tracking. It is very simple to join and intuitive to use. There are free and discounted options available. Student lists can be uploaded and then lessons can be presented as challenges. It is, in essence, a gamified version of a learning management system.

Youtopia is young—just over 2 years old. In February 2014 I interviewed Youtopia's founder and CEO, Simeon Schnapper. He explained that meaningful engagement is the goal. When it was formed as a start-up, the founders brainstormed its business model; they all liked gamification, behavioral psychology, learning, fun, and play. It has had moderate success. It has built up its customer base, and it's solving some unexpected problems. Some clients simply needed a way to digitize, while others needed help organizing and tracking students. "Some institutions were still stuck in the 90s, using pen and paper rather than computers," Schnapper said. For this market segment, the gamification piece was secondary to its learning management system. Youtopia was originally piloted in Philadelphia's school district.

Youtopia's headquarters are in Chicago, which put the company in the position of working with the Chicago City of Learning (the year-round version of 2013's nascent Summer of Learning). Citizens were encouraged to visit city parks, museums, and botanical gardens, all while learning and collecting badges. Students shared their accomplishments at a culminating summer event. In addition, at the Adler Planetarium in Chicago Youtopia collaborated with another start-up, For All Badges (part of For All Rubrics) and six or seven civic institutions in Chicago, including the planetarium and botanical gardens. Their purpose was to set up a badge network for STEM (science, technology, engineering, and math) learning. Earning a badge at Adler would have the same artifacts—digital badges, in this case—with evidence mapped to a particular activity. The pathway to achieve a badge would be in a shared curriculum. "So if you are at the Chicago Botanical Gardens, there might be a badge in the ecosystem of other institutions," Schnapper explained. "Building up a framework may soon include places nationally, like the Bronx Zoo." He also pointed out the work of the Hive Network, which uses badges for afterschool programs in several cities. Schnapper continued, "Cities and foundations get behind badges, at least for informal extended learning opportunities."

Schnapper was really excited about the involvement with the City of Learning. "If there is an open badge support, City of Learning will prove it. It's informal and across the city," he said. About 100 9th-grade students were at Adler learning STEM. There were badges for each activity. One program involved building a rover to launch into space and then landing it on the moon. Schnapper recalled, "There was a girl who had a problem logging in and was upset because she was at the bottom of the leaderboard. The teacher then pointed out that she simply had to do the activities. I don't know if that mechanic or the leaderboard will play out for everybody, but the transparency of competition was there." Badges on Youtopia can be displayed as they accumulate, and they can be assigned a point value. Doing so, however, shifts the game mechanic from sharing an accomplishment to competition. Youtopia is letting the users and the market lead the way. Schnapper told me about a teacher who emailed him asking to create a button to increase points for underperforming students. His goal isn't to trick people into being motivated; he wants to empower the teacher to do what they do.

Before we finished speaking, Schnapper shared with me how the MIRI utilized its service. MIRI is the Machine Intelligence Research Institute, the artificial intelligence nonprofit co-founded by Ray Kurzweil. It used Youtopia for badges, points, and recognition for about 100 people, and utilized the power of volunteer management. One of the founders, Ray Kurzweil, uploaded a TED-style video. If someone within the MIRI organization transcribed it, he or she earned a "Transcriber" badge. People worldwide competed for the "Translator" badge, adding captions in their own native languages. "It used to take months [to translate videos], now it takes less than a week—and the badge cost them nothing," Schnapper said. "There was a crowdsource ability layered on the gamification."

ClassBadges

James Sanders, co-founder of ClassBadges, is an advocate for badges and personalized learning. (ClassBadges became part of EdStart in May 2014.) We spoke in February 2014. Sanders started his career as a social studies and English teacher. He also worked as a paid consultant for Google, curating kindergarten through grade-12 content for its educational initiative, including Google Play for Education, YouTubeEDU, YouTube Teachers, and YouTube for School. While advising Google, he started ClassBadges with his cousin Duncan Winter and Esther Wojcicki. Sanders said, "Esther was the brains behind Google's early education initiatives." Wojcicki is a Stanford professor and the mother of Susan Wojcicki, the current CEO of YouTube, and Anne Wojcicki, founder of the genetic ancestry service 23andMe.

In June 2013 Sanders took a position at the White House as a Presidential Innovation Fellow, part of Barack Obama's education initiative for postsecondary agenda. While there, he worked to build the U.S. Department of Education's Open Data Initiative. Todd Park, the former White House chief technology officer, created the program. It seeks to bring in people from the private sector. "We're charged with going in, assessing problems, and developing lean solutions to those problems," Sanders explained. "We are judged on how much money we're saving the American people, or lives are we saving, or how many jobs are we creating."

James Sanders is a former KIPP (Knowledge Is Power Program) teacher. He was the innovation manager for KIPP Bay Schools, which is comprised of eight charter schools in the San Francisco Bay Area. He also tried to figure out how to personalize learning for each of its students. The KIPP network of schools has been featured on *60 Minutes* and in the best-selling book *How Children Succeed: Grit, Curiosity, and the Hidden Power of Character* (2012) by Paul Tough. The book's thesis is that children need to learn *how* to fail—and then come back with resilience. Persistence is ingrained in KIPP schools' character education program. "We have students who go to school and their perception is that the classroom or the lesson is something that happens to them," Sanders said. "They are passive participants in this scheme that we call education. Their role is measured by seat time or by grades. We can shift. In order to achieve the next goal or skill, students need clear, masters-based goals. Those character traits are necessary." Tenacity and perseverance are character traits that demonstrate ownership of learning. To Sanders, badges help transfer the responsibility to acquire knowledge. He said, "If feedback was more immediate and open, students may begin to own the results of negative and positive. The artifact, which could be a badge or a paper certificate, represents those learning experiences. Right now, to succeed in a classroom, you must possess the ability to sit, be patient, raise your hand, and speak when spoken to—that doesn't require curiosity, grit, and perseverance."

According to Sanders, nuances in the learning process impede students from being able to track how they're progressing. Mastering a set of skills can be recognized with something more permanent—and portable—than letter grades. On Xbox, for example, players see a visual representation for Achievements unlocked, as well as those they have yet to master. Shouldn't students be able to do the same with their learning goals? For Sanders, and many other reformers, the answer is digital badges. When the student is able to view his or her own weaknesses and foundational skills, he or she can be directed to digital content solutions that can then provide needed learning experiences. If students need more work on quadratic equations, they can go to Khan Academy, master the subject at their own pace, and earn a badge.

Without technology it's nearly impossible for teachers to differentiate in large groups. Sanders explained, "What I see happening is schools shifting from three or four grade levels in a single building to more of a centralized, free-forming space where students can get together in small and large groups, based on the needs of the activity." Discussing race in America would require a large and diverse group. Smaller projects such as developing a website would work better with pairs of students. This model would free the teacher to work with individual students. I asked Sanders how he envisions the "classroom of the future" (incidentally, that's the name of his blog). He said:

> I see ownership shift from teacher's grade books to students' learning dashboards. Students can log in and see how they're doing, what specific standards he or she has to make, or the specific goals needed to reach college. They can identify their areas of interest and explore opportunities outside of the classroom, completing their experiences there. Maybe it's their local Maker club, maybe it's an online course that they can complete and earn formalized recognition for it. We need to eliminate the idea that education is ephemeral—where we get rid of all of the student learning at the end of the year, throw away the report cards, wipe the grade books clean and start fresh in the fall. We are losing valuable information on how these students are progressing.

I teach in a middle school. Many of my colleagues intentionally ignore a student's previous year's grades. They do not want to prejudice their teaching style due to the changes students go through during adolescence.

Unlike teacher-assigned grades, personalized learning environments can give every student his or her own archive of the work he or she has completed. "The idea of 'My Educational Data' is becoming a bigger deal in education," Sanders said. Students would be given access to their data file generated when using a tool such as Khan Academy or an educational game. He continued, "Just giving kids a data dump is going to be useful. I could see an emergence of standards, or a schema, that would allow third party providers or data warehouse companies to provide tools where students can plug in and get a visual representation of how they're doing." Sanders used the Department of Health and Human Services' Blue Button Connector as an analogy. "The Blue Button allows you—as a recipient of health services—to see your data, because it's yours. And you can download it. Let's say you have an app on your Android phone. You can get recommendations based on the report that your doctor gave you the last time you were there. That's what I want to happen in education."

In order to accomplish personalized public education, funding is necessary to let teachers play and try new technologies. Sanders explained, "Schools are not providing teachers with enough personalized support. We still have this idea that we can do a professional development one day a week or one day a month and that's enough. I really want to see schools developing plans or a system that allows teachers to learn more and experiment in their classrooms." The role of the teacher is growing in importance. Sanders continued,

> Teachers are entrepreneurs in their classrooms. They're solely responsible to develop a product—in this case, a class or content—where their users are, for the most part, captive. There are certain metrics that they are going after, students' interests, test scores—a little mini-company. Classrooms don't have any competition or any reason to dramatically change their product because every student is required to go to school. We need to empower teachers to be the entrepreneurs.

As with any entrenched system, significant barriers exist. This isn't the first challenge to grading models, either. The difference now is the availability of connectivity tools to enable this level of personalization.

A ClassBadges account is relatively straightforward to create. Student names can be added to its virtual classrooms. Furthermore, it offers hundreds of free badge design options. Simply choose badge art, type a description, and link to a class. That's it! The tool set is intuitive, allowing teachers—and students—to create a more personalized learning experience. My students helped develop some of our badges, including the "Proofreader Badge" for catching mistakes in handouts and websites, and the "Outside-the-Box Thinker Badge" for creative responses. Badges level up in difficulty to earn, from "Noob" (newbie, or beginner) to "Master." There is no leaderboard, and students must sign in to see their badges (they get email notifications).

Open Badges

Mozilla, maker of the Firefox browser, is involved in creating a free and open digital badge platform. An open system implies that anyone could have access to the information. One of Mozilla's initiatives is to create a platform for digital badges to be shared in one location. Achievements earned on the Khan Academy or from a massive open online course could, theoretically, all appear on a user's Mozilla account. An employer or anyone else who wants to follow someone's career path could, in turn, review that page.

Mozilla's BadgeKit came out of 2013's Chicago Summer of Learning. About 100 organizations worked with Mayor Rahm Emanuel's office to design badge systems for informal learning during the summer months. Mozilla's Emily Goligoski explained how it worked with organizations, and saw the need for a centralized place to go to issue badges from a single portal. She said, "Learners can craft their own pathways and tell powerful stories." Mozilla is now user testing with other Chicago organizations. Institutions may want to bring their logos in a professional way to show to their members or students. Goligoski continued, "The vision is that educators across the city are in a shared learning network, have access to see and share the badges that others have designed, repurpose the criteria that their colleagues write. They do not need to start from scratch, so they can put the badge system to work for their students."

Then there is also the consumption side of badges, where employers review applicant achievements when making hiring decisions. I asked Goligoski if there was a risk of badges becoming an extrinsic reward, essentially a new name for grades. She clarified, "There is a risk that badges can be grade-like, but, the meta-data shows that hiring managers look at when badge was earned, the criteria, and the ramifications on their learning choices on their specific career." Although badges can seem like grades, experience has shown that employers read the narrative holistically. Rather than review the Photoshop badges a photographer may have earned, a magazine is more likely to review the potential employee's entire badge collection, including the order in which each was achieved.

There remains a disparity between what students learn and labor market demands. Open Badges conducted interviews from the point of view of employers, including the different entry points in professions. The team interviewed mainly health care, service, and technology professionals. The hope was to create cross-career, cross-industry badges aligned to 21st-century, or "soft," skills. They reached out to the community and explored research such as Personal Effectiveness Competencies and the Common Career Technical Core, as well as Angela Duckworth's and Christopher Peterson's research on grit and tenacity. Varelidi shared with me the most in-demand career skills. She said the workforce desires "resilience, self-control, the ability to feel like you have control over life and decisions, being excited, being engaged about work, team playing/being a team player, having optimism, having a positive attitude, the ability to tinker, being open to failure, curiosity, having initiative, engaging in critical thinking, the ability to communicate ideas to others, and flexibility." She stressed flexibility. She said, "It comes up again, to change to new requirements in the technology industry, as does the idea of learning how to learn and being open to new knowledge and skills."

Within Mozilla's Open Badges community is the emergence of exemplars, modeling best practices. "People see what works really well in meaningful ways," Chloe Varelidi explained. "Badges show different skills in constellations to show how to improve your learning. Pathways address the need for employers to find qualified employees and to assess what is a good career choice." This can be especially helpful for underprivileged youths who may not know what career path to take—or lack guidance. Varelidi compared a person's badge journey to a game. "Pathways are like building roles in a role-playing game," she said. "The massive trees have branches of engaged skill-sets."

Adaptive Assessments

Video games provide instant feedback to players. Players are awarded points or badges for doing things well, and face setbacks if they fail. You can't proceed to higher levels without displaying a level of mastery! Because digital games are incredibly adept at providing data, their usefulness as an assessment tool becomes increasingly apparent. In today's high-stakes testing culture, an educational game developer can't sell to schools without having an assessment piece. For example, the physics sandbox *Newton's Playground* includes "stealth assessments" embedded into its code. I contacted Val Shute, co-creator of *Newton's Playground* and the author of the concept of stealth assessments. We spoke in February 2014. She told me that the purpose is to blur the distinction between learning and assessment. Players are assessed without a break in the action. She explained:

> In a nutshell, stealth assessments are a methodology that uses evidence-centered design in order to bury the assessment deep into the code of the game. It determines what you want to capture and analyze, with a log file. It's automatic. At any time and at any grain size, I know how well you are doing. For example, creativity in general, or some aspect of creativity, like cognitive flexibility versus your divergent thinking. I know about all those things by virtue of what you are doing in the environment. Then I can pull out certain data from play to make meaning to certain constructs.

In games, you fail fast, and then try again. This builds persistence. It is truly failure reframed as iteration. Many children fail at games in their free time, sometimes just to hear the sound effect or see the animation. When playing *SimCityEDU: Pollution Challenge!*, my students realized that certain businesses tended to catch on fire. For fun, some opened fire-prone industries near each other to see what would happen. There is a feedback loop at work when failing. It can become a teachable moment to discuss on reflection. I asked Katie

Salen, founder of the Institute of Play and Quest to Learn, about using games for assessing student competencies. We spoke in February 2014. She said:

> Games really struggle with that still. I'm in the experience—then get pulled out—then in—then back out. We are trying some interesting things. The game points to the genre of simulation for game-based assessments because kids can build models [and] compare to others' models, like one a teacher would want to see. Simulation games are a good genre. From a development perspective, which I like to think about since I build things, there is still a lot to be learned. We need to build a common language between the assessment folks, the learning folks, and the game development folks. Also, we need to try to find a process that honors the speed at which the different groups think and build. The assessment folks' output tends to be slower than game developers', who tend to think very quickly. And you can't actually understand what's working in a game until you build it.

GlassLab (the Games, Learning, and Assessment Lab) built evidence-centered design assessments into *SimCityEDU: Pollution Challenge!* (2013). It seamlessly measures student mastery of systems thinking tasks. This style of assessment differs from chocolate-covered broccoli, which measures responses after play, by adding in problems and puzzles. Evidence-centered design is measured during the game, gathering data from player choices. Results can be exported and analyzed on scatter plot graphs to get a better picture of the learning process.

Assessing one's aptitude in working with systems is not as concrete as scoring multiple-choice standardized answers. GlassLab partnered with the Educational Testing Service to utilize the evidence-centered design assessment approach formalized by Robert Mislevy, Linda Steinberg, and Russell Almond in the late 1990s. This technique works "well for skills, competencies, and attributes that are difficult to assess" (Shechtman, DeBarger, Dornsife, Rosier, & Yarnall, 2013). After each student plays a mission, the teacher receives data based on evidence collected pertaining to successes and challenges in the virtual city.

Adaptive Engines for Learning

Digital games sometimes give players a choice of difficulty modes: easy, medium, or hard (first-person shooters can get creative: recruit, veteran, insane). The difference between easy and difficult can be the number of punches it takes to beat up a bad guy, or automatic versus manual aiming of a laser gun. Difficulty modes are a hot button issue for game designers because they are relinquishing choice to the player to move outside the flow channel.

If the user finds an experience too boring or, conversely, impossible—even when the game was carefully designed to be a fulfilling experience—then they may post a negative online review.

Many modern video games use sophisticated adaptive engines to automatically adjust the challenges based on player performance. Designers refer to the complicated mathematical algorithms coded into games as the Dynamic Difficulty Adjustment system. What if the mathematical formulas coded into games crossed over into computer-based learning? Dynamic Difficulty Adjustment in this setting is known as "adaptive learning," which attempts to create personalized learning environments for students. Challenges adjust as a student progresses through content. Jenova Chen's master's in fine arts thesis, based on his game *flOw* (linked at the end of Chapter 4), differentiated between "active" and "passive" Dynamic Difficulty Adjustment. Active Dynamic Difficulty Adjustment bears similarities to technology currently used in adaptive tests that grow in difficulty to match the test taker's ability (Chen, 2006). Passive Dynamic Difficulty Adjustment relinquishes control of challenges, allowing the difficulty to increase or decrease as the player sees fit. You can observe children working at their desired difficulty level in sandbox games such as *Minecraft*. Chen made a connection from games to designing tests in his thesis. Regarding tests, he recommended:

1. There is no cap for the total score. Students can gain as much score as possible during the test period. Therefore, even top students can still challenge themselves every time they take the test.
2. Students should be able to see scores gained through each question and feel the joy of answering them correctly, which encourages them to do more.
3. The difficulty and the score of each question should be related. More challenge equals more reward.
4. Students should be able to sense the difficulty of each question and have the control to skip hard questions. (Chen, 2006)

Chen's research showed that an active adaptive system for difficulty does not necessarily need to be in place. People can self-pace their challenges. In fact, many may desire that freedom. He also proposed more transparency in tests. Scores can add up the same way as in a video game—instantly and with no limit. Challenging students to perform better to beat their personal bests on assessments delivers an intrinsic satisfaction. It also builds persistence.

Knewton

Knewton is an adaptive learning company. It applies to online education the engines used to scale difficulty in video games. I interviewed David Liu, COO of Knewton, via an exchange of emails during March 2014. Knewton is a platform, or infrastructure, for third-party publishers. Companies can "create adaptive experiences for any type of content, in nearly any subject matter, for every student." Liu explained that when students go through online lessons, the Knewton platform "analyzes vast amounts of anonymized data to figure out what a student knows and how they learn best." Knewton recommends what to study next, helping students advance. The system offers "teachers real-time predictive analytics to detect gaps in knowledge and differentiate instruction." The teacher has access to student data points. Students who have different needs, interests, strengths, and weaknesses can work toward goals in a sequence and at a pace that continuously adjusts to fit their needs.

At this point you might be wondering, what does this all mean? Basically, it is part of a larger field called "predictive analytics." If you have an account on Netflix or Amazon you might already be accustomed to it ("If you liked *Toy Story,* you might like *Shrek*"). Coursera, the massive open online course platform, does the same. Take a course in Spanish and you might get an email recommending a class in French. The Internet-streaming site Pandora uses predictive analytics to guess musical tastes.

In essence, Knewton uses an online course's feedback system to adjust the difficulty of the delivered lessons. Because it is a platform company, it has the ability to "collect vast amounts of data as students progress through an educational game." This makes the learning experience both gamified and adaptive. Liu explained the process as follows: "As a student progresses through a digital course or educational game (for example, whenever a student watches a video, reads a lesson, answers a practice problem, takes a quiz, or takes an action within a game), anonymized data on what they know and the effectiveness of the content are analyzed in aggregate with millions of other anonymized students." Basically, data becomes anonymous and is combined with other learners. The process is similar to how Facebook and Google predict your likes and searches, combining your interests with other users'.

Companies who create educational games have the ability to partner with Knewton to use its adaptivity software. Currently, its existing partners include Pearson, Cambridge University Press, Cengage Learning, Houghton Mifflin Harcourt, and Macmillan Education. Knewton then created adaptive experiences based on the publisher's content. The company works with teachers and learning designers through institutional partnerships, such as one with Arizona State University. In addition, Knewton has teams of subject matter experts, former teachers, and other academics on staff.

I asked Liu about the metrics used to measure success. They can measure students' progress toward specific learning goals set by teachers, parents, and administrators. As a concrete example, he pointed out how the University of Alabama used a Knewton-powered course in the lower of its two remedial math courses. Liu explained, "Pass rates for the course increased from about 70% to 87% in the first semester using Knewton." While it will take time to demonstrate long-term outcomes, early evidence points to Knewton's efficacy. Liu continued, "Since math students at Arizona State University began using Knewton-powered courses, pass rates have risen from 64% to 75% and withdrawal rates have been cut in half. Almost half of students taking Knewton-powered math courses finished class 4 weeks early."

Games as Adaptive Assessments

The use of video games in the classroom shouldn't imply that the learning process, including assessments, becomes fully automated. Game-based learning requires the teacher to facilitate. When I use a game such as *SimCityEDU* to teach about interconnected systems, I take time for students to write, discuss, and reflect. A well-designed game should encourage replay and iteration. I find it counterproductive to grade how well a student plays a content- or skill-driven game. (In my opinion, creating in sandboxes such as *Minecraft* can be graded as an authentic assessment, with a rubric.) Furthermore, missions on games unlock only if the player succeeds and can level up. I recommend grading as pass/fail depending on whether the game was played. The grade should be a small part of the final assessment; written reflection about why decisions were made should have more value. Perhaps a good rule of thumb is 20% of the grade relating to completion of a part of a video game and the other 80% based on reflection and application on what was learned. The reflection piece should include a critical discussion of game mechanics, such as why certain choices had different consequences.

Filament Games's co-founder Dan White isn't completely "sold" on the notion of games as assessment tools. In January 2014 he told me, "I did a rant on this at Games for Change [in 2013]." His concern was, "Once something is used as a tool for assessment, it fundamentally changes the experience for the player. If I'm a player in a game and I know that I'm being assessed based on my gameplay, I'm not going to be failure agnostic." When people—not just children—play games, they try things in different ways and they experiment. This is an example of James Gee's Multiple Routes Principle. Gee wrote, "There are multiple ways to make progress or move ahead. This allows learners to make choices, rely on their own strengths and styles of learning and problem solving, while exploring alternative styles" (2007, p. 223).

According to White, students who are graded in a game don't experiment; instead, they take the shortest route to success. This may look great on paper because it demonstrates that the content was learned. The more fundamental issue is that the creativity it takes to arrive at multiple solutions becomes lost. "It's fine for games to collect data and be formative, but not summative of what somebody knows or to go in a grade book," White continued. "It's a slippery slope." The problem is when the teacher passes judgment as a grade of what a student does or does not know. (In 2014 Filament Games's *Argument Wars* became the first to partner with GlassLab. One goal will be to pull out data from player interactions.)

Market pressure could force developers to create simpler games designed to just deliver a content piece or a specific skill. Teachers are subject to accountability and may have very little leeway in how they structure lessons, especially with standardized testing. Taking a week to discuss the American Revolution in *Assassin's Creed III* may not help students fill out ScanTron sheets. Nonetheless, teacher facilitation of reflection is key to enabling students to make connections from virtual worlds to real life.

Kurt Squire from the Games + Learning + Society Center proposed a solution. We spoke in January 2014. He said, "A good metaphor for assessment might be like a raid in *World of Warcraft*. You want your failure matrix to be responsive." His answer was based on research on the game *ProgenitorX*. The best predictor of the outcome of learning was success rate on the final level. Squire sees time as a challenge in the field. "You don't get that much time to build and iterate to get things right," he said. There are several rounds to refine a game, and then get it ready for market. This includes user testing, playtesting, and design iteration.

Conclusions and Takeaways

Learning in a digital informal setting is often personalized. This is a result of adaptive algorithms that can automatically predict and level up learning. No technology can replace a teacher. Digital badges are an increasingly common tool to certify personalized learning. They create visible career and college pathways. For kindergarten through grade-12 students, badges exist in some city programs, museums, and cultural centers. To be most effective, intrinsic learning must come first and then be acknowledged with a digital badge.

Lesson Plan Ideas

Design a Badge System: Digital badges are used in games and websites to acknowledge accomplishments. Students can design a badge system for a historical figure's life. Mix in geolocation badges (such as those awarded on mobile apps such as Foursquare, Yelp, and Facebook location "check-ins") with badges for achievements. For example, what badges would George Washington earn? For checking in at Valley Forge (geo-location badge), attacking the Hessians? The badge should have a spirit of "fun" in its title (e.g., for George Washington—"Un-merry X-mas, Hessians!") and a few sentences describing how the badge is issued (e.g., for George Washington, mention what he would need to accomplish to earn the badge; in this case, for leading an attack on the Hessians after crossing the Delaware). Each badge must also include a paragraph integrating systems thinking—specifically, the feedback/causal loop involved in triggering a digital badge. Common Core State Standards can be met, depending on the topic you choose. Steps to complete the project: Go to www.MakeBadg.es; type the label for the badge's name; find a clip art image appropriate for the badge, save it and upload it to MakeBadges; download the completed badge; add it to a document with a caption.

Games

Aleks, an adaptive tool from McGraw-Hill—http://www.aleks.com

DragonBox, adaptive learning algebra and geometry—http://www.dragonboxapp.com

Dreambox adaptive learning—http://www.dreambox.com

DuoLingo, adaptive learning for language learning—http://www.duolingo.com/#

Fastt Math Next Generation, adaptive learning—http://fasttmath.cssu.org:55880/slms/student access/fmng

Grockit, adaptive and social test prep—https://grockit.com

Kahoot gamifies with a leaderboard and a timer. Create trivia games, drag and drop interface to quiz in real time—https://getkahoot.com

Lure of the Labyrinth, an adaptive algebraic mathematics puzzle game—http://labyrinth.think port.org

MySpanishLab, adaptive Spanish tool—http://www.myspanishlab.com

Zondle, create quiz games—https://www.zondle.com

Resources

BadgeKit, Mozilla's design tool kit—http://badgekit.openbadges.org

Case studies of badges—http://www.reconnectlearning.org/case-studies

Changing Education Paradigms, Ken Robinson's TED Talk—http://www.ted.com/talks/ken_robinson_changing_education_paradigms

Chicago City of Learning—http://chicagocityoflearning.org

Chicago Summer of Learning—http://www.chicagosummeroflearning.org

ClassBadges, easy-to-use badge system for schools—http://classbadges.com

ClassDojo, badge-based behavior modification system—http://www.classdojo.com

Classroom of the Future, James Sanders's blog—http://www.classroominthefuture.com/aboutme

Common Career Technical Core—http://www.careertech.org/career-technical-education/cctc/info.html

Common Core Initiative, link to the state standards linked in this book—http://www.core-standards.org

Discoverables, a U.K. platform to identify and build "soft," or 21st-century skills for employers in a range of industries—http://www.discoverabl.es

ForAllBadges, a simple tool kit that can export badges to Mozilla's Open Badges platform. It is now part of its sister service, ForAllRubrics—https://www.forallrubrics.com

Hive Learning Network, supporting city learning—http://hivelearningnetwork.org

HASTAC, digital media learning—http://www.hastac.org

Khan Academy's Learning Dashboard is where users can track mastery and progress. It is in Khan's Personalized Learning Environment—http://www.khanacademy.org/coach-res/become-a-coach/site-tour/v/the-learning-dashboard

Knewton, adaptive learning—http://www.knewton.com

MakeBadges, design your own badges. It's easy for students to use, too—http://www.makebadges/badge.html#

Moonshots in Education, James Sanders's Ignite talk about the classroom of the future, personalized learning, and digital badges—http://www.youtube.com/watch?v=Aege0UVf4uo

OpenBadges, learning pathways portal from the Mozilla Foundation—http://openbadges.org

Personal Effectiveness Competencies—http://ccetompkins.org/energy/green-jobs/personal-effectiveness

Teq Online Professional Development, with badges that can be exported to Mozilla's Open Badges platform—https://www.teq.com/teqonlinepd/badges

Youtopia, learning management system with game mechanics—http://www.youtopia.com

· 9 ·

UNIVERSITY GAME LABS

Research for this book brought me to a treasure trove of games readily adaptable to my classroom. The CUNY Games Network in New York City has a portal entirely dedicated to teaching with games. Jesse Schell leads Carnegie Mellon's innovative Entertainment Technology Center. Tiltfactor, the Mary Flanagan–led game lab at Dartmouth University, develops several digital and paper-based social impact titles. Tracy Fullerton heads the University of Southern California's influential Games Innovation Lab. The program graduated luminaries who have had games exhibited at the Museum of Modern Art.

Much of today's games and learning research is conducted at the University of Wisconsin–Madison. James Gee spent a decade as a professor at Madison. Kurt Squire and Constance Steinkuehler, who are husband and wife, extended the program by co-founding the Games + Learning + Society (GLS) Center. Each year it hosts the annual GLS Conference. Squire and Steinkuehler both led research on situated learning in games, describing how people learn informally in order to advance in a game. At the 11th Annual Games for Change Festival, Steinkuehler discussed many positive findings from well-designed games, especially those that build "academic" language, a literacy skill useful for college entrance exams. For example, research indicated that inner-city youth read above their reading level in order to advance in the game *Civilization*.

Squire co-founded the Education Arcade at MIT, with Henry Jenkins. It conducts research and development in games as part of MIT's Scheller Teacher Education Program (STEP). MIT has a long history in digital media learning, including its Media Lab, which produced the Logo programming language and, more recently, *Scratch*. Using color-coded bricks, *Scratch* is teaching thousands of students how to code. The Education Arcade developed the electromagnetism game *Supercharged!* in 2004. According to research detailed in Clive Thompson's book *Smarter Thank You Think*, students who played the science game "scored 20 percent better on tests of the concepts" (2013, p. 202).

The Learning Games Network is the offspring of MIT's Education Arcade and the GLS Center. It is "a non-profit institution trying to spark innovation in the design and use of learning games through promoting collaboration among scholars, teachers, developers, producers" (Squire, 2011, p. 217). One of the Learning Games Network's most recent projects was *Quandary*, a free online game that engages players in the ethical decision-making process of colonizing a new planet. Teachers can access *Quandary in the Classroom* to access Common Core–linked lesson plans. *Quandary* won a Game of the Year award at the Games for Change Festival. Other Learning Games Network titles include the mathematics puzzler *Lure of the Labyrinth* and the English language game *Xenos*. *Quandary* and *Lure of the Labyrinth* can also be played on the BrainPOP platform.

This chapter features interviews with Kurt Squire and with Alan Gershenfeld from the Center for Games and Impact at Arizona State University. I also spoke to researchers at the Games and Innovation Lab, led by Tracy Fullerton. The first section in this chapter is a profile of Robert Torres, former executive director of the Institute of Play. He is currently the senior program manager at the Bill & Melinda Gates Foundation. His role is crucial in funding some of the most effective projects. Torres's professional journey and advice is useful to anyone attempting to bring games into the classroom.

The Bill & Melinda Gates Foundation

As I interviewed people for this book, the Gates Foundation's Robert Torres kept coming up in conversation. The Cooney Center's Jessica Millstone referred to him as "a visionary" in the field. It is important to know who and why game-based research projects are being funded. Much of the grant money in this area comes from the Bill & Melinda Gates Foundation and/or the John T. and Catherine D. MacArthur Foundation. To understand Torres's point of view is to understand game-based learning. I had the opportunity to interview him in February 2014.

Torres began his teaching career 25 years ago working for Teach for America, the nonprofit started by Wendy Kopp. Teach for America has a highly competitive recruitment process. It places young teachers in low-income school districts. Kopp's idea stemmed from her 1989 thesis at Princeton University. Torres eventually became the managing director of Teach for America's faculty. While there, he joined the Learning Project think tank.

Eventually, Torres left Teach for America to become the principal of a school on the Lower East Side of Manhattan. He worked there for 5 years. Torres told me that while there, he became fascinated with the design of learning environments—how people learn, and what is effective design. By this point, he had been in the education field for more than 10 years and had been growing increasingly fatigued by the process of seeking foundation funding. He wanted to create a consulting firm that was based solely on work contracts, freeing him from reliance on foundations. This plan proved successful, and his firm was hired to design new schools.

At this time, the Gates Foundation, the Soros Foundation, and the Carnegie Foundation joined forces and attempted to "recreate" the American high school. Torres recalled the "flooding" of funds into the effort. In New York City, about 400 new schools were created. Torres's group wound up designing 30 schools, in collaboration with New Vision public schools. (New Vision had been one of the major recipients of the Gates funding.)

Torres felt like he was part of significant innovations. Teach for America grew in popularity across the county. The small schools he was creating were succumbing to old structures—mostly due to the "assessment regime" that drives education. "Assessments have theoretical assumptions that we don't actually think about as teachers, or administrators, or at any level," Torres said. He next explained how the theory of information processing—the cognitive theory that we can store facts in our head, like a computer's hard drive, and then recall the answers on an exam—is essentially the theory behind standardized tests. Teachers may feel pressure to deliver content by a certain date because there is so much yet to cover.

This system ultimately falls short for low-income students. The middle-class or upper-income child has a whole "ecology of support" at home. Torres used a lesson on the Russian Revolution to illustrate this. "It is possible that the Russian Revolution, discussed for 45 minutes in class, might reappear at the family's dining room table, or with the soccer coach, or with the army of tutors," he explained. "For the lower-income kid, it just wasn't going to work on so many levels."

By most measures, he had been a successful teacher and school principal. His students scored well on standardized tests, because they were taught to the test. At a crossroads of teaching and leading education reform—a multibillion-dollar industry—Torres decided to switch gears and go back to school. In his thirties, Torres entered graduate school to learn about the "learning sciences," an interdisciplinary field that merges computer science, neuroscience, cognitive science, and educational research. Unlike current practices of training teachers how to deliver instruction, this methodology assesses how students actually learn. Like a game, the process begins at inquiry and moves to mastery. Context plays a part in how people achieve mastery. A chemist applies his or her knowledge based on the different situations that he or she encounters. In order to succeed, mastery of chemistry content is required. It was then that Torres had a realization. "Games, of all things, mirrored the principle that we were seeing in how people were developing mastery," he explained. "Game designers had figured out the conditions to keep people compelled and persistent through very complex environments to solve sets of problems."

Connie Yowell, education director at the MacArthur Foundation, had a similar revelation. For about 100 years MacArthur had been funding educational reform. Torres explained how Yowell paid keen attention to what children are interested in doing—playing games. They both began to speak about games for learning at various conferences, including the first Games for Change Festival. Then, in 2006 the MacArthur Foundation invested $50 million to fund the games and learning space. As a result, Institute of Play and the Quest to Learn school were created.

Torres worked as the executive director of the Institute of Play. He had been a MacArthur grantee for about 6 years. He personally benefitted too— his dissertation was tied to a project, the systems thinking game design tool *Gamestar Mechanic*. MacArthur was the primary grantor for many educational technology spaces.

The Gates Foundation, founded by Microsoft's Bill Gates and his wife, Melinda, had been slower to join the educational technology sector. Nonetheless, the time had come. Torres eventually went to work for the

Gates Foundation, helping to strategize around technology and learning. The Foundation funds many educational technology projects, as well as other innovations in the game-based learning space.

Four years later, much has happened. For example, Torres authorized the funding of the GlassLab project (the Games, Learning, and Assessment Lab), originally established in 2012 by the Institute of Play. (It was spun off as an independent, grant-funded entity in July 2014.) It emerged out of a 2-day conference held at the University of Southern California, with 40 psychometricians (assessments scientists) and 40 game designers. The objective was to see if scientists and designers—people who speak different academic languages—could actually prototype a set of games. Torres presented it as a design challenge. GlassLab's current partner organizations include the Educational Testing Service and Pearson. It is headquartered on the campus of Electronic Arts in Redwood, California. *SimCityEDU* was its first project.

The Gates Foundation and the MacArthur Foundation supported many of the research projects discussed in this book. Both Torres and Yowell had the foresight to bring together researchers, assessment scientists, and game designers—no easy feat! The current crop of well-designed learning games owes much to their vision.

Games + Learning + Society Center

Kurt Squire is co-director of the Games + Learning + Society (GLS) Center at the Wisconsin Institute for Discovery. I interviewed him in January 2014. He is the author or editor of three books and more than 75 scholarly publications on learning with technology. He has directed several game-based learning projects, ranging from *ARIS*, a location-based, mobile app, to *ProgenitorX*, a game about harnessing stem cell technology in order to save the world from zombies. Squire's research has been supported by nearly $10 million in grants and gifts from the MacArthur Foundation, the National Science Foundation, the Gates Foundation, Microsoft, the Department of Education, the AMD Foundation, and the National Institutes of Health.

Squire began his teaching career as a Montessori teacher, when he led a discovery-based learning classroom. He next became an instructional technologist. He wrote an influential dissertation about using the game *Civilization* in an urban high school setting. This was back in 2004, when it was considered radical to play console-style games in school. To advance in the game, students were reading information from websites that were higher than their grade level (Squire, 2011).

In 2011 Squire published *Video Games and Learning: Teaching and Participatory Culture in the Digital Age,* featuring contributions from Henry Jenkins, with an introduction by James Gee. Jenkins is an expert on participatory cultures, where content creators—and gamers—meet in a situated learning setting. The book and his coursework were integrated into a massive open online course hosted on Coursera in the fall of 2013. Along with others in the GLS research department, Gee was recruited to contribute videos about his Learning Principles from video games.

Since publishing his book, he has continued his work on game-based research. His team builds games that blur the line of the classroom, bringing ordinary citizens in to play together with students. The development team mixes AAA (big budget) and indie (independent) backgrounds. There are about 20 Ph.D.s researching games and learning. GLS also has 10 to 15 full-time developers on staff. This approach ensures that games created for research projects still have engaging, fun mechanics. "As core developers we force ourselves to do a lot of playtesting, which is best practice, and then biweekly playtests and monthly builds with the target audience," Squire explained. It has also signed up teachers in the Playful Learning online community and conducts outreach to schools.

The lab has developers working at the Learning Games Network developing games for researchers and academics to create a "unified culture." "The goal is to get developers and academics working together," Squire stated. "A shared office space keeps it culturally the same." Unlike at commercial game companies, projects at GLS are built with the intent of being academic projects; however, many get distributed to the general public. The tests with its core audience are led by the developers so they can look the players in the eyes. Squire prefers the experience-based model to a lecture-based setting. This style focuses on what students do to attain information, as well as how they mobilize it in the context of problem solving.

Squire sees the barriers to game-based learning adoption as logistical, rather than teachers not wanting games in their classrooms. Perhaps it is generational. Younger teachers grew up playing games, especially *SimCity* and *Civilization.* Digital distribution—through platforms such as BrainPOP and iTunes—as well as teacher training and support can bring more games to students (GLS Center's *Citizen Science* can be played on BrainPOP). Squire explained, "Games help players build skill. A digital distribution system can lead to an explosion of games." So how should teachers use video games to extend learning? Squire suggested:

> Add games with interesting questions, a lot of enrichment, and high valued work. Games can then be used with academic value. One professor did something interesting, 16 weeks, 16 games; she got interesting results from a not very historically accurate game—*Age of Empires*. The professor then discussed what it does and what it doesn't do. It was used for a vehicle for interpretation and reflection, with writing prompts. That was really clever to me. There was also an ELA [English language arts] teacher who played *Skyrim*, in class, for 30 minutes and then did a whole writing unit afterwards.

The work of academics and nonprofits is being built upon and expanded. Squire remains cautiously optimistic. "One of the perennial challenges is not to care about games [themselves], but education, which games are a part of. We've done some work on that. We make sure that we have good models of how curriculum integration works. And, of course, empirical data."

Center for Games and Impact

The Center for Games and Impact was founded at the Mary Lou Fulton Teachers College at Arizona State University by Sasha Barab and James Gee in partnership with E-Line Media co-founders Alan Gershenfeld and Michael Angst. Barab was the lead investigator in the research project game *Quest Atlantis*. The Center provides Impact Guides, which give "players, parents and teachers the tools to understand play, inspire reflection and stimulate transformation with the goal of building a more knowledgeable, responsible and empathetic citizenship" (2014). I had the opportunity to interview both James Gee and Alan Gershenfeld in the spring of 2014.

There are very few academic centers that study the full life-cycle research of actual products and continued services. Gershenfeld and his E-Line business partner, Michael Angst, along with Sasha Barab and James Gee, discussed how there needed to be an alignment between game design, game mechanics, scientists, and good learning. "The Center was co-founded to integrate the thought process behind research, design, marketing, and distribution so that they become sustainable and can actually make an impact at scale, rather than result in just another research paper," Gershenfeld explained. "Research papers have been critical, but we've had years of them. We're trying to turn them into products and services."

The Center has a studio in Phoenix and a partnership with Arizona State University. The off-campus location is part of a joint venture with E-Line Media's Pathways Learning Project, tentatively called the Thrive Learning Platform. As of this writing, there are several projects going on in that space. Teachers can earn a certificate in Games and Impact from the Center. The web portal has Impact Guides for off-the-shelf games including *SimCity*, *Civilization V*, *Portal 2*, *Little Big Planet*, *Peacemaker*, *Journey*, and *Minecraft*. These are especially helpful for parents as well as teachers. In 2014 the Center introduced a new game, *Quest2Teach*. It is a role-playing game for pre-service teachers. The video game features a variety of situations that a new educator might face.

Games Innovation Lab

Tracy Fullerton is the chair of the Interactive Media & Games Division of the University of Southern California (USC) School of Cinematic Arts. She is also the director of the Game Innovation Lab and author of *Game Design Workshop: A Playcentric Approach to Creating Innovative Games*, now in its 3rd edition. I interviewed Fullerton as well as some of her research team. We spoke in March 2014. Her students' projects elicit more than fun—they often require introspection. Fullerton was the thesis advisor for Jenova Chen, whose company is expanding the emotional range people feel while playing games. Just about all of the members of Chen's company, Thatgamecompany, were students of Fullerton. The company's games include *flOw*, *Flower*, and *Journey*. Fullerton has also collaborated with Bill Viola, a MacArthur Genius grantee, on *The Night Journey*. The collaboration is an interactive game that has been exhibited in various galleries for the past 7 years. She described the game as "a spiritual journey."

Students at USC can earn a master's of fine arts degree in interactive entertainment and game design. Independent principal investigators choose research questions and then design a project. Next they put a team together— along with the funding—to realize their intervention. All games in the Game Innovation Lab have a participatory design element between multiple designers. The process includes paper prototyping and iteration until the mechanics are worked out. Digital is the last step. Sometimes, games stay in the nondigital stage.

Marienta Gotsis, a researcher at the Games Innovation Lab, explained the creation process in more detail. "Games are the deliverable. That is a work of art. It may not always be beautiful, but it aspires to be," she said. In the end, a student's research project is an actual product. Because of the aesthetic component, there are different talents required at each stage from pilot to production. A systems thinker observes the paper-based version and then transposes that to a digital platform. A designer, on the other hand, thinks about the player's experience, not just the systems and mechanics; 3D digital artists, who are proficient in applications, are also required.

Research projects struggle with finding funding. Without a steady cash flow, it can be difficult to innovate. The graduation schedule presents another limitation: The master's degree takes 3 years. For education or health games, the process can be even slower. "You need to manage the iterative stages of production," Gotsis explained. "The sad part in research is when you don't have the money to go from what you want to make to actually making it. It can take years, even if you know it works. It's not like there is venture capital money and it becomes scalable for commercial use."

Thoreau in a Sandbox: *Walden, the Game*

Walden, the Game is Tracy Fullerton's latest project. It is "a simulation of Thoreau's experience of living." In the classic book *Walden Pond,* author Henry David Thoreau attempted to balance a life of simplicity with a connection to nature. Fullerton's game is one of the first to be funded by the National Endowment of Arts in the category New Media Arts. She explained, "There has always been a strong connection between play and making art." The act of making art can be seen as a game, or at least as a playful activity. Fullerton also pointed out many early examples of games as works of art, including surrealistic game environments.

Walden, the Game is an engaging way to teach 19th-century literature experientially. Thoreau's book seems readily adaptable to a digital simulation. The protagonist depends on four basics of life: food, shelter, fuel, and clothing. These elements became part of the mechanics of play. Players collect or grow food, find firewood and then chop it, mend clothes, and build shelter. Failure to do so affects the player's ability to survive. Visuals and sounds become gloomy when work becomes a grind. If too much time is spent on these tasks, the player's life experience "becomes dull and dismal." Fullerton continued, "If the player can sustain a simplistic existence, then he or she can spend time wandering the woods, enjoying occurrences of inspiration with the natural life of animals, plants, the sounds of the forest and even society in the distance."

The challenges change with the seasons, too. It is fairly easy in summer, and then the difficulty levels up during the fall and winter months. Even in these "sparse seasons," some pleasures are presented, such as skating on Walden Pond. The game concludes with a celebration of the resurgence of spring. It is "experiential and poetic."

The underlying theme of *Walden Pond* is solitude, inspiration, and a sublime life. The challenge to Fullerton's team was how to achieve this in a game. There is a reward system to acknowledge when a player finds and collects pages of *Walden Pond*. Assembling the book provides further insight into Thoreau's thinking. The setting takes place over 1 year—though Thoreau was at Walden Pond for 2 years, 2 months, and 2 days. At end of the year, the player enters "sandbox mode," free to roam the wilderness as he or she pleases.

Nutritional Education with *Virtual Sprouts*

Virtual Sprouts is a research project that brought together investigators from USC's medical school, school of education, school of engineering, and world-famous film school. Nutritionists and other researchers also were brought in to help. The project was based on a real gardening program that was piloted in a Los Angeles elementary school. The garden was found to be just as useful in teaching nutrition as other metabolic interventions. It also hit multiple goals for education, including California's science standards. While putting a garden in every school is a lofty goal, realistically it is not feasible. Therefore, USC researchers created a digital gardening and cooking experience.

The alpha version (preliminary release) is being deployed into some schools. Researcher Marienta Gotsis explained how the team took a systems approach. She said, "Manage one thing and everything falls into place." In this regard, the core mechanic of gameplay is similar to that in *Reach for the Sun*, Filament's video game about mastering a plant's systems.

Virtual Sprouts is a first-person (perspective) role-playing gardening game. Students assist a gardener who is aspiring to be the top chef in a local contest. The goal is to help her cook and meet nutritional and taste standards. Gardening hints include "I'm craving protein" and "I'm craving sweets that are high in calcium." As the game progresses, the player is presented with healthy recipes. From there, he or she can grow an ingredient from scratch, such as garlic. The virtual garden experiences the four seasons, humidity, changes in sunlight, weeds, and other factors.

Once the plant is successfully grown, it can be harvested and brought to the kitchen. There is a pantry full of additional items to enable the player to make a wrap or a salad. The process includes a practical application of mathematics. Players need to think about making calculations as all ingredients are assembled. The feedback system assesses several dimension of play, including the gardener's missions, how much sugar and fiber they used in recipes, and the quality of grown produce. Students can use augmented reality apps, with an iPad camera, to take a "selfie" photograph with the trophy.

The game was playtested with an afterschool charity in December 2013. "Students were keen on replaying," Gotsis said. "The challenge is to fund a fully featured playable version." *Virtual Sprouts* comes with curriculum matched to California's teaching standards. "Teachers have limited time to cover curriculum. If they take time out, you have to make it up for them," she continued. Her team's goal is not to increase student's screen time; rather, they want to intervene and improve behaviors via short, meaningful, playful experiences. "You try a few times, and then come back to it." The teacher's lesson plan is the reinforcement activity. There are very few cooking and gardening games in Apple's App Store. Furthermore, the content is not connected to research. Gotsis explained that she sees a place for *Virtual Sprouts* as an eventual commercial release.

Adventurous Dreaming Highflying Dragon

Often times, researchers are in the third year of study, writing theses and looking for clinical interventions for projects. In this case, Marienta Gotsis connected a student investigator with a pediatrician and a psychiatrist. The deliverable, called *Adventurous Dreaming Highflying Dragon (ADHD)*, was a motion-controlled video game for children around age 11. The game is intended for those diagnosed with attention deficit hyperactive disorder (ADHD).

Adventurous Dreaming Highflying Dragon plays on an Xbox Kinect, where the player is literally the controller. Kinect is a motion-sensitive camera that reacts to player movement. Gotsis wanted the game to be completely original. "Earning points can be too conventional, especially for kids," she explained. "The reward-oriented model is problematic. Whatever you're doing should be intrinsically engaging. Points don't matter after a certain point." In the game, students role-play as a clumsy dragon that can't fly. The goal is to earn the skill of flying.

As with most games, the player has an infinite number of opportunities to learn. First the player is tasked with following a sequence of items, including yellow mushrooms, purple corn, and blue mushrooms. Next, the gamespace opens up to a large forest where many items are falling from trees. The challenge is to catch items in a sequential order. Gotsis remarked, "It is difficult to not get distracted and not catch everything that falls." Sequences and shapes increase in complexity, testing the player's memory. The second challenge has the player contorting his or her body—and then holding still—to stop cracks in a water tower. This, too, levels up, as more cracks appear in different locations. Gotsis laughed, "You have to be creative with poses to cover the cracks to heal the tower." The third task involves scratching off a cave wall to get to a gold nugget. It is both a visual-spatial challenge and a test of impulse control. The better the player gets, the smaller the nuggets become. Succeeding in all three tasks gives the dragon power to use its wings. While the game lacks the narrative of a commercial release, its core mechanics hold up. "The underlying mechanisms work for adults, too," Gotsis concluded. "Exercise and regulation can be transferred to other settings." *Adventurous Dreaming Highflying Dragon* is a game that puts sound educational research into practice. It is both fun and educational.

Gaming College Admissions: *FutureBound*

The process of getting into college is game-like: There is the arc of higher education and there are serious consequences. *FutureBound* turns those experiences into a game. It was collaboratively created by the Game and Innovation Lab and the School of Education. Zoe Corwin, a professor at the School of Education, led the project, along with Tracy Fullerton.

There are actually four games in the series: *FutureBound, Application Crunch, Mission: Admission,* and *Graduate Strike Force.* The idea stemmed from a perceived lack of college counseling, especially in underserved areas. They used iterative design with a high school–aged audience, including students at game design camp. The team was interested in a solution that students would find engaging, that spoke their own language. The games help students to build and present themselves in the best light. There were real-world questions Corwin wanted to infuse in the game. Is it beneficial to join a lot of clubs and be spread thin, or to be a leader in just a few clubs? What are the differences between a technical school and a liberal arts college? The games are the ultimate role-playing adventure: aspirations for life. "We indentified the moment—the tipping point—where kids go to college," Corwin explained. "Some kids were prepared for college and ready to go, but don't know the application process."

Tracy Fullerton elaborated further about how little many middle school students know about their futures. She said, "College and careers is a black box for many in middle school, how careers match up to challenges and aspirations." In *FutureBound*, the player is a middle school student haunted by a monster. The monster is fueled by fears and doubts. Fullerton explained, "The way you combat them is by powering up superpowers about career paths. You learn from characters about their passions and you use their powers." For example, soccer players use their powers to kick soccer balls at monsters. Players level up to attain more desirable careers. To become an airplane pilot or a neurosurgeon, you need to fight bigger monsters, attacking larger fears invading the school. The game is really about creating aspirations in an adventure game format, the core genre for that age group.

Two *FutureBound* games are geared directly to the application process: *Application Crunch*, a nondigital card game, and *Mission: Admission*, a Facebook game. *Application Crunch* is designed to help students complete college applications. It was not, however, intended to stay in its paper form. After paper prototyping and playtesting it with full classes, the team found the card-based game to be highly engaging. The playtesters did not want to stop playing and leave class. Therefore, Corwin's team decided to keep it paper-based.

Graduate Strike Force is targeted to a high school audience. The player evaluates colleges. Issues include weighing the cost of financial loans against the future opportunity the investment may—or may not—provide. Fullerton explained, "The world needs college graduates to fight monsters that are attacking us. Graduates need a range of skills and should be happy people not burdened by a lot of debt." The objective is to be part of the monster fighting force. Gameplay involves choosing schools, selecting financial aid packages, and seeing them through. Fullerton concluded, "If the player is depressed and burdened by debt, then they can't fight the robots attacking earth."

Corwin explained a three-pronged approach to the project's research. First are the qualitative components from observing students play, as well as from interviewing students. This is followed up with longitudinal interviews from students in their junior year of high school, then at the beginning of their senior year, and finally after they have applied to college. The idea is to see how the game affected their application process. The second prong is to perform quantitative pre- and post-tests. Corwin said, "We test changes in efficacies of students' beliefs that they can go to college, as well as being able to afford college." Finally, there are the measures built into the game itself, such as knowledge about college. A straightforward example is in *Mission Admission*. When students play for the first time, they typically go to the shortest college application in the game. After playing the game repeatedly, students tend to review more options. There is observational data in the card game, too. If a player makes a mistake the first time by missing an application deadline, they often adjust their strategy for the next time, paying closer attention to scholarship dates.

Sometimes, even the most "fun" game isn't played at home, just because it was played in school. The perception is that the game was "part of school," even if it was entertaining. Another problem was that *Mission: Admission* was on Facebook. Most young people tend to use the social media app on mobile devices that don't support Adobe's Flash Player. Perhaps the card-based game was the best platform to get across Corwin's message, after all. Corwin explained, "We go in classrooms and kids are excited to play games. They say they love it and would recommend to siblings, but they don't play at home." A familiar platform helps. Many educational titles are available on Steam, the streaming service from the Valve Corporation (*Portal, Dota 2*).

Conclusions and Takeaways

A lot of funding for game-based learning initiatives comes from the Gates Foundation and/or the MacArthur Foundation. The rationale is to follow what young people are interested in, such as play and games. University game labs are an excellent—and often, free—place to find games for learning. Some games intended for research projects are truly innovative. More and more universities are opening up game labs, so check them out online before the secret gets out!

Lesson Plan Ideas

Atlantis Remixed: Sasha Barab's research is linked to many content standards—http://www.atlantisremixed.org/site/view/Educators#6

Citizen Science: Playable on BrainPOP, which posts all applicable standards—http://www.brainpop.com/games/citizenscience

Quandary: Ethical decision-making game. There is a PDF with mapped standards, as well as a teacher's guide with lesson plans—http://www.quandarygame.org

Games

Adventurous Dreaming Highflying Dragon (ADHD), a self-regulation game for children diagnosed with attention deficit hyperactivity disorder—http://interactive.usc.edu/project/adventurous-dreaming-highflying-dragon

Anatomy Browser—http://www.gameslearningsociety.org/project_anatomy_browser.php

ARIS, a location-based game and app from Kurt Squire's lab—http://arisgames.org

Atlantis Remixed, Sasha Barab's science game—http://www.atlantisremixed.org

ChronoCards, a downloadable card game about history from the USC Game Innovation Lab. The first set is about World War I—http://www.gameinnovationlab.com/history

Citizen Science—http://www.gameslearningsociety.org/project_citizen_science.php

FutureBound, Application Crunch, Mission: Admission, and *Graduate Strike Force*—http://www.futureboundgames.com

Progenitor X, the zombies and health game—http://www.gameslearningsociety.org/px_microsite

Quandary, the award-winning game of interplanetary colonization—http://www.quandarygame.org

Quest 2 Teach, a role-playing game for pre-service teachers—http://quest2teach.strikingly.com

The Radix Endeavor, MIT's science-themed, MMO game—http://www.radixendeavor.org

Supercharged, an electronic particle game—http://education.mit.edu/projects/supercharged

Virtual Sprouts, a tablet game seeks to fight childhood obesity—http://virtualsprouts.com

Virulent, an educational health game—http://www.gameslearningsociety.org/project_virulent.php

Walden, the Game, to experience Walden Pond as Henry David Thoreau did—http://cinema.usc.edu/interactive/research/walden.cfm

Resources

Because Play Matters, Syracuse University's game lab—http://becauseplaymatters.com

Center for Games and Impact at Arizona State University—http://gamesandimpact.org

Creativity Lab at Indiana University—http://www.creativitylabs.com

The CUNY Games Network at Teacher's College—http://games.commons.gc.cuny.edu

Games and Innovation at the University of Southern California, headed by Tracy Fullerton—http://games.usc.edu

Games + Learning + Society Center—http://gameslearningsociety.org

Learning Games Lab at New Mexico State University—http://learninggameslab.org

Learning Games Network—http://www.learninggamesnetwork.org

MIT's Education Arcade—http://education.mit.edu

Play Forward—http://www.play2prevent.org/index.aspx

Playful Learning—http://beta.playfullearning.com

Reacting to the Past, Barnard College's game-based history program that dates back to the 1990s—https://reacting.barnard.edu

Tiltfactor, Mary Flanagan's social impact game design studio—http://www.tiltfactor.org

· 1 0 ·

VIDEO GAMES FOR LEARNING

In a telling interview with *Joystiq* magazine, Valve Corporation (developer of the Steam gaming platform) founder Gabe Newell stated that he did not "believe in a distinction between games and educational games. A lot of times [the label] 'educational games' is a way of being an excuse for bad game design or poor production values." Newell's statement came after years of poorly executed "edutainment" games, titles that focused on content, not delivery. Part of the fun of engaging in games is learning how to play the game itself. The learning should be part of the core mechanic, not just transposed on it.

This chapter features a "behind-the-scenes" look at several major educational game releases. GlassLab's lead designer, Erin Hoffman, shares the design process of its *SimCityEDU: Pollution Challenge!* game, which my students tested prior to release. She also details the making of *Mars Generation One: Argubot Academy*, GlassLab's tablet-based argumentation game. This chapter also includes interviews with the next generation of learning game developers. I had the opportunity to speak with Filament Games's Dan White, Schell Games's Jesse Schell, MangaHigh's Toby Rowland, and E-Line Media's Kate Reilly and co-founder Alan Gershenfeld. Finally, I review one the best platforms to find learning games: BrainPOP. Featured are notes from my tour of its New York City headquarters.

Filament Games

Filament Games is a Wisconsin-based development studio with a simple design philosophy: Learning itself is a fun act (unofficially, its motto is to make learning games "that don't suck"). Its games are designed with the same game mechanics as recreational games. If you master a Filament game, then you show mastery of the content it delivered. An example of Filament's approach is *Satisfraction*, a visual fraction game that uses a core mechanic reminiscent of the hands-on methodology used in Montessori learning. The game is visual, involving the player in cutting shapes into smaller pieces. The abstractness of fractions is turned into a puzzle game.

   Do I Have a Right? is one of Filament's most successful games. My students love it. The game, which teaches about the Bill of Rights, is part of the iCivics platform founded by retired Supreme Court Justice Sandra Day O'Connor. The game's objective is to run a law firm and make decisions based on a list of Constitutional rights. Prestige Points are added and used to grow the firm and to buy upgrades. Rather than learning disconnected facts, my students learned their rights through experiential play. The scoring system encouraged my students to iterate, trying over and over until they improved. The day after the activity, students came to tell me that they had played for hours at home and did even better. It is the only game many of my students will continue from home without being required to do so! By the time the test came around, they had a thorough knowledge of their Constitutional rights. My findings are, of course, purely anecdotal. The Cooney Center shared a Baylor University study showing an increase in students' test scores after playing *Do I Have a Right?* over students who hadn't played the game. I shared this anecdote with James Gee when we spoke in April 2014. "When you're incorporating games into a curriculum, you are encouraging people to play the game multiple times, to think of different ways to do better, to play collaboratively," he said. "Playing it to beat it is fine initially, but again, we want those experiences in school to go over to kid's thinking of the game as a designed object." This is Gee's Design Principle, in which "learning about and coming to appreciate design and design principles is core to the learning experience" (2007, p. 221).

   Although many students may play with the game outside of school, a participation gap still remains. Playing games and drawing connections is dependent on a student's support system at home. Gee explained, "It depends on the conduit's home. Privileged homes are where the parent scaffolds not only books, but also digital media. This gets kids to make connections. And then you have other homes where you don't. It's part of a larger issue. If games only go to some homes, then you've doubled the learning opportunity for some kids but not the others."

Filament Games co-founder Dan White has a deep connection to the games and learning space. In January 2014 I contacted him to learn more about his and his company's philosophy. White's journey began as an undergraduate student at Cornell University. He used a National Science Foundation grant to create an online virtual museum. The project was called *Active World*. "It was very primitive compared to *Second Life*," he said. *Active World* was initially playtested with the local 4H and Boys & Girls Clubs. White recalled, "I was taken with how kids engaged with it, even though [it was] primitive." After the project, White earned his master's degree in educational technology. Kurt Squire was one of his advisors; James Gee funded the project. He then parlayed his project-based thesis into a prototype of an ocean science game.

Filament Games came next. White explained, "Game technology should be authentic, constructivist, inquiry-based—not flash card-based—because learning is inherently fun. Don't take something that sucks and sugarcoat it with sparkles." His philosophy lets players "inhabit new identities and interact with systems, to learn the subject matter." White wants to move education to constructivist, project-based learning. Filament's games, therefore, are authentic spaces of learning.

In *Gamasutra*, a game industry magazine, White compared the process of getting games into schools to the rigors of rock climbing (White, 2014). Games get created, and then rewritten to integrate teaching styles, the Common Core State Standards, and other modifications (2014). These demands can distract from the designed core mechanic (2014). White proposed playtesting with teachers to bring the end users into the process (2014). This was the approach GlassLab used with *SimCityEDU*. It was pre-released to teachers and students (including myself), with accompanying feedback surveys. E-Line Media's *Historia* was developed the same way, with teachers and students brought in as co-designers. The teacher ultimately facilitates knowledge transfer from a game in a classroom. Leading follow-up discussions and reflections round out a game-based learning approach. Filament Games provides lesson plans for many of its releases.

There is an advisory panel comprised of half a dozen teachers. It also works with the National Science Foundation Research Experiences for Teachers (RET). The fellow assists in the development of a set of middle school science games. Filament has two teachers in residence and a learning specialist, too.

Including teachers in the design phase generates more feedback. The result is a better product.

Filament uses two metrics for measuring a game's success: usage by downloads and industry recognition. White said that iCivics games have had over 15 million plays at over 5 minutes each. This indicates that teachers derive value from its games. *Reach for Sun* was a critical hit, winning the Best Gameplay award at Games for Change. It is a life science game that puts the player in the role of a growing plant. The mechanic is systems thinking: Balance the plant's life cycle system to win. The game is available on Steam, a popular streaming game platform for entertainment titles, and BrainPOP.

Schell Games

Carnegie Mellon's Professor of Entertainment Technology Jesse Schell is also the founder of Schell Games. In March 2014 I spoke to him to about the process of educational game design. As a result of a talk he gave at the Games for Change Festival, his company linked up with Amplify, a for-profit educational curriculum company. Amplify plans on incorporating Schell Games into its Android-powered tablet.

Jesse Schell was always interested in games and entertainment. He began at the Walt Disney Company's virtual reality studio. He moved up the ranks from computer programmer to become creative director. Twelve years ago he came to Carnegie Mellon, drafted by fellow Disney employee Randy Pausch (famous to many for his memoir and video *The Last Lecture*. Pausch's Carnegie Mellon team created the digital animation tool Alice). Schell explained, "Randy Pausch and I started working at Disney in '95. We stayed in touch and he brought me to Carnegie Mellon. I teach his classes now."

Schell's textbook *The Art of Game Design: A Book of Lenses* is now in its 2nd edition. He explained to me where entertainment games fit into educational settings. "All entertainment works when it has found a way to make you care about something," he said.

> When it doesn't work, it didn't make you care. Education is the same way. You've got to find a way to make people care. If I don't care about doing these math problems, some fake thing about saving the princess may not work. In most cases, saving the princess and the math problem has so little to do with one another that it doesn't seem meaningful or real.

I then asked Schell how teachers should integrate games into their classrooms. "Teachers should look for problems they are trying to solve with a particular game," he said. "Games for games' sake doesn't make any sense." The same could be said of educational technology. It's a tool, not the lesson.

To Schell, game content is too scattered across the Web. It can be a confusing—almost daunting—process to find, test, and implement a game into a classroom. He stated, "There is no marketplace to sell it into schools. It's a miracle that anything happens at all." There is also no ubiquitous platform. "If kids use the same device in school, stick it in their pocket, they might play at home. If they go home, then have to find the website, and then install it—it's not going to happen." I had this issue with *SimCityEDU*, which required a download. Even the most engaged students in class shied away from playing it from home. *Do I Have a Right?*, on the other hand, plays on a computer's browser, on BrainPOP, and by an iPad app. Schell continued, "When my daughter was in elementary school, she was into *Poptropica*. Pearson [the textbook publisher] gave the kids handouts to tell how to download it. The handouts served as a reminder."

In addition to the lack of ubiquitous technology in schools, there really are no standards at all (for games and technology). It is not always obvious how a game fits in with curriculum. Bringing something such as *MinecraftEdu* into a class requires a lot of professional development because teachers need to see how it can be used to teach to Common Core State Standards. Schell foresees a standardized platform and a marketplace for schools. He explained his efforts with Amplify. He said, "Amplify is going for a curriculum and a collection of interesting games at the same time. Amplify looks at it, believes games are powerful, and will be a market differentiator for them." As a teacher, I plan to regularly check Schell Games' websites for future projects!

GlassLab: Games, Learning, and Assessment

The Games, Learning, and Assessment Lab, or GlassLab, was founded in 2012 with a $10.3 million grant from the Bill & Melinda Gates Foundation and the MacArthur Foundation. GlassLab was a division of the Institute of Play; it became an independent studio in July 2014. GlassLab is located on the campus of Electronic Arts in Redwood Shores, California. The Entertainment Software Association originally brokered the deal connecting foundation monies. Games meet the Common Core State Standards; projects must have formative assessments based on student play. Challenges are designed to be just ahead of where students are, which should guide them to higher and higher levels of competency. The Education Testing Service created the evidence-centered design model that is built into the games. It provides seamless feedback to teachers. The initiative brings together known quantities in the education space to help with assessment and telemetry. This gets data out of the game to help teachers assess how students are doing in the game. GlassLab also partnered with Pearson. Electronic Arts was GlassLab's first partner. The partnership is not exclusive, and can extend to other publishers such as Activision or Valve. Part of its mission is to take existing AAA games and modify them; basically, pulling out the education that already exists. The other part of its mission is to design original games linked to Common Core assessments.

In the course of writing this book, I spoke frequently with Erin Hoffman, game design lead on the first two GlassLab projects. We began speaking in January 2014. Hoffman started her career designing online and console games, as well as massively multiplayer online virtual worlds. She has worked for the social gaming company Zynga (*Farmville, Draw Something*), which is credited with designing *FrontierVille*. Hoffman is also a published fantasy fiction author of the Chaos Knight fantasy series from Pyr Books. She reflected on GlassLab's process of learning with games. She said, "We thought of our principles: a love of games can be a love of learning. My interest was the cognitive state that is learning. It is an engaging and positive emotion."

SimCityEDU: Pollution Challenge!

Figure 1. *SimCityEDU* screenshot. Image courtesy of Institute of Play.

Figure 2. Students using the systems mapping tool from the *SimCityEDU* beta test. Image courtesy of Institute of Play.

SimCityEDU: Pollution Challenge! is a modification of the 2013 commercial release *SimCity*. GlassLab was given the actual source code and customized it by adding an educational focus on science, English language arts, and 21st-century standards. The experience put structured problems in a sandbox space (like creating challenges with LEGO bricks, rather than allowing children to freely play). In other words, GlassLab built the cities, and then transposed environmental impact challenges. The game assesses in real time during play. An assessment engine processes all player choices—from bulldozing power plants to zoning. Student competencies are reported to teachers, detailing how well students can make systems diagrams. "From a design standpoint, with a large sample, you get a lot of patterns," Hoffman said. "You can make correlations to data. If you see a behavior happening, you can pair it to other behaviors." *SimCityEDU* is pattern-based, and scaffolds skills. The seemingly simple system of virtual city planning quickly becomes complex.

My students took part in playtesting the pre-release version. It was to be the first in a series of *SimCity*-modified games. Students assume the role of the mayor and must balance a city's systems. We joined the beta in August 2013; the release was scheduled for early November 2013. I deployed the game in early September, making the activity double as an icebreaker for the new school year. I borrowed laptops from neighboring teachers to create a 1:1 setting. Ultimately, the experience framed the entire school year by creating an authentic reference point for systems thinking concepts. I was able to analogize historical interactions as a causal feedback loop; students understood interrelationships from their *SimCityEDU* experiences. "Meta-gaming"— using games as a model for real-world comparisons—became a useful teaching tool. It can work for all disciplines: Characters have interconnections in novels, numbers affect each other in math, and life sciences evaluate the fragility of ecosystems.

SimCityEDU has a leaderboard that aggregates student performance with points and badges. Games are open-ended and have many paths to the "right" answer. There are, in fact, many "right" answers. Many students replayed and shared strategies to better their personal scores or to beat their classmates. This illustrated Gee's Probing Principle, in which players test and hypothesize solutions, as in the scientific method (2007).

The final release features six missions. Missions are further divided into "Gameplay" and "Challenges." Gameplay involved balancing a virtual city's systems. Some challenges are mind maps that reinforce systems thinking concepts from missions. Other challenges are text-based—words are clicked and dragged from paragraphs onto a systems map. Each mission levels up in difficulty to encourage mastery. The first mission, Parktown, tests player strategy in placing bus stops throughout the city. Too many bus stops are inefficient; too few will not transport enough children to school. Students experimented by placing one bus stop in the center of the city, and then waited to see what would happen. The second mission, Little Alexandria, tasks the player with increasing the number of jobs in the city. Later missions are pollution-related, specifically, coal versus solar. The final mission is the boss level. Coal creates jobs, but also increases pollution. Players must decide how to boost employment without harming the city's environment. It is a difficult challenge and involves many overlapping causal loops. Students must apply all that they learned to overcome the hardest challenge. (This mission was actually deemed too challenging in the beta version, and was scaled back in difficulty.) Lesson plans for the missions ended with self-reflection writing prompts.

The pilot was several months long. The alpha testers helped create lesson plans that the beta teachers implemented. About 1,200 students and their 27 teachers participated. All students were surveyed, as were teachers, via SurveyMonkey. Professional development videos were provided to give teachers more background information on gameplay. After all, not all teachers are avid gamers. Documents were added featuring "cheats," hints for students, and completed mission walkthroughs.

I did not use the prepackaged formative assessments to grade my students. I did require everyone to complete the game, which meant that each mission had to be unlocked as they played. The leveling up system superseded the idea of grading. Assessing play can take away from the intrinsic satisfaction and fun.

Doing so can make the learning extrinsic and can inadvertently encourage students to take the quickest route to what they perceive is a desired answer. I expanded the GlassLab's writing prompts into full paragraph writing assignments. The printed portfolio became the game's authentic assessment. The objective of *SimCityEDU* is different than surviving in a zombie game. Students were asked to reflect on what was required to succeed and to describe how they accomplished each task. I created a bulletin board to display the portfolios. This became a culminating activity in a unit that had a lot of embedded assessments.

I personally played through the game to get myself acclimated to the challenges. I gave very little assistance to students so they could figure it out for themselves. Some students failed just for fun. For example, some noticed that certain businesses were prone to fires (donut shops, Chinese restaurants). They began to build them near each other to test what would occur. Other students were slow to zone. The result was a protest at city hall. These instances illustrated negative feedback loops.

The game took 10 hours to play, over the course of 2 weeks. Students had a hands-on, constructivist learning experience of causal loops and systems thinking tasks. The beta version's daily electronic surveys increased the students' buy-in; they knew their responses affected the final release. During each day of the *SimCityEDU* beta test, I had to ask students to leave at the bell—even if lunch and recess was the next period. No one signed out of class to use the bathroom.

Mars Generation One: Argubot Academy

In August 2013, a few months before *SimCityEDU's* release, Hoffman stepped off and led the concept of GlassLab's first original game. She was running tests for a product code-named *Hiro*. It was initially prototyped as a text-based, interactive fiction game, before graphical elements were added (the iterative design process was detailed in Chapter 4). At the time of my first interview with Hoffman, it was called *Argubot Attacks*. It was officially released as *Mars Generation One: Argubot Academy* in the spring of 2014. It is a tablet game that teaches argumentation evidence as part of the Common Core State Standards. The objective is to teach students how to evaluate and create an argument by connecting data and evidence to support a claim.

GlassLab worked with NASA to ensure the authenticity of a Martian setting. The player is part of the first generation of a human city on Mars. Their society resolves conflict using argument robots. Players equip their robot with an argumentation claim, and then evidence, and eventually other dimensions of arguments. In the tutorial, you argue about ice cream flavors. The dispute is settled by dragging a claim, along with supporting evidence, to the robot. Both pieces interlock as a completed puzzle. Some evidence is off-topic, which can cause defeat in battle.

Argumentation is a commonly used game mechanic, especially in board games such as *Apples to Apples* and *Taboo*. When arguing, there are particular kinds of emotions one experiences from participating. There is actually a dramatic feeling in an argument. The game, therefore, must capture the essence of the interpersonal drama one feels from arguing.

The challenge was to match the game mechanic with the competency of argumentative thinking. Herein lies the trap of "edutainment," or chocolate-covered broccoli. Hoffman's solution was to "find the fun within the competency itself." The team started with a competency map. "I dove into the mechanics of argumentation, how it's being taught, the difficulties of how it's taught, and then I associated the competencies to proven game mechanics," Hoffman said. GlassLab's learning director recommended the pedagogy of Stephen Toulmin. This methodology states that there really is no such thing as a false argument; rather, there are different schemes appropriate to an argument. If you have a scheme, or argument, and if it can stand up to critical question attacks—such as experts agreeing or other supporting evidence—then the argument is valid.

Hoffman realized that Toulmin's argument schemes were similar to those at play in the trading card game *Pokémon*. Because each Pokémon has a different ability, the player needs to strategize about how to duel with his or her opponent. She explained, "You have to determine the scheme, what the appropriate attacks are for that scheme, then what attack you're using in your *Pokémon*/argumentative scheme. There were a lot of parallels so we developed the game structures that connected the core feeling of the competency itself of the game mechanic we knew would work with kids."

The app was officially unveiled at the 11th Annual Games for Change Festival in New York City. Hoffman participated in the panel's discussions led by GlassLab's Jessica Lindl. GlassLab's added support goes beyond the game as a stand-alone experience. Like *SimCityEDU*, *Argubot* has a website that features links to game-based research and lesson plans. Teachers can import student lists and track student progress on the dashboard. Tablets simply need a student name with a log-on code—no emails are necessary. The support website originally included printable *Pokémon*-style trading cards enabling teachers and students to modify and create their own argumentation games for any content area.

E-Line Media

E-Line Media is a game-based company with diverse connections: Alaska native leaders, game designers, and learning scientists (from Arizona State University and the Center for Games and Impact). A big part of E-Line's philosophy is to scale up classroom games; it is bringing a digital version of the fun, paper-based *Historia* to potentially millions of users. It is worth reviewing the company's philosophy and dedication to the game-based learning sector. Like GlassLab, E-Line has teacher support that is tremendously resourceful. It has been very responsive in addressing technical issues and providing lesson plans for my students. In June 2014 Kate Reilly, *Historia's* project manager, personally visited my classroom! In this regard, it is a service company focused on student learning.

The company is cautious with its partnerships. When I initially interviewed Reilly, in January 2014, she told me that it took over a year and a half for E-Line to link up with Jason Darnell and Rick Brennan, *Historia's* teacher-designers. It just began working with TeacherGaming, distributors of *MinecraftEdu*. Other partners include the social impact game *Half the Sky* and the video game authoring tool *Gamestar Mechanic*. It also co-sponsors the National STEM Video Game Challenge (discussed in Chapter 13).

More recently, E-Line began working with the Cook Inlet Tribal Council in Anchorage, Alaska. The Council formed Upper One Games. It is a partner in the *Historia* project, as well as *Never Alone*, a puzzle game about Iñupiat folklore. The Council is seeking to change education by infusing its values of resiliency into comprehensive products. "To them, *Historia* was a great fit," Reilly explained. "It emphasized the importance of interdependence and collaboration to the success of a people. The game is about building a better world—the boundless opportunities of young people."

I spoke with Alan Gershenfeld, the co-founder of E-Line Media, in May 2014. Gershenfeld started his career in film, working in China in the late 1980s. In 1992 he was recruited to Activision, the video game software company. When he arrived, it had just gone through bankruptcy and had very few employees. This is in stark contrast to today; Activision is a multibillion-dollar publishing powerhouse known for the *Call of Duty* series. The studio soon moved to Hollywood. Gershenfeld's film background—along with the company's relocation to Hollywood—brought a new vision and sensibility for games, film, and digital entertainment. This was in the early 1990s, when CD-ROMs entered the market. CD-ROMs offered more storage, which led to more robust games. Gershenfeld's role in the company grew from head of creative affairs to the head of the Los Angeles Studio.

During the late 1990s Activision grew dramatically. Gershenfeld now had experience growing and managing a large commercial game studio. He knew how to design, develop, publish, and distribute content. By 2000, however, he wanted to move to the New York metropolitan area and change direction. He wanted to empower youth through digital media—not just earn profits. He and his friend started a film company focused on documenting refugee camps. Next, he started one of the first "double-bottom-line businesses," focused on social impact *and* making a financial return. Then he met Suzanne Seggerman, co-founder of Games for Change (this organization and its annual festival are discussed in Chapter 13). He joined the board and eventually became its chairman.

In the mid-2000s there was a community of practice emerging about games for impact. Gershenfeld saw hundreds of millions of dollars from governments, agencies, nonprofits, and foundations seeking to harness learning from games. The problem as he saw it was that a lot of products and services from the research pipeline were not commercially viable enterprises. Some research projects are intended for dissertation studies, not for general consumption (though some are used that way). E-Line Ventures, with Gershenfeld's film school friend Michael Angst, was created to close that gap. The original intent was to do "angel investing" (funding start-up companies). Eventually, they switched from their investment focus to become a publishing company. E-Line Ventures became E-Line Media. "E-Line Media seeks to provide repeatable, scalable mechanisms to do multistakeholder partnerships," Gershenfeld said. "We integrate research, design, development, marketing, distribution, assessment in both consumer and educational channels." In other words, E-Line takes research projects and turns them into long-term, viable assets that are marketable.

E-Line Media is in the consumer space, too, with a separate office in Seattle. Gershenfeld compared the northwest studio to Participant Media, the independent film company responsible for *An Inconvenient Truth* (2006) and *The Help* (2011). Gershenfeld is interested in how brains can change through games and play, too. The educational, transformational space is currently called

Pathways. He said, "We plan to do consumer games that attack meaty themes in really interesting ways. Cultural storytelling, expanded through games."

The company has a passion for harnessing the power of games. Geshenfeld is currently a board member of the Cooney Center and Games for Change. "E-Line Media's service leverages game design, game mechanics, and other learning modalities," he said. "It's not like we just build games. We also build ecosystems, services, creating communities around games used for trajectories." This model is transforming the idea of what a learning game studio can achieve.

MangaHigh

Toby Rowland is the CEO and founder of MangaHigh, one of the more popular producers of adaptive math games. The company currently has a staff of 18, including teacher advisors.

In February 2014 I spoke to Rowland via Skype. His background includes many start-ups, from e-commerce to online dating to social gaming. He co-founded the casual social game site King.com in 2003, which had a runaway hit with the social game *Candy Crush Saga*. In 2008 he resigned to start MangaHigh. Rowland saw potential in how online learning can transform the way education is delivered, not just in the developed world but all around the world. "The special sauce I could bring was engagement," Rowland said. "Not just with games, but competition systems and tournaments, to make people want to play again and again."

MangaHigh uses an adaptive learning engine with a mathematical algorithm coded into the game, with the goal of putting the best lesson in front of the student. Rowland explained, "It understands students' computational ability and changes the complexity of the questions to get the best out of them. In the background, every student gets a constant evaluation, whether they can go forward or consolidate previous lessons before going on." The website boasts several math-themed games. You can click in and out of the puzzle challenges or you can play for hours.

Mastery of puzzles indicates students understood the math. A *Tangled Web*, which has about 160 levels, starts with simple questions about, for example, angles around a point, and progresses up to polygons. The player controls "Itzi, the spider" around a spinning clock. The game's complexity evolves with the mathematics. Rowland said, "The game takes a mathematical problem and makes the revolution of that problem into an interesting puzzle."

Rowland told me that between 2 and 4 million questions are answered in its games, every school day. MangaHigh has a "try and test" model to entice users, as well as "freemium" plans ("freemium" is a portmanteau of "free" and "premium"). "The starting principle has to be that people check things out before buying into them," Rowland explained. "We're very generous with our freemium terms. We know that when people see the games, they will like them." A *Tangled Web* can be played on BrainPOP's platform.

Rowland feels that there is a place for game-based incentives. "It can bring flavor to something that otherwise might be dry," he said. "I've seen students, even not at grade level, becoming fascinated with the math. They are debating, solving puzzles, being engaged in mathematical thinking."

Games—even those so closely linked to content standards—can still be a tough sell for administrators and school districts. There are very established and entrenched purchasing systems that have to be considered. "It's difficult to manage for start-ups," Rowland said. "It's about budget and long-term adoption. People can find market entrance quite disheartening." For now, MangaHigh plans on continuing its development of math games. "We're curious about other content, but we like math the most."

BrainPOP

Figure 3. The character of Moby the robot is also a trademark of BrainPOP. ©2014 BrainPOP and/or its related companies. All rights reserved. Reprinted by permission. The character of Moby the robot is also a trademark of BrainPOP.

Many of the games in this chapter—and in this book—are playable on BrainPOP's GameUp platform. I visited the New York City headquarters in May 2014, along with my 3-year-old son, Spencer. When we arrived in the lobby he complained, "This isn't BrainPOP. This is an office!" It took some convincing to assure him that we were, in fact, at BrainPOP! Eventually, we were led into a game room, a kid-friendly space for my interview. As it happened, the company was hosting an office celebration that day: The 100th game had been added to GameUp.

BrainPOP is a well respected brand for teachers and parents. Started in 1999 by pediatrician Avraham Kadar, it is now in about 20% of American schools. BrainPOP has more than 1,000 short, educational videos featuring Moby, the beeping robot, and Tim. BrainPOP, Jr., the early elementary portal, features Moby and Annie. I met with Karina Linch, senior vice president of product management, Allisyn Levy, vice president of GameUp, researcher Katya Hott, and Games and Education Project Manager Scott Price. Hott and Price formerly worked at E-Line Media developing *Gamestar Mechanic*. BrainPOP also sponsored some of the games and learning research conducted by the Cooney Center. Employees call themselves "BrainPOPpers"; teacher advisors are called "BrainPOPstars."

The game room, where we met, was filled with hand-drawn pictures of Tim, Annie, and Moby that kids had mailed in. During our meeting I discovered that Linch—who oversaw the launch of BrainPOP, Jr.—is also the voice of Annie in the Moby videos. She brought my son and I into the booth where all of the videos are recorded. While there, we screamed at the top of our lungs; after all, it was soundproof! In the animations, Moby has no voice, just a series of beeps. His background remains a mystery. Maybe he is an alien? Maybe he is just a robot? Linch explained that the original Moby videos, from about 15 years ago, were shorter in length due to the limited bandwidth schools had at that time. As a result, Tim (voiced by BrainPOP's creative director) had to speak very fast. Moby's beeps were also a result of technical limitations. It used to be challenging to have multiple speaking characters in videos (again, a technology limitation of the early millennium). When technology improved, the team re-recorded Tim's dialogue and redid the accompanying quizzes. Interestingly, Moby still beeps. It turned out that children guess and infer his dialogue based on the pauses and perceived social cues.

BrainPOP's dedicated digital game platform, GameUp, was launched in 2011. It is a collection of vetted learning games. You can play games related to science, math, social studies, health, English language arts, and technology. One of the "rules" with GameUp is that it has to be extremely easy for a teacher to implement—no downloads or installations required. Of course, this limits the games it can add. Nonetheless, it provides a trusted portal for teachers to sample learning games. BrainPOP includes research and lesson plan suggestions with games.

BrainPOP provides samples of games to whet teachers' and students' appetites. If they want a deeper experience, such as playing the full version of the acclaimed *Lure of the Labyrinth*, they can go to the Learning Game Network's website and download the full version. BrainPOP feels that teachers may not want—or even need—a big commitment that involves permission requests to install software.

The team explained to me that BrainPOP doesn't want to send the message that games should be assessment tools. Instead, it posts a brief essential question that the student can answer. An example of a self-reflection question for a systems thinking game, is: What's one method you used? Newer games have seamless, integrated checks for understanding; you don't want to stop the action of play to ask questions. As a result, BrainPOP began to implement its SnapThought reflection tool. Students take a screenshot of gameplay and answer a question about why they made certain decisions. Games also include a quiz about what was learned, and lesson plans for implementation, with alignment to Common Core State Standards.

The games are playable only on computer browsers (e.g., Internet Explorer, Safari, Chrome). Flash, the application that runs most of the games, isn't supported on most mobile devices. The stand-alone apps for BrainPOP and BrainPOP, Jr. are just for movies and quizzes. When I inquired about other ways to build games, such as with the HTML 5 language that works on iPad's Safari browser, I was informed that it could be problematic. Video games are much more complex than touch-enabled websites. BrainPOP is currently looking for a solution as technology advances. The goal remains to have the simplest interface for the teacher, thus lowering barriers to adoption.

One new game that works on mobile is *Sortify*. It is a proprietary interactive where students choose from topics, create sorting bins, and move objects to where they belong. Options include parts of speech, the Constitution, natural resources, and musical instruments. My students sorted the American Revolution and the Constitution. When they clicked "Submit to teacher," I was able to view how each student performed on my Teacher Dashboard. There is also a downloadable document for students to create and play their own paper-based version.

When you play a game on BrainPOP, you see connected topics on the bottom of the page. The idea is for teachers and students—who may be driven crazy with standardized assessments—to see where a game fits into the scheme of the class. It makes recommendations for related games within the BrainPOP "Educator" login and "Lesson Plan" pages. BrainPOP doesn't tell teachers what to do or how to implement the games. In the end, it is still the teacher's role to contextualize the games. Best practices and research are also freely available. The opinion is that teachers want to know the best ways to implement games, and prefer not be told what to do. Student-created games are also featured, including those made with *Gamestar Mechanic*.

Katya Hott shared a 3-year study with New York City public schools and *Gamestar Mechanic*. Students designed and played games during assigned class periods, in unassigned class periods, and from home. Hott reported that a good portion—over 50%—used it in school as a resource, even if it was unassigned. At home, however, there was a precipitous drop. Nearly 1% used *Gamestar Mechanic* from home, and those were the students engaged in the details of design. That number was much lower than expected. She explained, "Even though they really loved it and it was play and fun, it happened at school, so it felt like school." Linch added, "Plus, there is so much competition with other games at home." Of course, times are changing. It may also depend on the age group of students and the game itself. Not every topic and medium is going to reach every child, hence the need to address multiple modalities. Nonetheless, BrainPOP is fulfilling the need for a one-stop source for games, videos, teacher support, and ease of use.

Conclusions and Takeaways

Developer websites are an excellent resource for learning games, research, and lesson plans. There is a renaissance in educational game design, with a lot of developers trying to create truly innovative experiences. Many vetted learning games are available to sample on BrainPOP's GameUp platform. Play the games in this chapter (many are free or available on GameUp). A useful tool is student reflection on in-game decisions.

Lesson Plan Ideas

Colonial Africa: A colleague of mine created a simulation game to teach 6th graders about the European colonization of Africa in the 1800s. Students each received a card when entering class. The card had either a European country on it or an African kingdom. Next, students got three resource cards, which depicted gold, cacao beans, rubber trees, or other African resources. The rules, displayed on the whiteboard, stated that students with African cards were allowed to trade only with other African kingdoms. Students with European country cards were then instructed to take two Resource cards from whomever they wished. Students took turns in the order of the strongest European country to the weakest. The European country with the most amount of money at the end won. Students who had African Kingdom cards were then told to pair up and share a seat in the back of the class. Following the simulation game students shared how they felt during the simulation and then connected that to why there are problems in Africa today. The reflection piece is essential to relate the interconnectedness of systems. Social studies standards apply.

Compare and Contrast as a Trading Card Game: Debate techniques are the building blocks of argumentative thinking. Typically, students are given T-charts or graphic organizers to analyze differing viewpoints. Too often, the passion of argumentation is lost when using traditional assessment techniques such as graphic organizers. In this case, argumentation, judging, and voting mechanics are used because each mirrored the actions used to debate issues. Students will create trading cards, along with evidence and claim cards. To create trading cards, two options are available: using the *Trading Cards* iPad app or drawing cards by hand. Each student should have five trading cards. Next, students create claims and evidence cards similar to those found in GlassLab's argumentation iPad game, *Mars Generation One: Argubot Academy.* Students will make at least one claim card per trading card; each claim card needs two or three accompanying evidence cards. Evidence cards are student-ranked from 1 to 3, 1 being the least important (similar to how battle cards are numbered in *Magic: The Gathering*). Students play in groups of five: Two students "duel," and three students judge and keep score. The game begins with drawing a card to see with whom they are battling in the duel. If players draw the same card—or if a card is from the same point of view—that card is returned to the deck. Students next put down their claims and evidence, one at a time, to "attack" each other's claim. The judges vote on whether the attack is effective. Once the round ends, another pair faces off. Students' trading cards, along with claims and evidence cards, are graded by rubric. Common Core State Standards pertaining to argumentative reading and writing apply.

Ether: The gravity game. Next Generation Science Standards apply—http://iridescentlearning .org/programs/the-gravity-ether

SimCityEDU: Pollution Challenge!: I used GlassLab's reflection questions and writing prompts to create a project with a culminating deliverable: a student portfolio. This style of grading can work for any long-form video game. (Of course, students can download it and play from home, too, to replay missions!) Because the only way to unlock the next mission is to complete current challenges, performance in the game need not be graded. What should be graded is the portfolio of written work that accompanies the game. Standards for the game, which include Next Generation Science Standards and Common Core State Standards, are available—http://www.sharemylesson.com/teaching-resource/ simcityedu-lesson-plans-50028746/

Sortify Game: This is the printable, design-your-own lesson plan from BrainPOP. Standards vary, depending on the discipline or content area—http://www.brainpop.com/educators/community/printable/sortify-design-game

Games

BrainPOP's GameUp, the platform to play many well-designed learning games in a browser, complete with lesson plans and teacher support—http://www.brainpop.com/games

Ether, the gravity game from Iridescent, with teacher resources—http://iridescentlearning.org/programs/the-gravity-ether

Gen i Revolution, a multiplayer financial literacy game from the Council for Economic Education, complete with lesson plans and teacher resources—http://www.genirevolution.org

iCivics, featuring lesson plans and learning games, both digital and paper-based—https://www.icivics.org

Magic 2015, follow the tutorial to learn the rules of *Magic: The Gathering,* on an iPad—https://appsto.re/i6gP5VB

Mars Generation One: Argubot Academy, the portal to download the tablet app and manage students via the teacher dashboard. Common Core–linked lesson plans and videos are also included to support teachers, as well as printable trading cards to extend learning—http://www.playfully.org

Mathbreakers is a 3D virtual world in which players apply mathematical concepts. For example, the fraction ¼ may be required as a key for a door. The player then must use a sword to cut an object to fit the size. *Mathbreakers* is a crowdfunded Kickstarter project—https://www.mathbreakers.com

NationStates is a game where players can build nations with different governments, flags and mottos. It is an online simulation based on books from author Max Barry. The game has a lot in common with Model United Nations clubs, creating rules and encouraging interactions—http://www.nationstates.net

Pokémon Trading Card Game, playable online—http://www.pokemon.com/us/pokemon-tcg

Poptropica—http://www.poptropica.com

Reach for the Sun from Filament Games is a Games for Change award winner. It is also an effective way to teach systems thinking—https://www.filamentgames.com/products/reach-sun-product

Satisfraction, the fraction game, from Filament Games—http://www.filamentgames.com/sites/default/files/games/Satisfraction_v1.1/index.html

SimCityEDU—http://www.simcityedu.org

Sortify, from BrainPOP—http://www.brainpop.com/games/sortify

A Tangled Web, MangaHigh's game of geometric angles (also playable on BrainPOP's GameUp)—http://www.mangahigh.com/en-us/games/atangledweb

Trading Cards, authoring tool for tablets, published by the International Reading Association. Free for iPad—https://appsto.re/i6gP5VS and Android—http://goo.gl/YJB5KQ

Resources

BrainPOP's SnapThought photo reflection tool enables students to take a screenshot and then submit an open-ended response to the teacher—http://www.brainpop.com/educators/community/video/snapthought-aphoto-reflection-tool

Do I Have a Right?, the popular Bill of Rights law firm game, also available for iPad (search: Pocket Law Firm)—https://www.icivics.org/games/do-i-have-right

E-Line Media, publishers of *Historia, Half the Sky, Gamestar Mechanic*—http://elinemedia.com

FableVision Studios, the digital art company founded by children's author Peter H. Reynolds. FableVision has worked on games and interactives from *Quandary* and *Lure of the Labyrinth* to *Dora the Explorer*—http://www.fablevisionstudios.com

Filament Games, learning games studio based in Wisconsin—https://www.filamentgames.com

Playfully.org, GlassLab's ubiquitous learning management service for educational games—http://www.playfully.org

Schell Games, Jesse Schell's game design studio—http://www.schellgames.com

Stephen Toulmin's argument methodology, a major influence in GlassLab's approach to its argumentation game *Mars Generation One: Argubot Academy*—http://www-rohan.sdsu.edu/~digger/305/toulmin_model.htm

· 1 1 ·

COMMUNITIES OF PLAY

Game and learning academic James Gee refers to offline game-based communities as "affinity groups." This is where people are "bonded primarily through shared endeavors, goals, and practices and not shared race, gender, nation, ethnicity, or culture" (2007, p. 212). Wikis—websites that anyone can edit—are an example. The website IGN Entertainment features wikis about video games. I have often turned to IGN to find user-created "walkthroughs" of games when I get stuck on a level or can't figure out a solution to a problem.

If students can engage in higher-order discourse on a topic they are interested in, perhaps it should be brought into formal learning settings. One such space was the Joystick101.org community (now defunct). Kurt Squire started writing for it as a graduate student and discovered that readers were active (2011). Squire wrote, "Knowing how to identify, navigate, and even *start* affinity spaces such as Joystick101.org is an essential skill for furthering one's professional development" (2011, p. 69). He continued, "It may be less games as a technology and more games as a cultural practice that encourages experimentation, systemic thinking, and authentic participation" (Squire, 2011, p. 71). In other words, gamer cultures have members who discuss and reflect, as well as critique, content. Also debated are heuristics, defined as analyzing "what moves were most effective, what decisions could have been made differently, what the correct winning strategies are" (Elias, Garfield, & Gutschera, 2012, p. 29). Think: Monday morning quarterback.

Apprenticeship training is a situated learning experience in which new initiates learn in a "community of practice" (Lave & Wenger, 1991). To learn, one moves from the periphery of a social and authentic setting to the center, where mastery is demonstrated. Lave and Wenger called this "legitimate peripheral participation" (1991). Learning can be incidental; it can just happen, by the learner simply being present in a setting. Much research has been conducted linking situated cognition to online communities. Fans join and participate in game-based discussion forums because of the intrinsic desire to learn more about a game. In forums and wikis, learners pick up more information from other members.

This chapter describes what happens offline, outside of a game. It also covers how fans generate and remix content within affinity groups and participatory cultures. Examples in this chapter all come with unusual monikers. These include: game-related fan fiction, Let's Play, eSports, machinima, and modding forums. These strange names (machinima?) emanate from the "community of practice" each one has.

Game-Related Fan Fiction

In *Convergence Culture: Where Old and New Media Collide* (2006) Henry Jenkins described "fan fiction," or "fanfic." This genre of participatory writing refers to "any prose retelling of stories and characters drawn from mass media content" (Jenkins, 2006a, p. 285). Jenkins analyzed "participatory" fan communities such as FanFiction.net and the unofficial Harry Potter fan site MuggleNet. Video game-themed fan fiction is a popular subgenre on FanFiction.net. A casual search of the "Games" subsection showed thousands of stories, mostly for *Pokémon*, *The Legend of Zelda*, *Mass Effect*, and *Assassin's Creed*. There were some intriguing fan-created historical fiction stories about the game *Civilization*. I wondered how game-related fan fiction would work in my classroom.

I decided to combine fan fiction with a character web, thus mashing up storytelling with the dynamics of systems thinking (everything is interconnected). I constructed *The Assassin's Creed: Renaissance Character Web Project*, a project-based learning unit. Students were tasked to add Renaissance-era characters to the video game. Titles in the series have featured Leonardo da Vinci, Niccolò Machiavelli, Nicolaus Copernicus, several popes, and members of the Borgia and Medici families. Also included in the game are "databases," in which players are given historical information about people and places from the time period. The unit was tied to historical fiction, which can make history more "real" and relatable to middle school students. The culminating activity was to create a functioning fan fiction wiki of characters, similar to the *Assassin's Creed* wiki: http://assassinscreed.wikia.com.

When I launched the project, I informally asked my students to tell me if they had ever written or read fan fiction. Only a few hands went up—although most said that they had heard of it. When I interviewed Henry Jenkins in May 2014, I asked about the state of fanfic's current popularity (remember, *Convergence Culture* came out in 2006). "Sixth grade is the earliest that people engage in fan fiction," he said. "Most people I talked to were in high school or older; a high percentage in my grad school have read or written it."

Jenkins coined the term "participatory culture." This is the situated learning space where "fans and other consumers are invited to actively participate in the creation and circulation of new content" (Jenkins, 2006a, p. 290). Participatory cultures are relatively easy to join. When a new member creates content by, for example, posting game footage on YouTube, other members offer feedback. Jenkins has done experiments bringing fan fiction around canonical literature into the classroom. "I think all of the tools are there," he explained. "The challenge is to get young people to make connections. People learn outside of school. Some of these activities may not be valued in the classroom."

I asked Jenkins for advice on using game wikis as a teaching tool. For example, *Assassin's Creed* is rated M for mature content, mainly due to violence. Students weren't playing the game in school; however, they were engaged in remixing its content. Jenkins told me about the ethics of participatory culture practices. Not every educator can see the value in a child's hobbies, including cartoons, comic books, and video games. Some student interests may not be perceived as "appropriate" by teachers. Jenkins explained:

> Teachers can't simply invite it [student's interests and hobbies] in and then impose their own hierarchy on the behaviors that young people choose to be involved with. In many ways, it has to do with the ethical environment within the classroom, as much—or more—than the specific activities that form a participatory culture. It should be a safe space. A safe space isn't just defined by the way we normally use that term, like sexual issues or gender issues. It also has to be culturally safe, so kids don't get put down for the popular culture they like, or the activities they engage with.

Teachers should keep an open mind and look at the ways that those can be valuable sites of learning and be meaningfully connected to the classroom.

Jenkins discussed a book he co-edited, *Reading in Participatory Culture* (2013), which "described instructional activities we developed around remix in a participatory culture." It was shaped by the work of Ricardo Pitts-Wiley, an African American playwright who got incarcerated youth to read *Moby-Dick* by getting them to rewrite *Moby-Dick*—essentially, creating fan fiction. Jenkins said, "These are kids who are reading below grade level [and] not just at risk—already in prison. They read a book that the school system generally saw as too difficult to teach because of its complexity."

Pitts-Wiley had students write fan fiction characters, thus remixing *Moby-Dick*. He asked them to imagine what these characters would be like in the 21st century, and they transformed *Moby-Dick* from a story about the whaling trade to a story about the drug trade. "It becomes [about] a gang leader bent on vengeance at the expense of dealing drugs," Jenkins explained. "And the question of the story is, how far will a young crew follow into the mouth of hell and vengeance when they recognize that it's going to lead into their own destruction. It's very important to introduce these kinds of remix activities because it not only teaches kids to read critically, but to read creatively." It was *Grand Theft Auto* meets Herman Melville.

Let's Play!

In June 2014 the *Wall Street Journal* reported that Internet sensation PewDiePie earned over $4 million from his YouTube channel. PewDiePie—who boasts more than 27 million subscribers—specializes in a trend called "Let's Play." This genre of video involves users who record and share comedic voice-overs of their game play. According to the website Let's Play Archive, people post "screenshots of themselves playing various old fondly-remembered video games (such as *Oregon Trail* and *Pokémon*) and include their own humorous commentary."

YouTube can be a competitive marketplace—not just for attaining popularity, but also for commerce. When I searched for "*Minecraft*" on the video streaming service, I got more than 20 million results. (One could argue that YouTube is a game; the scoreboard is the total number of subscribers and views.) Videos of games help market video games. *Minecraft* has never used traditional advertising such as television commercials. Instead, Let's Play boosts the grassroots following for the game (Goldberg & Larsson, 2013, p. 147). Jordan Maron—also known as CaptainSparklez—was one of the most popular Let's Play channels. He has more than 6 million subscribers! The more viewers that watch CaptainSparklez's Let's Play posts, the more monetized revenue Maron earns. Maron's tips on how to play even made their way into a book from Scholastic, *Minecraft: Essential Handbook* (2013). Paul Soares, Jr., another contributor to the Scholastic book, creates in the Let's Play universe. He hosts several *Minecraft* shows on YouTube from the perspective of a father and a gamer. Soares currently has about 1 million subscribers.

As with any participatory culture, there are rules for sharing. Most Let's Play videos are around 15 minutes in length and are broken up into parts. The Let's Play community discourages "blind playthroughs," in which first-time playing is recorded and uploaded. It is expected that the games were played several times and are flawless in execution. Watching someone die over and over is a waste of a viewer's time. The community of practice encourages waiting 3 months to make a Let's Play video for a new game ("How to Do a Let's Play," 2014; "LP Guide for Newbies," 2014). This guideline is intended to prevent spoilers about game content.

In December 2013, Google (the owner of YouTube) took steps to remove Let's Play video content due to copyright violations: Game titles often include licensed music. I can virtually drive around the fictional city of Los Santos in *Grand Theft Auto V* while listening to "One Vision" by Queen on the car's stereo. If I record my gameplay and post it on YouTube, am I violating copyright law? Is it against YouTube's terms of service? Are Let's Play videos "derivative works" or wholly original, based on remixed content? The issue may stem from the fact that videos are monetized with ads. Let's Play content creators earn money—and Internet fame—from posting videos of popular games. Some saw the crackdown as a raid, especially because Let's Play isn't just watching walkthroughs. Some videos are humorous entertainment, having more in common with satirized news clips presented by late night comedians. A proposed solution was the Let's Playlist. Producers and fans can curate games that are friendly to Let's Play. Most game developers now allow uploaded content, with the exception of, most notably, Nintendo (Campbell, 2013).

Let's Play is a seamless way for students to reflect and share what they have learned from problem solving in video game worlds, as well as to explain what they have created in sandbox games (e.g., *Minecraft*). Let's Play meets Common Core State Standards, too, especially when concepts need to be explained. The ability to teach and to explain information in an engaging way can make one highly marketable in today's global economy. Nowadays, job interviews, as well as many business meetings, are sometimes conducted via videoconferencing tools including Skype, Google Hangout, and GoToMeeting.

Many recording tools are free or have low-cost options. One of my former students had his father record his *Minecraft* project simply by holding a smartphone camera in front of the computer screen! More advanced users may opt to try screencasting tools—software that records what plays on a computer's screen. There are many options for recording software, including the FRAPS Game Capture and LoiLo Game Recorder. Bandicam is a tool that specializes in *Minecraft* videos. Keep in mind that screencasting video games can make a school-issued computer lag in performance and speed. It can work better to use lower power, browser-based screencast tools such as Screencast-O-Matic. For tablets, simply take a screenshot (on an iPad, hold the power button and the home button simultaneously). Then import the image into a word processing app—or even iMovie—for postproduction and written reflection.

eSports

SuperData Research (published in an article on Quartz's website) reported that in 2013, "71 million people watched other people play video games" (Mirani, 2014). This is almost twice the viewership of the 2013 Major League Baseball World Series (Mirani, 2014)! There is even a Major League Gaming channel. Electronic sports, or eSports, are clearly very popular.

To some it might seem boring to watch other people play video games. Isn't it more fun to play than to watch? All you need is a controller; no helmets, no pads, no training required. The low barrier to entry is one of the reasons so many people play video games.

Duel matchups are the most followed eSports. It is not unlike watching two people face off in a chess tournament. The World Series of Poker is another game televised as a sport. The most watched eSports are multiplayer online battle arena (MOBA) games, in which "teams of five players compete to strategically attack an enemy team's guarded base" (Magdaleno, 2014). *League of Legends* and Steam's *Dota 2* are two MOBA strategy games. ESPN 3 televised the 2014 *Dota 2* championship.

High-stakes battle arenas can be too competitive for the classroom. Nonetheless, it is a genre worth mentioning because its community is so strong. The video game–streaming channel Twitch boasts 55 million visitors per month! In August 2014, Amazon purchased Twitch (Shear, 2014). The popularity of eSports may someday eclipse major league sports.

Machinima

Quake (1996) is known for being more than a follow-up to iD Software's *Doom* (1992). Players began to use *Quake*'s world as a filmmaking platform. This genre, formerly known as "*Quake* films," has expanded to what is now known as "machinima," a portmanteau of "machine" and "cinema." Machinima predates Let's Play and has grown to become a popular niche with its own YouTube and Xbox Live channels, and even an annual film festival. *Anna* (2003), mentioned in Chapter 1, is an example of an award-winning machinima film.

The rise of machinima occurred at the same time as the growth of massively multiplayer role-play games. Multiplayer worlds give players free time to explore and interact. *Halo*'s setting and characters were used to create comedic stories for the series *Red vs. Blue*. More recently, *Seedlings* followed the adventures of characters in *Minecraft*'s blocky world. "Seedlings" refer to residents of a "seeded," or predesigned, world in *Minecraft*. According to its website, *Seedlings* "follows a group of non-player characters (NPCs) who live in a remote village on a server where they've been undisturbed by human players." The setup is reminiscent of *Toy Story* (what happens when the toys are left in a room alone) or *Wreck-it Ralph* (what game characters do after the arcade closes for the night).

Machinima can be an engaging tool for students. Shakespearean plays, historical events, or anything else that can be told using film can be created as machinima. Students can create a "music video, social commentary, advertisement, drama, or comedy" (Luckman & Potanin, 2010, pp. 155–156). My students made *Minecraft* machinima for a 13 Colonies project. It was set in the British TV show, *Doctor Who*: http://vimeo.com/113181899.

Many of the same tools used for Let's Play work for machinima (e.g., FRAPS Game Capture). Once the images are captured, open a movie editing application such as iMovie or Windows Movie Maker and add the narrative content. An even easier option is Valve's Source Filmmaker (SFM). Introduced in 2012, this free tool enables anyone to do more than simply record and edit games. Source Filmmaker includes a robust suite of tools to change camera angles, tweak character poses, sync dialogue to animations, and add props. It has a community of practice, with a wiki to informally learn the tools and a place to publish and share content.

Modding Communities: *From Doom to Minecraft*

In 2013 a young man named Alexander Velicky created an immersive world known as Falskaar. It was an expansion of Bethesda Game Studios's medieval-themed *Elder Scrolls: Skyrim* (2011). He employed over 100 people to record dialogue and to assist in its development (Birnbaum, 2013). Velicky, however, was not an employee of Bethesda—he was a fan creating a "mod," or modification. The Falskaar mod was one of the largest fan-made expansions of all time. It is, in a way, a love letter to the world of *Skyrim*. Of course, it can also be said that the mod was Velicky's résumé to become employed by Bethesda. That plan worked, too—well, sort of. Eventually, Velicky did get a job as a game designer, but he did not take a position with Bethesda. Instead, he formally began his game design career with a competitor, Bungie, maker of the original *Halo* games.

Velicky is part of a large and vibrant community of game "modders." They create and share content for reasons other than the promise of a career in game design. Many, as it would seem, simply love the craft of game design. Video game modding is an extension of hacker culture, whereby "closed" content is opened for all to access (Salen & Zimmerman, 2003). The book *Rules of Play* categorized different types of game mods:

- *Alterations* change the representational or interactive structures of a game
- *Juxtapositions* place unlikely elements together in the same game space
- *Reinventions* more radically redesign the structure of a game. (Salen & Zimmerman, 2003, p. 569)

The Falskaar mod falls under the category of reinvention, adding to the world in the same way a fan fiction adds content to books without the author's direct consent. The other categories, alterations and juxtapositions, are also common in modding and remixing cultures. A fan might wonder how a first-person shooter, such as *Call of Duty*, would play if it were designed as an 8-bit game, such as those on the Nintendo Entertainment System.

People began to mod digital games because the barriers to entry were lowered as the technology improved. The history of modding dates back to the early 1990s. Two decades ago, hackers realized that game data was saved in a separate file location than its game engine. Each is built on a framework, like a car's chassis. Examples of game engines include the Unreal Engine, Frostbite, Source, and Unity 3D. The Unreal Engine runs games from competing publishers, such as Warner Brothers Interactive Entertainment's *Batman: Arkham City* (2011) and 2K Games's *Bioshock: Infinite* (2013). Some engines are proprietary to publishers, such as Ubisoft's Anvil engine. Its *Prince of Persia: Sands of Time* (2010) used *Assassin's Creed II*'s (2009) artificial intelligence (AI) engine. A helpful analogy is to think of the engine as an application and the game as a dependent file. The application Microsoft Word is stored on one part of a computer's hard drive, while its documents are saved elsewhere, perhaps in folders. Discovering this file-application relationship meant that fans could mod games. Early mods ranged from changing rules, such as having unlimited weapon ammunition, to adding levels.

The first "viral" mod was Justin Fisher's *Aliens TC*, a remix of *Doom* ("TC" stands for "total conversion," alluding to the complete overhaul of the game's content). *Aliens: TC* was inspired by Fisher's love of James Cameron's film *Aliens* (1986). *Doom* was one of the first 3D game worlds. It was considered to be shockingly violent at the time it was released. It lacked a story structure; the player was dropped in a maze filled with dangerous enemies. The simple mechanic of survival lends itself to artistic modification. Its code was also freely accessible and shared over the emerging Internet. Because *Doom* was a PC game, its code was created separately from its engine. *Doom*'s creator, iD's John Carmack, reportedly made the data open and easily accessible (Carmack currently is the chief technology officer for Oculus Rift, the virtual reality company). Basically, he embraced hacker culture. Hackers and modders nicknamed *Doom*'s engine a "WAD," meaning "Where's all the data?" ("5 Years of Doom," n.d.). Like modifying a Word document, *Doom* modders simply needed to locate the outside data to make game customizations.

Doom modding communities remain strong to this day. Some fans continue the violent imagery while others remix in characters from other games, such as Sonic, Mario, and Lara Croft. ModDB is one of the more popular modding forums. In addition to *Doom*, ModDB features remixes of other titles from *Grand Theft Auto* to *Minecraft*. The forums are a working example of a community of practice, an informal learning community in which more experienced users apprentice newer members (Lave & Wenger, 1991).

Like *Doom*, part of *Minecraft*'s success is its embrace of fan-created mods. In fact, the entire game is a mod. Creator Markus "Notch" Perrson rewrote the *Infiniminer*, changing the player perspective to first-person (Goldberg & Larsson, 2013, p. 92). *Infiniminer* designer Zachary Barth echoed the spirit of mods and remix culture in the book *Minecraft: The Unlikely Tale of Markus "Notch" Persson and the Game that Changed Everything*. He stated, "The act of borrowing ideas is integral to the creative process" (Goldberg & Larsson, 2013, p. 95).

An idea to bring modding into the classroom is through discussion and reflection. For example, in 2014 a mod of *Civilization V* was released to coincide with the FIFA World Cup. It used the nation-building game as a platform to teach about the alleged bribery that takes place when cities vie to host the soccer tournament. The mod, called *FIFA World Cup Resolution*, places values on migrant workers and cheap laborers as pawns for corrupt nations. The World Cup mod uses the dark side of a bidding war to get across its social message.

When I use visual coding languages, such as *Scratch* (detailed in Chapter 12), I pre-assess to find out who the modders are. I have had several instances of students who take their game modding skills and apply them to game coding. In a sense, modding is a scaffolded step that could build to mastering more advanced coding skills.

Modding is typical in informal learning spaces; it may be challenging to bring the ethos of hacking into the classroom. Not every mod can be linked to curriculums (as *FIFA World Cup Resolution* can be linked to world politics). Game hacking forums often contain content that is not appropriate for school. Nonetheless, students may find themselves spending hours after school creating, testing, and sharing games. They may also be active in game communities, such as those in the Steam platform. A possible middle ground is to have students write e-books on proposed mods. When I searched for *Minecraft* books in Amazon and on Apple's iBookstore, I found several self-published titles. Encourage students to devise mods to their favorite games. What rules would they change? Why? Modding presents a teachable moment to encourage critical thinking skills.

Conclusions and Takeaways

Gamers learn and participate together in online communities of practice. This is an example of situated learning. Placing students in authentic settings (e.g., fan fiction, Let's Play, eSports, machinima, modding communities) can teach skills not ordinarily taught in schools. Doing so gives students an opportunity to engage in storytelling that interests them. Furthermore, it turns students into creators of digital content, rather than consumers.

Lesson Plan Ideas

Game Wikis: Construct a project-based, character web project. It should be framed around creating additional characters for an existing (or invented) video game series via downloadable content. The culminating activity is uploading the student-created character pages on a wiki. Common Core State Standards for English language arts apply, as well as whichever discipline and content area this activity is modified to fit. Here are links to my student's finished wiki pages: farber7th.pbworks.com/ACRen1 and farber7th.pbworks.com/ACRen2

"Me-chinima": iMovie for Mac or a green screen iPad application enables students to use game footage as a backdrop. First, record the student and game content separately. Be sure to use a green screen (fabric or poster paper works, too) behind the student. Next, add in game footage on the application's film editor.

Modding 2048: The popular number sliding game and mobile app can be played for free online—http://gabrielecirulli.github.io/2048 (It should be noted that 2048 generated controversy because its mechanic closely resembled the paid app *Threes!*) Students can mod their own version—https://www.udacity.com/course/ud248. Udacity, the online class provider, suggested making a mod using U.S. presidents. A better mod is one that fits the mechanic of combinations and/or geometric math with content, such as chemical bonds in the *Isotopic 256* remix—http://jamesdonnelly.github.io/Isotopic256—and *Circle of Fifths*, which teaches musical progressions—http://calebhugo.com/musical-games-interact-with-sound/2048-circle-of-fifths

Spec Scripts: Many video games feature cut scenes, or short interludes between levels. Students can act out cut scenes from games relating to content. As an exercise in transmedia storytelling, students can create a "spec script" using the characters and situations from a game. This is a popular genre on fanfiction.net, where users write and share episodic stories. Common Core State Standards for English language arts apply, as well as whichever discipline and content area this activity is modified to fit. Preview samples for appropriateness—https://www.fanfiction.net/game

Walkthroughs: Write a walkthrough of a game you play. Create a walkthrough about an original game. Common Core State Standards for English language arts apply, as well as whichever discipline and content area this activity is modified to fit.

Games

Aliens TC—http://www.moddb.com/mods/aliens-tc/downloads/aliens-tc-full
DOTA 2, massive online battle arena game—http://www.playdota.com

Falskaar Mod for Skyrim—http://www.nexusmods.com/skyrim/mods/37994

FIFA *World Cup Host Resolution Mod for Civilization V*—http://steamcommunity.com/
   sharedfiles/filedetails/?id=286563387

Kongregate Game Community (be sure to review game appropriateness first)—http://www
   .kongregate.com

League of Legends, massive online battle arena game—http://na.leagueoflegends.com

Steam Workshop, a place to share and play fan-created mods—http://steamcommunity.com/
   workshop

Resources

Bandicam, a popular screencasting tool specializing in *Minecraft* videos—http://www
   .bandicam.com

Camtasia screen recorder—http://www.techsmith.com/camtasia.html

CaptainSparklez *Minecraft* Let's Play channel—www.captainsparklezblog.com and http://www
   .youtube.com/user/CaptainSparklez (preview videos for content appropriateness first)

Confronting the Challenges of Participatory Cultures, by Henry Jenkins et al.—http://mitpress
   .mit.edu/sites/default/files/titles/free_download/9780262513623_Confronting_the_
   Challenges.pdf

DeviantART, fanart (fan-made art) and "cosplay" (portmanteau of "costume play")—http://
   www.deviantart.com

8-Bit Cinema, movie classics reimagined as 8-bit arcade games—http://www.youtube.com/
   playlist?list=PL1AXWu-gGX6LNsfQ-KkeGPxL76CFONTom

FanFiction.net's game-related stories—https://www.fanfiction.net/game

FRAPS Game Capture, Let's Play screencasting tool—http://fraps.com

IGN, video game cheats, walkthroughs, wikis, and guides—http://www.ign.com

Let's Play Exemplar: *Washington Monuments in Minecraft!*, made by one of my former students using *Minecraft*. It was filmed using a smartphone—http://youtu.be/
   Yu2E_3FrcFQ?list=UUnM3k1zeaUk8uVZoBfEDVXg

Let's Play Guide for Newbies—http://letsplay.wikia.com/wiki/LP_guide_for_newbies

Let's Playlist, wiki of game developers friendly to LP producers—letsplaylist.wikia.com

LoiLo Game Recorder—http://loilo.tv/us/product/game_recorder

Machinima—https://www.machinima.com

Major League Gaming, featuring a variety of eSports—http://tv.majorleaguegaming.com

Minecraft—Star Wars—'A New Hope'—Breath Trailer, an example of a fan film using machinima—http://paradisedecay.wordpress.com

PewDiePie, Let's Play channel that is not school appropriate—http://www.youtube.com/user/
   PewDiePie/about

Real-Life Mario Kart, fan film of Nintendo's Mario Kart, in the real world—http://youtu
   .be/-h4zTEwgCpQ

Red vs. Blue, machinima in the virtual world of *Halo*—http://www.youtube.com/show/redvsblue

Screencast-O-Matic, screencasting tool for Let's Play videos—http://www.screencast-o-matic
.com

Seedlings, machinima set in *Minecraft*—http://seedlingsshow.com

Paul Soares, Jr.'s *Minecraft* channel (preview videos for content appropriateness first)—https://
www.youtube.com/user/paulsoaresjr

Source Filmmaker (SFM), a free, robust machinima tool—http://www.sourcefilmmaker.com

TIG Forums, discussion boards about game making and modding—http://forums.tigsource.com

T Is for Transmedia: Learning through Transmedia Play, Cooney Center report, with an introduction from Henry Jenkins—http://www.joanganzcooneycenter.org/publication/t-is-for-
transmedia

Twitch, video gaming as a spectator sport—http://www.twitch.tv

Wikia—A wiki for movies, film, video games, and other popular cultural topics—http://www
.wikia.com

· 1 2 ·

CREATING DIGITAL GAMES

In an interview with journalist Robert X. Cringley, Apple co-founder Steve Jobs said, "I think everyone in this country should learn to program a computer. Everyone should learn a computer language because it teaches you how to think. I think of computer science as a liberal art." This quote, from the documentary *Steve Jobs: The Lost Interview* (2012), was recorded in 1996, just prior to Jobs's return to Apple. This book is not about computer programming, but I would be remiss if I didn't discuss applications to create digital games.

The educational foundation of coding can be traced to Jean Piaget protégé Seymour Papert. He pioneered the learning theory known as constructionism. Similar to constructivism's tenet of "learn by doing," the theory of constructionism can be summed up as "learn by making." Papert's seminal book *Mindstorms: Children, Computers, and Powerful Ideas*, first published in 1980, details constructionism and the kid-friendly programming language Logo, created by his MIT lab. In the preface to *Mindstorms* Papert stated, "a modern-day Montessori might propose, if convinced by my story, to create a gear set for children" (1993, p. xx). Programming to Papert was not about the language, but rather the tool set to create a working system.

Expectations for widespread school adoption of the "Logo Turtle," a small, programmable robot, were promising at the time. I remember using

Logo for Apple II in the early 1980s, but it seemed like a novelty compared to the BASIC language taught in schools. In 1993 MicroWorlds was released, integrating the language with robotic-controlled interlocking LEGO bricks. About a decade later, "a new Logo programming environment called *Scratch* emerged from the Lifelong Kindergarten Group at the MIT Media Lab" (Logo Foundation, 2011). Papert's vision is still strong today in today's Maker movement. The LEGO-robot collaboration lives on with Mindstorms, a top seller that uses advanced tablet applications to program movements.

Digital game design is a fast-growing field. According to a report from the Entertainment Software Association, "The U.S. computer and video game software publishing industry directly employs more than 32,000 people in 34 states" (Siwek, 2010, p. 1). This chapter includes an interview with Alan Gershenfeld from E-Line Media about the National STEM Video Game Challenge. Several easy-to-use coding apps, including *Scratch*, are reviewed. They are separated into different categories: click-and-drag games and visual programming languages. I spoke to New Jersey teacher Steve Isaacs about GameMaker: Studio, a robust authoring tool. My aim is to highlight tools that are easy to use and require little to no background knowledge. In addition to Gershenfeld, I also interviewed Hopscotch CEO Jocelyn Leavitt and Tynker CEO Krishna Vedati. Lastly, I review the educational applications of MaKey MaKey, the do-it-yourself (DIY) game controller kit. It can be used as an assistive technology device, thus enabling everyone, of all abilities, to play.

The National STEM Video Game Challenge

One of the most moving highlights of the 11th Annual Games for Change Festival was the celebration of the 2013 National STEM Video Game Challenge award winners. It was a genuine thrill to see the young students' reactions at being acknowledged by a roomful of accomplished game designers. Jesse Schell presented the awards. He also gave James Gee the Game Changer of the Year Award. Gee jokingly promised to keep his acceptance speech brief!

Alan Gershenfeld is the co-founder of E-Line Media and a board member of the Cooney Center. The two organizations co-host the annual contest. The Challenge began in 2010 and it has grown in size each year. I asked Gershenfeld about where game design fits into interest-driven learning. We spoke in May 2014. He said, "We can tap into a kid's natural interests and align them with literacies and skills they'll need to thrive in the 21st century. We identified four interest-driven areas: youth game design, youth entrepreneurship, youth social entrepreneurship, youth digital fabrication/making things." (Digital fabrication is the emerging literacy of 3D printing.) Interest-driven learning is also one of the key components to flow, or optimal happiness. If a student works on a project that he or she is passionate about, then it may not seem like a chore. Writing a book about games is not as "fun" for me as playing our Xbox; it is a topic that interests me. Children have passionate interests, too.

A long-term goal for the Challenge is to create a nationwide network of fledgling game designers. Students would then be able to find programs near their homes and follow their interest-driven passion in game design, like any afterschool club or sport. Gershenfeld continued, "This competition becomes a nice organizing way to urge that into existence. We intend to do that with all of the interest-driven products and services."

Winners of past Challenges have visited the White House and even met President Barack Obama. There are three entry categories: middle school, college, and developer. Gershenfeld described to me how the idea came to fruition. He said:

> It was natural for us, when we were talking to Michael Levine [founding director of the Cooney Center]. There should be a national video game design challenge. We approached the White House and said we raise the money privately and show research why making games actually fits Obama's Educate to Innovate Challenge—which we knew he was going to announce. When he announced it, we got a lot of partners. It had that exposure. We're in the fourth year running it. Ultimately, our goal is to fly the kids in for big events, like the White House Science Fair. We flew them in for Games for Change. Two-thirds of the families had never been to New York City, and they got to go with their child—a designer of really wonderful games.

There are a variety of applications available that teach game creation at an early age without requiring prior knowledge of how to code. The contest recommends designing with many of the applications discussed in this chapter, including *Scratch* and *Gamestar Mechanic*. Many of the tools use a click-and-drag interface, while others use interlocking bricks, similar to LEGO bricks, to create programming instructions. More advanced students may opt for GameMaker: Studio. Unity 3D, a professional suite, is another option.

Click-and-Drag with *Sploder* and *Gamestar Mechanic*

Several authoring tools are available to create games by simply pointing, clicking, and dragging objects onto a canvas. No coding is involved. For example, *Sploder* uses a click-and-drag (sometimes called "drag-and-drop") interface: click characters, blocks, or enemies, and then drag them onto a template. Published projects look like old-school, 8-bit arcade games. There are four categories of design: Retro Arcade (with a side-scrolling view similar to that in *Super Mario Bros.*), the Platform Creator, the Physics Puzzle Maker (think: *Angry Birds* slingshots and gravity), and the Classic Shooter, a space game. It is very simple to use. I particularly liked the Platform Creator, which features portal doors, power-ups, and plenty of bad guys. *Sploder* is free to use and has a community to share and comment on projects. A nice addition to the website is the Parents/Teacher page. The website was originally targeted to the gamer community, not classrooms. The community comments can be switched off to keep the learning environment more restricted.

Gamestar Mechanic, mentioned several times throughout this book, is more robust than *Sploder*. It was launched in the late 2000s and is now published by E-Line Media (it was co-created by E-Line Media and the Institute of Play, originally funded by the MacArthur Foundation). The Gates Foundation's Robert Torres used it for his doctoral dissertation about systems thinking. At the time, he was the executive director of the Institute of Play, one of *Gamestar Mechanic*'s partners. Torres's dissertation is posted on *Gamestar Mechanic*'s homepage.

When E-Line Media purchased *Gamestar Mechanic*, it focused on teacher discoverability, or "bottoms-up," word-of-mouth marketing. Gershenfeld explained, "There was early efficacy in the classroom with teacher-to-teacher recommendations." Due to its ease of use and well-run ecosystem, the platform keeps growing. "We're in 7,000 to 8,000 schools and afterschool programs," he elaborated. "It's purely bottoms-up, and I think we're going to see that grow significantly. There is an entire curricular service, there are also tools to create games, there's a community that we run, and there is also a flexible, modular curriculum."

To help teachers implement the tool, the Institute of Play published a *Gamestar Mechanic Learning Guide* (linked at the end of this chapter). Users of *Gamestar Mechanic* can also take a course in game design, or just freely play. Classes are offered online as well as in local and regional programs. The tool itself is gamified and quest-based, with levels, challenges, and missions unlocking as users proceed. There are also badges to accumulate. According to the website's portal, there are more than 250,000 user-designed games. *Gamestar Mechanic* is an excellent tool to encourage design thinking, systems thinking, and problem solving. There are deep discounts available to educators and classrooms and a virtual store to purchase game add-ons.

Visual Programming Languages

Scratch is descended from the Logo language. According to the MIT Media Lab, *Scratch* is intended to help "young people learn important mathematical and computational ideas, while also gaining a deeper understanding of the process of design." No knowledge of Flash, Java, or other actual coding is required; programming commands are embedded in color-coded bricks. Each brick is assigned a function. A blue one might say, "turn 15 degrees" or "move 15 steps." Logic statements (if-then) are on yellow bricks. Certain bricks snap into place with others, creating an interlocking computer language. When everything is assembled, simply click the green flag icon to see if the project works.

Coding gives an authentic context to mathematical language. In the book *Smarter Than You Think*, writer Clive Thompson gave an example of how children *discovered* calculus principles when attempting to draw a circle in *Scratch* by using a series of small, slightly turned lines (2013, p. 191). Students then ran their program to test its success. The intrinsic satisfaction is seeing the code turn into a workable system.

Remixing with *Scratch*

Scratch has a large and active user base. There are shared projects that range from animations to complex games. You can create, remix, and publish, as well as learn informally via its participatory community. *Scratch* has a "See Inside" feature that enables anyone to "open the hood" and view the bricks that were used in a particular project. I have found this feature to be an effective teaching tool for new users. It is empowering to see students make simple changes and then have the ability to call the project their own.

My 6th-grade social studies students remix video games using *Scratch*. Each is assigned to research a topic—in this case, medieval Europe. The remixed game should fit the theme. Examples ranged from a trivia game to a role-playing adventure about a baker's guild. I use a flipped classroom approach, giving the class links to YouTube tutorials for students to view from home, saving face-to-face class time for projects. I recommend the "I do, we do, you do" approach, modeling the app first on an interactive whiteboard. I keep my direct instruction to a minimum. This approach can motivate students to seek out additional how-to videos in informal learning spaces (e.g., the *Scratch* community, more in-depth YouTube videos). A brief self-reflection essay is also part of the assignment. The idea is for students to explain how their game relates to their researched topic.

Teaching coding is like implementing other educational technologies. It should be integrated into the curriculum, not used as an add-on. As with a game, students are quite adept at figuring out *Scratch* as they go. Many get "lost in the moment" of design, similar to what happens when building in *Minecraft*. There are helpful resources for teachers on the ScratchEd page, including remix and project ideas for all disciplines. Rubrics are also available.

Puzzle Challenges with Tynker

Tynker is a coding tool accessible on computer browsers and tablets. It offers an entire suite of instructor tools, including a teacher dashboard and an online grade book. Harnessing a Vygotskian approach, Tynker scaffolds learning, moving from interlocking bricks to more advanced concepts such as syntax-driven programming. Tynker offers a Starter Pack with lesson plans and project ideas.

I interviewed Krishna Vedati, Tynker's CEO and founder, to learn more about what differentiates it from other visual coding apps. We spoke in March 2014. Vedati has been a technology entrepreneur for more than 13 years. He took inspiration from *Scratch*, Alice (the coding language from Carnegie Mellon), and Kodu (from Microsoft). Each had something to offer, but they "were not built as systems of self-learning." Some applications, such as *Scratch*, rely on a community of practice, in which users learn from shared projects. Tynker is gamified as an adaptive learning tool. Each task is presented as an increasingly complex puzzle. This avoids the need to incorporate an open online community where outsiders can critique projects. After all, in a school there are privacy concerns. "Even with all of the social options available, many students simply opt to work with one or two of their own friends," Vedati explained.

Vedati hoped to bring technology skills to students in a fun way. The answer was to build a game-like structure to promote progress. Tynker's gamification techniques work because its puzzles function as part of a larger system of learning. Vedati explained, "In our case, the underlying mission is to teach programming, then gamify." Challenges include fixing a robot and saving a puppy. "Kids become immersed and emotionally involved. We've learned a lot from that," he continued. Vedati observed his two children consuming media from mobile devices. He felt that they needed to become creators and makers of media. "My kids are 10 and 7 and—if you ask them—programming is not on top of their minds," Vedati said. "Fun is."

"Tynker" was chosen as the product's name. "Kids like to tinker with things," Vedati stated. (Vedati told me that the word "tinker" was hard to acquire. The misspelled moniker was chosen to convey a spirit of fun.) Many of the teachers who use Tynker have no programming experience, which makes their feedback valuable. The company visits classrooms several times a week. It also tests with parents and offers online courses, giving parents a full view of their children's progress.

The built-in tutoring system constantly tests. It observes how fast students solve adaptive puzzles, what and how many blocks are required to execute a series of commands, and how many steps and tries are required. Higher-level tasks challenge students to reverse engineer (figure out how a project works). There are skill-level badges. Examples of digital awards include the Gamer Badge, the Storyteller Badge, and the Robot Maker Badge. To win a badge, certain skills must be observed by the system. The reward system is holistic, taking into account all of the steps learners need to do to master an achievement.

More than 8,000 schools used Tynker in 2013. Like other coding tools, it can be integrated into any discipline. It is used in project-based science classes (experimentation), in math (fractals), and art (digital animation). Tynker can teach 1st and 2nd graders mini-animations, and science and engineering to students in middle grades. There is even an *Angry Birds*-style physics challenge. "Be creative—with programming as the glue," Vedati stated. In higher grades, Tynker becomes a JavaScript language that can be used to build realistic apps. Students sequence, create conditions, loops, and combinations, and build simple Turing machines. The task of debugging is also covered. Vedati described weather apps and mash-ups that were created in high school classrooms. "We take them from where they don't know anything, give them computational thinking skills, and then make them build complex things to transition to mainstream programming," he explained. "Visual programming is a starting point."

Coding on a Tablet with Hopscotch

Hopscotch is a visual coding app tailor-made for mobile devices. According to its iTunes page, children can program "characters to move, draw, and collide with each other, and use shaking, tilting, or even shouting at the iPad to control them." Like Tynker and *Scratch*, it uses a visual coding language. It is not based on adaptive puzzle challenges, like Tynker; the "Community" is where ideas are exchanged. Hopscotch uses the Community to release company news, as well as an "Idea of the Week." Practical applications of math are deeply ingrained in the shared projects. One example is the Sydney Opera House, featuring flying robots that trace out the famous Australian landmark. By clicking "Edit," the angles and directions that were coded become revealed. It is intuitive and easy to use.

I spoke with Jocelyn Leavitt, the CEO and co-founder, in May 2014. The company's philosophy is constructionism—to use technology as a creative tool for expression. "The whole idea is children teaching computers, rather than computers teaching children." The approach is similar to *Scratch*'s, the coding tool influenced by the constructionist work of Seymour Papert.

Leavitt has a background as a social studies teacher. Originally from Hawaii, she worked at the Dalton School in New York City. Her interest is in experiential education. "I was influenced by the indigenous people in Hawaii and the way project-based learning figured in to indigenous education," she stated.

Hopscotch's co-founder, Samantha John, whom Leavitt met through mutual friends, had an engineering background. Both shared a passion about women in software. They discussed how there were not enough female engineers in the software field. Leavitt explained, "We were passionate about building a toy that we would have been passionate about growing up with. We saw that a lot of our friends were software engineers with similar backgrounds: white, male, and nerdy growing up." Many engineers began programming for fun when they were in middle school. Leavitt continued, "We wanted to get girls to have the same experiences. We saw huge potential for a mobile programming language with the iPad becoming more popular."

I asked Leavitt how competition has increased, especially since the widely publicized Hour of Code launched in December 2013. The first Hour of Code took place during Computer Science Education Week. The goal was to get 10 million students to try computer science for 1 hour that week—regardless of their grade, class, or discipline. About 15 million students wound up participating! Leavitt said, "It raises awareness for need for kids to code and access this type of learning. It's a mixed bag. On one hand it's harder with more competitors, but, the field is expanding, too."

I next asked how they market the app to girls as well as boys. It can be tricky, and it may appear that you are pandering to your audience if you adjust the look of a toy traditionally made for a boy. Leavitt explained the process:

> We deliberately tried to make it not overly girly, to make it gender-neutral. Early on, we made decisions to make it feel welcoming and opening to girls. For instance, the basic things like choice of colors. We went back and forth with designers five to six times. The initial set of illustrations looked too boyish; we wanted it to appeal to girls too. I took the app into the classroom to have kids play with it. I asked the boys and girls, "Do you think it's an app made for boys, an app made for girls, or unisex?" All the girls said it was an app made for girls and all the boys said it was unisex. That perfectly illustrates the line we're trying to walk.

Hopscotch seeks to get all children to build their own software, even those who do not consider themselves to be engineers. By creating a gender-neutral experience, every user becomes empowered. Leavitt elaborated, "At the end of the day, being able to build your own computer programs and your own software is deeply empowering. It's kind of an extension of human capabilities." Middle school was the chosen target group because research showed that children at this age are more able to grasp coding concepts. The app is designed for informal learning (outside of school); however, it is frequently used in the classroom. Information is not tracked due to the intended age of users. As a result, Hopscotch relies on anecdotal data from pictures and stories teachers send in.

The company's first foray into coding began in 2011 with *Daisy the Dinosaur*. Its very simple interface enabled young children to control an animated dinosaur. *Daisy the Dinosaur* teaches coding by challenging children to make Daisy perform tasks. Hopscotch was launched about a year later. The business model is now focused solely on the Hopscotch app. Simply put, Hopscotch has more power. Leavitt said, "We saw things that worked in *Daisy*, but wanted to move on." Because people still enjoy and find utility with *Daisy*, it remains in Apple's App Store.

Designing in Hopscotch is completely open-ended, like a sandbox. Similar to *Scratch*, there is a toolbox of commands and functions. Leavitt explained the company's approach to me. "We don't do a ton of hand-holding," she explained:

> Teachers recognize Hopscotch's value as a tool. We have a shared community, kids upload projects, games, and apps. Other kids take inspiration from what they can make or do. We see a lot of games. Kids like to play the thing they made and see other kids

enjoy the things they made. We wanted a toy for the iPad because of the form factor and it made a lot of sense to have a touch screen interface for a visual programming language.

After playtesting, Hopscotch discovered that many students went home and continued their projects on their own time. It is very driven by how testers—both children and adults—use the program. Leavitt said the reception has very positive. She said, "Kids really are delighted when they discover they can make their own things. It is empowering when they have an idea for a game or something they want to make and they can do it."

The Hopscotch 2.0 update was released in the spring of 2014. The interface is now even easier to use, sacrificing none of its functionality. There are now "Rules" that can be assigned to characters. Each rule creates new "Abilities." Hopscotch School Edition was released in late August 2014. It is a paid version with teacher tools, like a dashboard to enable assessments.

Hopscotch is an engaging tool to create content on a tablet that takes advantage of a mobile device's motion sensors. Animations can react from being tapped, tilted, or shaken. Its broad appeal may inspire a future engineer—boy or girl!

GameMaker: Studio

Mark Overmars, a professor from the Netherlands, originally created the authoring tool GameMaker: Studio. He eventually sold it to YoYo Games, which has scaled up its use. More and more schools are using it because it is robust, yet easy to use.

To learn more about GameMaker: Studio's classroom implementation, I met up with Steve Isaacs, a computer teacher at William Annin Middle School in Basking Ridge, New Jersey. We spoke in July 2014. Isaacs teaches video game design to 7th and 8th graders. He has spoken about teaching with GameMaker: Studio at several conferences, including the Serious Play Conference.

Isaacs started using GameMaker: Studio in his classroom about 15 years ago. He was clearly an early adopter; it wasn't originally intended to be a teaching tool. As a result, Isaacs began to aggregate and develop his own resources, including video tutorials. A few years ago, he started sharing his tutorials on Twitter. YoYo Games's CEO took notice and commented on his postings. Isaacs was seen as the perfect conduit to get GameMaker: Studio into students' hands. Isaacs, along with Mark Suter, an Ohio-based computer technology teacher, worked with YoYo Games to create a "Learn" section on its site.

Like many authoring tools in this chapter, GameMaker: Studio has a drag-and-drop interface. It's an easy entry point to teach about game development.

Each clickable object has a "conditional statement" (e.g., if clicked, then go left—the classic "if-then" programming logic couplet). Objects are programmed as "events" or "actions." Users can then define the actions that sprites (movable objects), rooms, sounds, and backgrounds have. For example, *if* a sprite collides with a wall, *then* it stops. "It's very intuitive," Isaacs said. "It's structured in a way that a programmer would think. It's a great introduction to computer science in an unintimidating manner." Advanced students can eventually code in GameMaker Language (GML).

To get a sense of game mechanics, Isaacs has students try out games from different genres. "I give a little bit of instruction and a lot of support," he said. "I show the kids the basic syntax of how typical things work, like adventure-type games. I give a number of 15-minute demo lessons. My goal is that they understand how things work, and then go to the online community. I don't want their games to look like my demo." Isaacs's methodology describes my (unintentional) first experience using *Scratch*. I showed the basics of *Scratch* to my class; many went to YouTube, from home, to learn more. Isaacs's approach whets students' appetites to lead them to learn informally, from the community.

Isaacs's students first prepare a "road map" to plan their games. This occurs before using GameMaker: Studio. They fill out a simplified version of a professional design document. Doing this serves to help students map out their games, as well as to keep the assignments authentic. Next, students write up the game's narrative storyline and character outlines, describing physical attributes and abilities (e.g., strong fighter, enemy). Then students sketch out the level design, scoring mechanisms, and win/loss scenarios.

As in a professional studio, an iterative design approach works best. Isaacs encourages a lot of peer testing. "The goal is to provide constructive, concrete feedback," he explained. "What would make your game better?" Middle school students can be prone to telling others how to play their game. To remedy this, Isaacs assigns a student to watch the playtest. He elaborated, "I have to tell kids to 'sit on their hands' and not help. Students watch their game played through someone else's eyes. At that age, students think that something is obvious to do because they planned it. If it's obvious to the designer, it may not be obvious to the player. If five people go left when you want them to go right, then they have to go back and iterate."

GameMaker: Studio is currently Windows-only; however, projects can be easily ported (exported copy) to other platforms. Isaacs's students have published games for Mac, iOS, Android, and HTML5. The tool is available as a free download, with paid add-ons. The Learn section is constantly growing, as is its community of practice. GameMaker: Studio is an effective tool to engage students in the iterative design process of game creation. "The point of entry is low, but the potential is huge!" Isaacs concluded.

Conclusions and Takeaways

Coding is different than constructing (as in *Minecraft*) because the system is intended to be interactive. Game design applies systems thinking and design thinking competencies. It is a practical application of math and science, along with the humanities. There are dozens of apps for students to create digital games. Visual coding languages are compelling because they apply Seymour Papert's theory of constructionism, or learning by making. Some tools are click-and-drag, while others use interlocking blocks. Some coding sites use games and puzzles to teach, creating a community of practice in the classroom. Others use an open canvas and an online community.

Lesson Plan Ideas

DIY Assistive Game Controllers: MaKey MaKey is an electronics kit that came to market in 2013. With it, ordinary objects become input devices for a computer. The website features bananas played as piano keys and Play-Doh used as a *Super Mario Bros.* game controller. The possibilities of do-it-yourself (DIY) game controllers are truly limitless! It costs $50 and comes in a small green box. In addition to the Arduino circuit board, the kit includes colored alligator clips, a USB plug, and stickers that say things such as "Be Stoked" and "Construction Kit." It is essentially a switch—actually, several switches. Switch interfaces are commonly used in assistive technology. Review the AbleGamers Foundation's Game Accessibility Guidelines to learn more about remapping keyboards. WASD and arrow keys are common in PC-based games. Because the keys are so close together, a disabled person would have difficulty being precise—even when using a keyboard overlay. The AbleGamers Foundation is a nonprofit organization that "aims to improve the overall quality of life for those with disabilities through the power of video games" (The AbleGamers Foundation, 2014). The AbleGamer Foundation's Game Accessibility Guidelines—http://www.includification.com; MaKey MaKey—http://makeymakey.com

Gamestar Mechanic Learning Guide: Lesson plan ideas are suitable for any content area. Coding is a tool, not the lesson—http://www.instituteofplay.org/wp-content/uploads/2011/02/Gamestar_Mechanic_Learning_Guide_v1.1.pdf

Hour of Code Lessons: Standards depend on the discipline and content area—http://csedweek.org/learn

Scholastic Arts and Writing Award Contest: Games created with *Gamestar Mechanic*, as well as *Scratch*, Game Salad, or GameMaker: Studio, can be submitted to the Scholastic Arts and Writing Awards in the video game category. E-Line Media is a partner in the contest (the relationship is posted on the website). *Gamestar Mechanic* contest submissions simply need to be linked, not downloaded or exported into different file types. Because it is a writing contest, a text description is also required. Up to five students can collaborate. This is an excellent opportunity to teach game design in any subject area, just like any other educational technology. Like other digital media, games can be used to tell stories and present information; why not make the experience even more engaging with a student-created interactive design?

Scratch Lesson Plans: The *Scratch*ED community shared content—http://scratched.media.mit .edu/resources

This is a Remix: Rather than start from a blank page (or, literally, from *scratch*), why not remix an existing project on *Scratch*? Go to http://scratch.mit.edu and then select "Explore" or "Search." Find and test a game (some projects are partially completed; it is important to test functionality and whether a game is fun prior to remixing). Click "See Inside" to view the blocks that made the program (it's like checking under the hood of a car). Next, click "Remix." *Scratch* autosaves the project with a new name. To start, change the backgrounds and sprites (digital characters) using *Scratch*'s library. There is a paint feature, as well as an upload folder. Digital pictures can be searched on Google Image. Additional sound effects can be downloaded on SoundBible.com. Once your project is remixed, include instructions for play and click "Share." Any content area can be turned into a game. Standards depend on discipline and content area. Review other projects to get a feel for how yours should look. The *Scratch* team has templates at http://Scratch .MIT.edu/users/scratchteam

Tynker Lesson Plans: Available for multiple disciplines and content areas—http://www.tynker .com/courses/programming-101.html

Games

Game Developer Tycoon, a business simulation game where the player designs and brings games to market. Level 1 begins in the 1980s—http://www.greenheartgames.com/app/ game-dev-tycoon

GameMaker: Studio, an authoring tool to create games. Prices range from free to professional— https://www.yoyogames.com/studio

GameSalad, a game creator for mobile, downloadable for free—http://gamesalad.com

Gamestar Mechanic, systems thinking games and game design tools from the Institute of Play and E-Line Media—http://gamestarmechanic.com

Goldie Blox, a nondigital game marketed to teach STEM skills to girls—http://www .goldieblox.com

Hopscotch, coding with color-coded blocks, made for a tablet—http://www.gethopscotch.com

Hopscotch School Edition, released in late August 2014. It is a paid version with teacher tools, like a dashboard to enable assessments.

Kodu, from Microsoft, to create games for Xbox—http://research.microsoft.com/en-us/projects/kodu

MaKey MaKey projects on *Scratch*—http://scratch.mit.edu/studios/230629/projects

MaKey MaKey as assistive technology—http://makeymakey.com/guides/assistive.php

Robot Turtles, a board game with tiles and illustrated cards to teach programming and coding logic to early elementary school children. The turtle was inspired by Logo—http://www.thinkfun.com/robotturtles

Scratch, to play, remix, and create games and digital animations—http://scratch.mit.edu

Scratch, Jr., early childhood coding on iPad—http://www.scratchjr.org

Sploder, to test and create 8-bit retro arcade games—http://www.sploder.com

Unity, a professional-grade game rendering tool—http://unity3d.com

Resources

The Able Gamers Foundation, gaming for people of all abilities—http://www.ablegamers.com

Boy Scout Game Design Workbook, by David Mullich—http://boyslifeorg.files.wordpress.com/2013/03/gamedesign.pdf

Code.org, a nonprofit that offers cross-curricular support to teachers—http://code.org

Code to Learn Foundation, supporters of several projects, including *Scratch*, Jr.—http://codetolearn.org

GameDevMap, a "live" map of game developers worldwide—http://www.gamedevmap.com

Gamestar Mechanic Learning Guide—http://www.instituteofplay.org/wp-content/uploads/2011/02/Gamestar_Mechanic_Learning_Guide_v1.1.pdf

Global Game Jam, marathon sessions of collaborative game design—http://globalgamejam.org

Hour of Code during Computer Science Education Week—http://code.org/educate/hoc

Khan Academy, coding projects ready to remix, known as "spin-offs"—https://www.khanacademy.org

Includification, game accessibility PDF from AbleGamers—http://www.includification.com/AbleGamers_Includification.pdf

Logo Foundation, the little turtle that started it all—http://el.media.mit.edu/logo-foundation

MaKey MaKey kit—http://www.makeymakey.com

National STEM Video Game Challenge—http://www.stemchallenge.org

OUYA, Android-powered console funded by Kickstarter, available at retailers such as Target—https://www.ouya.tv

Scholastic Arts & Writing Awards for Video Games—http://www.artandwriting.org/the-awards/categories/#VideoGames

YoYo Games on YouTube, tutorials and more for GameMaker: Studio—https://www.youtube.com/user/yoyogamesltd

· 13 ·

GAMES TO CHANGE THE WORLD

Social impact games are different than educational and serious games: The intent is not necessarily to teach a content area or a skill. As mentioned in Chapter 3, games are built with reward mechanisms. What if game feedback could effect positive change? This genre pushes the medium past childhood toys to cultural artifacts. Designer Jesse Schell refers to the sector as transformational. His studio, Schell Games, moved from creating only entertainment titles to creating both educational and transformational games. I interviewed him in March 2014. To Schell, transformational games are "designed to change a person." He elaborated:

> I like the term better than "serious games," which is a broken term. I've been proselytizing a bit that serious games imply a serious goal: If you are having fun, you're doing it wrong. I'm from an entertainment background; entertainment is a serious business. From the realm of art or entertainment, saying their work isn't serious is insulting. The goal isn't to be serious, but to transform people. Most of the design failings of transformative games happen when they spend too much time on the game's content, or the information they want to come across, and not enough on how they want to transform a person.

An example of a transformational gaming project is the Half the Sky movement. In the United States, the Facebook game *Half the Game* was published to raise Americans' awareness of international women's rights. It is based on a documentary that detailed the oppression of women in some developing countries. Related to the Half the Sky movement, the United States Agency for International Development (USAID) released three mobile games: the family-planning awareness titles 9-*Minutes* and *Family Choices* and the digestive health game *Worm Attacks*.

This chapter reviews how to implement social impact games in the classroom. I spoke to several developers of social impact games, including Abby Speight, senior product manager at Zynga.org. I also had the opportunity to attend the 11th Annual Games for Change Festival. This chapter features a profile of its current president, Asi Burak. At the festival, I observed game designers and developers exchange ideas about creating impactful experiences. A successful game delivers its message through both aesthetics and mechanics. When both work in harmony, it is truly an art.

Mission US and Social History

Mission US: A Cheyenne Odyssey, won the Most Significant Impact award at the 11th Annual Games for Change Festival. This is the third game (or mission) in a series produced by the Center for Public Television. For the past few years, my students have played through the first mission, *For Crown or Colony*, set in pre-Revolutionary Boston. The second title, *Flight to Freedom*, is about the Underground Railroad. The mission unfolds on the perilous trip runaway slaves took to the free Northern states. In *A Cheyenne Odyssey*, the player takes on the role of Little Fox, a young Native American boy. The team collaborated with advisors from the Northern Cheyenne Reservation to create an authentic experience. The fall of 2014 will see a fourth mission, this time about a young immigrant's journey through Ellis Island. The interactive role-playing games are free and include lesson plans. Each has a point-and-click interface.

I met with the series' design team, David Langendoen and Spencer Grey, both partners at Electric Funstuff in New York City. Our interview took place in May 2014. I also met with Leah Potter. She was previously with the American Social History Project and now works at Electric Funstuff. Also in attendance were Bill Tally and Jim Diamond from the Education Development Center's Center for Children and Technology, and Jill Peters and Chris Czajk from Thirteen/WNET, part of the Corporation for Public Broadcasting.

Peters's role is to connect all of the pieces of the project together, especially with fundraising.

First I spoke to Chris Czajk, who oversees the educational outreach program, including lesson plan integration and the inclusion of primary source documents. *Mission 1: For Crown and Colony*, which came out in 2008, has the most lesson plans that I have ever seen packaged with a game. Because it was a pilot, there were a lot of conversations with educators about what kind of games they would like and what should be included. The result was an abundance of support materials. *Mission 2* and *3* scaled back teacher materials.

I next asked Electric Funstuff's David Langendoen about the design process. He is a game designer, writer, and executive producer. He explained, "Writing games is not only interesting to me, but an activity that can translate into the classroom." Langendoen and his partner, Spencer Grey, had shared experiences growing up; they both played role-playing games. They each wrote threaded stories and, many years ago, reverse engineered the game engine of *Neverwinter Nights* (a role-playing adventure game from 2002). They tried to map out the choices and consequences loops. Threaded stories (also mentioned in Chapter 4, pertaining interactive fiction) involve more than the arc of storytelling. Game writers must be cognizant of their target audience's reading level, as well as ways to steer players into story branches. Computer logic informs those branches. The major challenge is to make the choices seem like they matter. Building the *Mission US* games required a dialogue editor to figure out the multiple actions and conditions.

Mission US games focus on social history, rather than political history. They are not just about specific events, but about the experiences people had. Jill Potter's role is to review the logic of how people answered the historical narrative's questions. Unlike the game *Civilization*, which remixes history, *Mission US* has a rule that what has happened cannot be changed. The choices must then involve a character's personal interests. These include emotional decisions and romantic involvements. I asked Langendoen how they make it feel like decisions actually matter. He explained how causal loops grew in complexity with every added mission in the series. *Mission 1* is the simplest, with the smallest number of cause-and-effect loops. For example, angering a character can result in a lost round. The short-term penalty is to scrub an outhouse, followed by a quick return to the main storyline. *Mission 2* is more sophisticated and features a badge system. The badges you earn tell a story at the end. In *Mission 3* there are even more options in dialogue and actions, including ethical choices. Players can decide whether to be brave. For authenticity, the reward system is based on the virtues of the Cheyenne people, such as bravery and generosity. The payoff for taking chances is delayed. In the Battle of Little Big Horn, survival is heavily dependent on whether the player was wise, brave, or generous.

Each game takes about 90 minutes to play. Some teachers play part of a mission in class and assign the remainder for homework. Often, students continue from home and complete all of the mission's parts. Chris Czajk told me about a student in Florida who replayed more than 40 times. Czajk told the teacher that it was perfectly fine. Jill Peters then pointed out, "When kids have different experiences, it prompts rich class discussions." This echoed a point from James Gee about games being open-ended experiences. Teachers can assign a game for homework and then have students play in teams in class. When students go back and replay missions, the class can discuss the other choices they made. The teacher's role is contextualization and facilitation on content *and* game decisions.

The Education Development Center conducts research and evaluation on *Mission US* games. It studies students' prior knowledge and assumptions about history and gameplay. The goal is to see where a game fits in a classroom that has multiple layers of expectations. The Education Development Center's Jim Diamond's dissertation was on historical empathy. He studied how young people gauge the mindsets of people from the past; people make game decisions with particular notions. He said he found no correlation.

Mission US curriculum materials serve to connect player decisions to historical events. The kind of history a game covers determines the causes and effects it can present. What would a young person's perspective be? What kind of actions could a teenager take? The major national events in the *Mission US* games happen in the background of the narrative. (Conversely, in *Assassin's Creed III*, the player rides along with Paul Revere and is at the Boston Massacre. So much U.S. history is intertwined with game missions that the game was criticized as being like *Forrest Gump*.) Langendoen explained how *Mission 3* was originally to be about the railroad expansion. The issue was player agency. Is the player a 14-year-old Irish surveyor or a teenage Chinese immigrant? What actions could he or she realistically take? Player agency is also a concern when trying to elicit emotions such as empathy. It was at that moment that the Native American theme was chosen. A 12-year-old Cheyenne boy character gives players more freedom and choice. Teachers should consider agency when designing an authentic project-based learning activity.

Games empower people—often more so than real life can. This helps to make the experience fun. A player's character may be more skilled or luckier than others. In a historical game, however, power needs to be balanced with realism. In *Mission 1: For Crown or Colony*, the design team initially assumed that the player would want to be a Patriot. This notion turned out to be a misconception; not everyone in colonial Boston wanted to get involved in a revolution. The team decided to intentionally make the lead character, Royce, a little dislikable. Constance, the Loyalist (a colonist siding with Britain) was more sympathetic. She was introduced as she searched for her lost dog. Narrative storytelling built empathy for her character. (The team pointed out that there was a real newspaper clipping from the time about a missing dog. The primary source document is included in the game.)

Students project themselves onto characters. The teacher must "unpack" these experiences. "The game without the conversation about what happened diminishes the experiences," Langendoen explained. "The *Mission US* games are really conversation starters." Langendoen told me an in-joke teachers use to assess student progress in *Mission 1*. He said, "They ask the class, 'How many students had tea with Constance?'" This is a reference asking who went against the political affiliations of the time. Remember: Royce is a Patriot and Constance is a Loyalist.

The game teaches consequences by gamifying personal choices. In *Mission 2*, Lucy has opportunities to sabotage her master's dress, which has consequences a few steps later. A teacher can connect that to unknown consequences and broader effects. Langendoen said that about 5% of players took that particular story path. "A few well-crafted pieces that players stumble onto give the illusion that decisions matter," he explained.

I asked the design team about "fail states"—the consequences from losing in the game. Langendoen explained that there was controversy over losing due to the fact that class times are typically brief. Starting over from scratch isn't feasible in a 40-minute bell schedule. In *Mission 1*, consequences mean Royce has more chores to do. After that, the player can keep going. In parts of *Mission 2*, the designers *wanted* students to fail. They wanted to elicit feelings of frustration. The escape from the slave plantation must be difficult to do the first time. About 75% of players failed the first time. The game then "rewinds" the player to the start to try again. In this case, the mechanic delivered the message. It also builds persistence. When they initially playtested, an unintended issue occurred: Students weren't resisting—ever. More feedback was added, along with a badge system to relay the message that choosing resistance is an acceptable choice. Getting wounded in *Mission 3* causes the player to wake up after particular events have passed.

Mission US is simple to roll out in a class and works in a computer browser (*Mission 3* is playable on the BrainPOP platform). Students can create usernames and passwords without email addresses or personal information. The purpose of the accounts is to create a save point for play to continue from home. By talking to teachers, the *Mission US* team discovered the need for smaller games that don't take long to play. A 40-hour game isn't feasible for a teacher who is required to teach 350 years of American history. Everything is playable on a computer's browser, and no downloads or installations are required. *Mission US* has videos to help teachers implement the game.

Social Impact Gaming

Over the years, many video games with social themes have been developed. In 2005 the United Nations World Food Programme released *Food Force*, developed by Konami. It was a downloadable game in which players delivered food to people in need. Another game for social change was MTV's *Darfur Is Dying* (the chase mechanic was discussed in Chapter 3, with Google's Noah Falstein). Released in 2006, this online game put players in the role of a refugee in civil war–torn Darfur. In my social studies classroom I have implemented games with social themes, including *Ayiti: The Cost of Life*, a role-playing game set in Haiti. Other games to teach poverty include *Third World Farmer*.

Brian Kehrer wrote an article for *Gamasutra* detailing the process of creating a social impact game. He designed *Nightmare: Malaria*, a tablet game with a similar mechanic as the popular side-scroller *Limbo*, in which the character floats from one part of the screen to another. The difference here is its message: Malaria is dangerous and kills, especially in developing nations. Academy Award–winning actress Susan Sarandon voiced the opening cut scene. The gameplay takes place within an infected young girl's blood vessels and brain. The objective is to save teddy bears while avoiding mosquitoes. Creating games with social messages can be as delicate as creating educational projects. The issue was balancing the game's message with the core mechanics (Kehrer, 2013). Kehrer described the priorities of design elements, ranking what is engaging to do. He wrote:

1. The game must be fun first
2. The player's only objective is to stay alive, the player cannot kill

3. Each level will end quickly, either in success, or death
4. Players are safe under a net
5. The game's environment should feel viscous
6. Mosquitoes should be terrifying. (Kehrer, 2013)

The result is a dark and chilling experience that is still engaging to play. No easy feat! When you die, facts about malaria pop up. There is also a plea to donate money to buy actual mosquito nets. It levels up in challenge as missions are unlocked. The project was done *pro bono* (free) for a charity (Kehrer, 2013). Kehrer also cited a TED Talk by Peter Singer, *The Why and How of Effective Altruism*, as his inspiration. Playing the game with students can lead to a discussion of the game's mechanics. Singer's TED Talk, linked at the end of this chapter, can be used to extend the conversation.

In 2014 the social awareness game *Get Water!* was released. It is a mobile game to teach children about the water crisis and the education of young girls. The game is about Maya, a young girl who keeps getting pulled out of school to collect water for her family. The mechanic uses a touch screen's interface to move Maya across the virtual world. Unlike the tense and dark *Nightmare: Malaria*, *Get Water!* is light, colorful, and optimistic. Even the music is catchy. The aesthetics are intended to first engage players, and then to educate them.

Get Water! was developed by Decode as an experimental project. It was concepted with a fellowship of international students and grew from there. In March 2014 I interviewed Decode's Nicole Darabian, who told me how the project moved forward. She said, "We saw potential of introducing it to classes, so we connected with school boards in Montreal and Quebec, Canada." Teachers brought the game into their classrooms and then they followed with a questionnaire 2 weeks later. Playtest questions included: What did you think about the game? What did you think about the story about the girl (Maya)? "We saw they definitely got it," Darabian said. There are lesson plans provided on its web portal to contextualize the experience. She continued, "Lessons are needed to bring structure. Learning objectives and outcomes can facilitate teachers to see games as a learning tool."

Game design applies behavioral psychology to create rewarding experiences for players. Gamification in the classroom seeks to engage students with similar techniques. Transformational gaming goes even further, using behavioral science to drive social change.

Zynga.org

Playing games together—with a positive purpose—can effect change for the better. This is especially true at Zynga.org, the nonprofit organization started by social gaming giant Zynga (*Words with Friends*, *Farmville*, and *Draw Something*, to name a few). Its motto is: "Play good, do good." I spoke with Abby Speight, Zynga.org's senior product manager in July 2014. She has previously worked for FORGE, a small nonprofit, as well as for Yahoo's social responsibility initiatives. Speight also was a panelist at the 11th Annual Games for Change Festival.

Zynga.org began in 2009 as a "grass-roots initiative" among Zynga.com's employees. "Employees saw games as a great place to engage players in social causes," Speight said. The first campaign was in the game *YoVille* (2008), a virtual world played on Facebook and MySpace (*YoVille* is now called *YoWorld*). A *YoVille* Pet Shelter was added to raise money for the San Francisco Society for the Prevention of Cruelty to Animals (SPCA). "Players loved the approach—there was fundraising and it raised awareness about the SPCA," explained Speight. The Pet Shelter led to more initiatives. After Haiti's devastating earthquake in January 2010, an existing Haitian campaign was expanded across other Zynga games such as *Farmville*. Then in 2011, Ken Weber, former COO of the ONE Campaign (the charity co-founded by Bono), joined as executive director.

In 2013 the "Holiday Lights" campaign was added to *Farmville*. "It was an expansion of a new farm themed around players giving back for the holidays," Speight said. "Players had the opportunity to purchase items in their farms to benefit Feeding America." Participants were able to see a real-time, visual representation of their efforts in virtual lights. Initially, Zynga.org hoped to raise $500,000. Players met the challenge so quickly that the goal was doubled (that, too, was easily reached). "You see the world light up as players engaged for a group goal," Speight continued. "Players responded in extraordinary fashion. They saw what it looked like when they gave back."

According to Speight, Zynga.org has raised nearly $20 million through 150 game campaigns. In addition to its fundraising efforts, it also helps in the educational sector. For example, game design is now taught in the San Francisco Unified School District. In 2013 it launched co.lab with the NewSchools Venture Fund to help educational technology start-ups. The partnership helps turn people's visions into reality; industry "thought leaders"—either from Zynga or from external companies—are matched with start-up talent.

"It is Zynga's learning games accelerator," Speight explained. "Co.lab helps promising educational technology companies take the next big step forward, to enable them to move more quickly in their work."

Zynga.org's website is a helpful resource to find social impact games for the classroom, including *Half the Sky*. Clicking the "Results" tab shows which charities benefitted from Zynga titles such as *Mafia Wars*. It has worked with more than 15 nonprofit companies.

It can be a challenge to deploy social games in a classroom. It may look good on paper: non-zero-sum cooperative games, which often involve virtual gifting. The reality is that many of the titles play on platforms commonly blocked by school administrators, such as Facebook. Many titles, such as *Words with Friends*, can be played on a stand-alone app; however, due to the Children's Online Privacy Protection Act (COPPA), registered users must be 13 years old. Educational game companies work around COPPA by having teachers "host" student accounts in a private classroom. Another solution is for students to provide little more than a username. Nonetheless, educational versions of Zynga games remain "in the consideration stage."

Games for Change

Since 2004, Games for Change has sponsored a festival in New York City. Its mission is simple: to catalyze social impact through digital games. Games for Change is a relatively small nonprofit. Its philosophy is that games—like other art forms—can be more than just for entertainment. Previous keynote speakers have included Supreme Court Justice Sandra Day O'Conner, former Vice President Al Gore, and Valve Corporation founder Gabe Newell (Valve published *Portal 2* and runs the Steam platform). While there, Newell announced Teach with Portals, the initiative to bring the physics puzzler into the classroom. Jesse Schell has also keynoted. As a result, the educational curriculum company Amplify hired Schell's studio, Schell Games, to create content for its tablets.

I spoke with Asi Burak, president of Games for Change, prior to attending the 11th annual festival. We spoke prior to the festival, in March 2014. Games for Change stemmed from the Serious Games Initiative. (Burak, like Schell, told me that he does not care for the moniker "serious games.") The first event, about a decade ago, had about 40 people in attendance. It was held in Washington, D.C. The past few years have seen an increased profile. It has grown in ambition, attempting to elevate the medium of impactful games the same way the Sundance and Tribeca Film Festivals have done with independent films.

Burak told me that the social impact sector is still fragmented. It is difficult to classify content. He said, "The awareness piece is communication-based; civic learning is education-based, like iCivics; behavior change is part of the health discipline; building social movements is community organization. We're trying to categorize them. Social impact games are different; each does something different."

The Advisory Board and the Board of Directors are strong supporters of the movement. Members include James Gee, Jane McGonigal, and Ken Weber from Zynga.org. They meet four times a year, giving the organization broader reach and perspective. There are, of course, other organizations and conferences in the sector, such as the Digital Media Learning (DML) Conference and the Games + Learning + Society (GLS) Conference. Most of them concentrate on educational topics. As much as learning is on the agenda, it's not Games for Change's sole focus. The essence of a social impact game is one that pertains to the role of government in people's lives, politics, and social events. These topics aren't as clear-cut as content-driven educational games. Many do fit social studies standards.

Before Games for Change, Burak helped developed the game *Peacemaker* (2007). It was an early example of a social impact game designed for general consumption, not necessarily for use in schools. *Peacemaker* is essentially two games, with two different points of view: Israeli and Palestinian. "It was powerful, depending on if you are part of the conflict," Burak explained. The game used real footage from the news, licensed from Reuters. Upon its release, Burak observed how teachers used it with discussion and how it became part of a larger program. He recalled, "Very early I saw games as piece of a larger concept, not a stand-alone." *Peacemaker* cost over half a million dollars to produce, and it can be played for hours. Schools in the West Bank may avoid discussing politics in class, but they do play games. "The game provides a safe environment," he continued. "Kids talk about the role-playing element, like, 'what I did when I was the Israeli prime minister.'"

Like many game developers, Burak grew up with games. His goal with Games for Change is to make compelling experiences. If movies and novels can make you cry and feel emotion, why can't games? "With social impact games you don't compete with the classroom, but other media and blockbuster games," he said. "You need to be more compelling and exciting or you will be perceived as preachy." Designers don't want to lose the audience by doing something superficial, either. The art is to create an engaging experience that people will want to play.

Allying with the Tribeca Film Festival in 2014 opened a new direction with the public sector: Family Day. The Saturday following the festival featured a family-friendly street fair. Burak said, "Games were never represented on that day in years past. There were sports, face painting, but no games." While there, the public discovered games from Quest to Learn and the Come Out and Play organization.

Distributing content directly on Steam, iTunes, and Facebook means that designers no longer need a major publisher. Low-budget games from independent developers need to be innovative to stand out. Burak is hopeful about the future. "Games will be obviously much more impactful and immersive," he predicted. "Look at the Oculus Rift [the virtual reality headset]. Games will be better and more compelling than reality. We'll get there." There is also the rising sector of independent empathy games, titles that are more emotionally compelling than fun. *Papers, Please; That Dragon, Cancer;* and *Gone Home* are examples. Burak contined, "The opportunities are limitless. Tell things about reality and your own life; not just entertainment pieces, but meaningful issues."

The Cooney Center is partnered with Games for Change. It has curated a Games for Learning session featuring James Gee and Katie Salen at a roundtable discussion. The goal was to create a conversation about how games are changing education. The main topic was how to make classrooms more play-based and student-focused. Public education can bring social impact games into the mainstream, as could a good distribution platform. The challenge remains for Burak and Games for Change. "Documentaries are a genre. I want to see Games for Change as a genre," Burak concluded.

The 11th Annual Games for Change Festival

In April 2014 I attended the 11th Annual Games for Change Festival in New York City. It was like the boss level of writing this book! In order to coincide with the Tribeca Film Festival, the Games for Change Festival was moved to early spring (previously it had been in June). There were many takeaways for me, including games to bring into my classroom. Sessions met on separate floors in a building on the New York University campus. The main talks and panels took place in the main auditorium. The lobby had every nominated game on display for guests to play. One game utilized Oculus Rift's virtual reality goggles. There were program breaks that turned the lobby into a forum for business card exchanges. I had the opportunity to meet many of the people I had interviewed, face-to-face, for the first time.

The Festival is a true idea forum. Each morning began with small group sessions in which game designers brainstormed and discussed creative topics. I sat in on a paper-prototyping workshop where the group remixed Monopoly into Philanthro-poly. The remixed game's objective was to become the biggest philanthropist, not a Gilded Age tycoon. I also observed the Game Verbs for Change workshop. It focused on building a design grammar for impactful games. As a teacher, I noticed that many of the action verbs were similar to those in Bloom's Taxonomy of Higher Thinking (e.g., create, collaborate).

There were several compelling speakers and panelists. Google's chief game designer Noah Falstein spoke, as did Jesse Schell. GlassLab unveiled Mars Generation One: Argubot Academy and announced a deal to partner with other educational developers. GlassLab's Jessica Lindl told the crowd that approximately one in five games makes it into a student's hands. GlassLab will now offer services to help educational game developers get through the barriers of school adoption. As of this writing, the initiative is called Playfully. There also was a fascinating talk about the Block-by-Block program, the United Nations's UN-Habitat program that partnered with game developer Mojang. Block-by-Block uses Minecraft to enable citizens in the developing world to plan architectural projects.

Jane McGonigal's Keynote

The Festival opened with Jane McGonigal as the first keynote speaker. Her book Reality Is Broken: Why Games Make Us Better and How They Can Change the World (2011) had been a New York Times bestseller. In 2013 McGonigal keynoted the International Society for Technology Education (ISTE) Conference in San Antonio, Texas. While there, she led an auditorium of teachers in a massive thumb-wrestling tournament. Currently, McGonigal works with the Institute for the Future. She detailed her past projects, including "Top Secret Dance Off," in which players uploaded silly pictures of themselves dancing. The community created an accompanying badge system. What McGonigal did was create game mechanics that were awarded socially, from player to player, rather than via the typical top-down structure. This is a good lesson on how to create a positive culture in the classroom: Students create the reward system. Her anecdote concluded with a description of her game *Evoke*, also featured in her book *Reality Is Broken*. In the game, players peer-evaluated one another. It went on to win an award at Games for Change.

The topic of McGonigal's keynote was *Games for Change: 2024*. In the speech, she connected stories from her book with her work with the Institute for the Future. She detailed five fictitious nominees for Game of the Year 2024. One was *Everwin*, about save-to-win lottery accounts. Some banks incentivize saving accounts by applying a percentage saved to state lotteries. She combined this trend with the rise in social gambling. The next nominee pertained to 3D printers that make food using corn-based "ink." It was tied with research about animal simulators and empathy. Participants wore virtual reality headsets to "see" life from the animal's point of view. McGonigal reported that several of the research subjects gave up eating meat. Other nominees included a mash-up of the Oculus Rift virtual reality headset, StoryCorps, the one-on-one podcast website, and Global Lives, a "24 hours in the life" website. Perhaps one day we can all walk in someone else's shoes. Her next prediction was "MegaNFL," in which power-ups are given to professional teams whose fans accomplish positive achievements. For example, one team could have an advantage if its fans ran a certain number of miles. The final prediction was "Socrates 2.0," a gamified and socialized blend of informal learning. The audience voted for the winner via SurveyMonkey (I voted for "Socrates 2.0"). As a teacher, I found her predictions to be engaging and optimistic. I shared her talk with my students, as well as the Institute for the Future's website. After all, they are the future!

Well Played Talks

Each year the Festival features a "Well Played" series of talks. The talks are based on the *Well Played Journal*, published by Carnegie Mellon University Entertainment Technology Center. It is "a forum for in-depth close readings of video games that parse out the various meanings to be found in the experience of playing a game" ("*Well Played Journal*," 2011). (The Games + Learning + Society Conference in Madison, Wisconsin, also features Well Played talks.) The journal is accessible for free and features written evaluations of video games. The Well Played talks are essentially live walkthroughs of games given by designers not associated with the production of the titles. This style of analysis is like hearing authors read and discuss their favorite books with an audience. The Well Played talks can be an effective, interest-driven method to teach students how to critique media.

Tracy Fullerton, chair of the University of Southern California Game Innovation Lab, led the first Well Played talk. It was about the exploration game *Gone Home* (2013). She discussed the game's first-person, point-and-click mechanics, which are similar to those of 1990s games such as *Myst* (1993). The game is set in 1995, making the style of play part of the story. *Gone Home* looks like a prototypical horror game, with an empty, creepy house. It is filled with "pointless interactions." This was the designer's intent. Players can manipulate everyday objects, some of which have no relation to the overall story arc. Fullerton described *Gone Home* as "traditional storytelling within an interactive structure."

Gone Home really isn't the haunted house game it purports to be. It is actually a coming-out story of a LGBT (lesbian, gay, bisexual, transsexual) teenager. Fullerton called it "the everyday nightmare of coming out." The story, which unfolds in a series of found notebooks, journal pages, and audiocassettes, is slower than a typical video game. Fullerton suggested that it should be "read" like a long novel. Fullerton summed up the game as "the ordinary horrors of an ordinary family." It was marketed as a horror game, likely because streaming platforms such as Valve's Steam Community rely on user votes when content is added. As a result, some of the user comments were negative because the game turned out to be different than expected. Most realized that innovative games could be about real-life issues, and they pushed it to become a critical success. *Gone Home* went on to win the Game of the Year award.

At the Festival's second Well Played talk, designer Nick Fortugno compared the ethical decisions presented in the award-winning *Papers, Please* to the philosophy of Immanuel Kant. When one thinks about ethics, the terms "right" and "wrong" come to mind; of course, there are many shades of gray in between. According to Fortugno, moral dilemmas are "not a mathematical system of good and evil." In other words, doing "good" does not have an immediate payoff. The mechanic of a delayed reward led *Papers, Please* to win the Most Innovative Game and Best Game Play awards at the Games for Change Festival. It also won a BAFTA award for Best Strategy and Sim.

Papers, Please is set in 1982, and the visual aesthetics reflect games from that era. In the game, you assume the role of immigration officer at the border of a fictional Communist country, Arstotzka. Rules for immigration—including requiring entrance tickets and passports—constantly change, or level up, until mastery is reached. Player decisions in *Papers, Please* are not "black or white." Ethical quandaries are front and center. You can accept bribes or let in "less desirable" immigrants. When I first played, my character was repeatedly penalized for allowing immigrants with falsified documents to enter. Penalties led to my not being able to cover my rent or heating bill, which resulted in my character's wife, son, uncle, and mother-in-law getting sick. I was eventually jailed for unpaid debts and my family was sent away. Because of the variety of moral dilemmas presented, Fortugno called it "one of the best serious games ever made."

When students play video games, they project themselves onto characters. The teacher's role is to contextualize and facilitate discussions on story content *and* game decisions. *Papers, Please*'s "mature content" can be toggled off to make the game more appropriate for school settings. As with any media, it is best for teachers to preview materials first. For a deeper understanding of the interplay of ethics and video games, I highly recommend viewing Nick Fortugno's Well Played talk about *Papers, Please*: http://youtu.be/kQR3xh-C9hJA. After viewing it with your class, facilitate a discussion about morals and dilemmas.

Games and Empathy

Mary Flanagan is the Sherman Fairchild Distinguished Professor in Digital Humanities at Dartmouth College. Her design studio, Tiltfactor, has many impactful game titles. She spoke on the second day of the Festival. Flanagan is a long-time proponent of creating games that promote social change. She spoke about games for health, and specifically about zombies and vaccinations. *Pox* (also mentioned in Chapter 2) is one example. It is a board game as well as a free iPad download. There is no heavy-handed pandering; the mechanic is the message. The player chooses spaces to contain an infectious outbreak and people to save. Playing to win enforces the idea of vaccination circles, like when an entire family gets a flu shot.

Video games can engage with more emotions than just fun and thrills. One of the most moving games in that respect is *That Dragon, Cancer*. It is "an adventure game that acts as a living painting; a poem; an interactive retelling of Ryan and Amy Green's experience raising their son Joel, a 4-year old currently fighting his third year of terminal cancer. Players relive memories, share heartache, and discover the overwhelming hope that can be found in the face of death" (Green, 2014). Joel succumbed to cancer on March 13, 2014, before the project was completed, 1 month prior to the Games for Change Festival. The project is also the subject of a documentary, *Thank You for Playing*. It is an empathy-art game about the most serious of topics. As of this writing, the game has yet to be released.

The Festival concluded with a talk from Jenova Chen titled *Blank Canvas: Designing a New Era of Emotional Storytelling through Games*. Chen wants games to do more than tell a simple story. "Compared to a Saturday morning cartoon," he told the crowd, "I'd rather watch a Pixar film." Chen observed how so-called adult games are for "a child in a man's body." Games for adults shouldn't just mean more mature content. He remarked on how a lot of his friends who used to play games stopped "because it's for kids." Those same people, however, still read books, go to the movies, and visit theme parks. Why do other forms of entertainment offer a greater range of emotions than what games currently do?

Thatgamecompany, which Chen co-founded, partnered with Sony to distribute its games via the PlayStation Network. Chen created *flOw* (the game about flow, mentioned in Chapter 3); Thatgamecompany designed *Flower*, now on display in museums. Its latest title, *Journey*, is an interpretation of Joseph Campbell's Hero's Journey, or monomyth. It stems from the book *A Hero with a Thousand Faces* (1949), in which Campbell realized that all mythological hero stories take the same cyclical path. Chen's team used Campbell's Hero's Journey as a template, which they applied to the aptly titled *Journey*. Everything—from background color to music—followed the story's hero's arc.

Emotional depth in other media uses a process called catharsis, or relief from drama and tension. Chen used the typical three-act movie as an example. There is an increasing emotional intensity, and then it drops. Chen stated that the story is next followed by a "second act twist, followed by a dramatic lift at the end." He feels that catharsis is the key to infusing a greater range of emotions into games. As I listened to Chen speak, I immediately thought about playing *Journey* in a school setting, followed by a class discussion about mythology.

Games have come a long way from the cultural artifacts of *Mancala*, *Go*, and *Senet* to the elevated medium of art in *Gone Home*; *Papers, Please*; and *Journey*. Unlike painting, sculpture, photography, music, and film, games demand interaction from participants. The innovative designers and developers celebrated by Games for Change are driving social change and pushing the medium to new heights.

The Future

What will the future of gaming bring? Wearable devices open up a world of possibility for serious and educational gaming. Oculus Rift and Sony's Project Morpheus may finally bring virtual reality to the mainstream. If animal simulators are any indication, the future for empathy games seems wide open. Another technological advancement is Google Glass, a computer projected in front of a user's eye. It creates a hands-free, augmented reality experience.

I asked Noah Falstein, Google's chief game designer, about how he would utilize Google Glass in the classroom. As it turned out, he wrote an article on its potential for the magazine *Gamasutra* in October 2013. We spoke in May 2014. He envisions students playing role-playing games in a classroom. "I can see a group of people re-enacting scenes from history or an incident from social studies like a cultural invasion of another," he explained. "Each is given a role, but they don't know what they're supposed to say until the moment they have to say it." With Google Glass, the text appears almost as if on a teleprompter—always there right in front of the wearer. Its microphone knows when the user is speaking, and it can prompt dialogue at precisely the right time.

At the 2014 Game Development Conference, Manveer Heir, a designer for the popular *Mass Effect* science fiction games, spoke about stereotypes in the industry. *Mass Effect 3* had featured a homosexual male nonplayable character aboard the protagonist's space ship. The third game in the trilogy gave the player the ability to play as a male or female character. Nonetheless, gender stereotypes persist. It was disheartening to see that Ubisoft's *Assassin's Creed Unity* (2014), a game set during the French Revolution, will have a multiplayer mode that includes only male characters. When confronted by reporters at the E3 Conference, where the game was revealed, developers said it was too difficult to animate female avatars (Farokhmanesh, 2014). Perhaps the Internet uproar in fan communities can remedy this imbalance. Games are still an immature medium undergoing growing pains. Market biases and shortcomings can be used as a teachable moment with students. After all, today's student gamers are tomorrow's designers!

Conclusions and Takeaways

Social impact games push the envelope of entertainment. As the medium matures, so should the content. That is, themes shouldn't become more adult; rather, a deeper range of player emotions, such as empathy, needs to figure in the games. Try implementing games from sites such as Games for Health, Games for Change, and other portals that feature social impact or transformational games.

Lesson Plan Ideas

Get Water!: Lesson Plans for World Water Day—http://getwatergame.com/learning. Next Generation Science Standards would apply, as would applicable social studies standards pertaining to world cultures.

Hero's Journey: Play through *Journey* as a class, or watch the Let's Play walkthroughs on YouTube. Make comparisons to this infographic of Joseph Campbell's monomyth—http://upload.wikimedia.org/wikipedia/commons/1/1b/Heroesjourney.svg. Standards include English language arts.

Idea Challenge: OpenIDEO crowdsources solutions to world problems. This site can make authentic narratives in problem-based learning truly real world. For a project-based lesson, have students go to this site to choose their own problems to solve (rather than a teacher-assigned problem). This lesson is not content-specific. Standards depend on how you use this tool—http://www.openideo.com/challenge

Mission US: Lesson plans for the social studies interactive. This lesson meets English language arts Common Core State Standards—http://www.mission-us.org

Well Played: Classroom Edition: Student lead a Well Played talk about a version of a game they are interested in, modded for a content topic. For example, students can describe a point-and-click style game, such as *Myst* or *Gone Home*, set in a book's famous location, such as a district in *The Hunger Games*. Other examples might include a talk about something the students built using *Minecraft*. Common Core State Standards include English language arts, especially those pertaining to "explain."

Games

Ayiti: The Cost of Life, a social impact game about poverty in Haiti—http://ayiti.globalkids.org/game

Blind Side, which won the Most Innovative Game award at the 2013 G4C Conference, is a mobile thriller that "gives players the experience of living without sight as they hear their way through a danger-filled city" (Games for Change, 2014)—http://www.blindsidegame.com

Data Dealer, a web-based game that raises awareness about online privacy concerns—https://datadealer.com

EyeWire, a massively multiplayer online game from MIT to map neurons in the human brain—http://eyewire.org

GetWater!, a social impact game for Charity Water—www.getwatergame.com

Gone Home, the exploration game about the horrors of ordinary life—http://www.gonehome-game.com

Grow-A-Game, brainstorming cards to create kindergarten through grade-12 social impact games, available using paper cards or on iPad—http://www.tiltfactor.org/growagame

Half the Sky, the social game for women's rights, playable on Facebook—https://www.facebook.com/HalftheGame

The Migrant Trail. Tied to a documentary, this game lets players assume the role of a migrant or a patrol agent—http://theundocumented.com

Mission US games, including *Mission 1: For Crown or Country, Mission 2: Flight to Freedom*, and the Games for Change winner *Mission 3: A Cheyenne Odyssey* are free on a web browser (*Mission 3* is also on BrainPOP)—http://www.mission-us.org

Never Alone, from E-Line Media and Upper One Games, "a beautifully illustrated puzzle-adventure game depicting a young Iñupiat protagonist and her arctic fox companion"—http://neveralonegame.com

Nightmare: Malaria, a social awareness game about malaria—http://nightmare.againstmalaria.com

Papers, Please, winner of the Most Innovative Game award at Games for Change 2014. The game is about making ethical decisions, choosing who can enter a country and who cannot. Wrong choices penalize the player's family. In a Well Played game analysis at the Games for Change Festival, Nick Fortugno compared the player decisions to philosophy and ethics questions posed by Immanuel Kant—http://papersplea.se

Papo & Yo. According to the developer's website, players "will need to learn to use Monster's emotions, both good and bad, to their advantage if they want to complete their search for a cure and save their pal"—http://www.wearemimority.com/papo-yo

Peacemaker. Play as Palestine or Israel—http://www.peacemakergame.com

SICKO (Surgical Improvement of Clinical Knowledge Ops), a game-based simulation for medical students. (It should be noted that problem-based learning originally began on medical school campuses.) The game was created at Stanford School of Medicine and is free to play—http://cme.stanford.edu/sicko/

Start the Talk, a game developed by the U.S. Substance Abuse and Mental Health Services Administration to help parents discuss underage drinking with their children—http://samhsa.gov/underagedrinking

SuperBetter, on Jane McGonigal's (author of *Realty Is Broken*) site, launched after she recovered from a concussive injury—https://www.superbetter.com

The Stanley Parable, a first-person "nonviolent" exploration game—http://www.stanleyparable.com

That Dragon, Cancer, Ryan Green's tribute to his son, Joel—http://thatdragoncancer.com and the documentary, *Thank You for Playing*—http://www.thankyouforplayingfilm.com

Third World Farmer, a simulation game—http://www.3rdworldfarmer.com

Uplifted, the "happiness" game—https://itunes.apple.com/gb/app/uplifted/id582248097

WeTopia, the social game for good—https://www.facebook.com/appcenter/wetopia

Xenos, the English language learning game—http://www.xenos-isle.com

Resources

Block by Block, the United Nations' UN-Habitat program that partnered with Mojang to use *Minecraft* to plan urban development in developing nations—http://blockbyblock.org

Center for Games and Science—http://centerforgamescience.org/games

co.lab, mentoring new educational technology start-ups—http://playcolab.com

Critical Play, Mary Flanagan's TEDx Dartmouth Talk about games as art—http://www.dart
mouth.edu/~tedx/maryflanaganvideo

DonorsChoose.org, helping teachers fund class projects—http://www.donorschoose.org

Fred Rogers Center's Play & Learn, early childhood apps, a focus at the 2014 Games for Change
Festival—http://www.fredrogerscenter.org/resources/play-and-learn

Games for Change—http://www.gamesforchange.org

Games for Change on YouTube—https://www.youtube.com/user/GamesForChange

Games for Health—http://gamesforhealth.org

Games for Peace—http://gamesforpeace.org

Institute for the Future—http://www.iftf.org/home/, and its 10-year forecast—http://www.iftf
.org/our-work/global-landscape/ten-year-forecast

Kickstarter, helping designers to crowdfund projects and ideas from the public—https://www
.kickstarter.com

Kids+Creativity Network in Pittsburgh, a focus at the 2014 Games for Change Festival—http://
remakelearning.org

NewSchools Venture Fund, helping fund several educational technology start-ups, including
those in the gaming sector such as Tynker and ClassDojo—http://www.newschools.org/
ventures

Tetris as therapy for post-traumatic stress disorder (PTSD), as described to attendees at
the Games for Change by Jane McGonigal—http://janemcgonigal.com/2014/03/27/
help-prevent-ptsd

Thatgamecompany, the Jenova Chen-led studio (*Cloud, flOw, Flower, Journey*)—http://
thatgamecompany.com

Values at Play, adding human values into games—http://valuesatplay.org

Well Played Journal. Volumes are accessible for free and feature in-depth analysis of video
games—http://press.etc.cmu.edu/wellplayed

The Why and How of Effective Altruism, by Peter Singer—http://www.ted.com/talks/peter_
singer_the_why_and_how_of_effective_altruism.html

Zynga.org, where the social gaming giant (*Draw Something, Farmville*) meets the social good—
http://zynga.org

REFERENCES

The AbleGamers Foundation. (2014). Retrieved July 28, 2014, from http://www.ablegamers.com

Abt, C. C. (1987). *Serious games.* Lanham, MD: University Press of America.

Anderson, J., & Rainie, L. (2012, May 18). *The future of gamification.* Retrieved January 19, 2014, from Pew Internet & American Life Project website: http://www.pewinternet.org/Reports/2012/Future-of-Gamification.aspx

The art of video games. (2012). Retrieved December 24, 2013, from Smithsonian Institute website: http://americanart.si.edu/exhibitions/archive/2012/games/

Assassin's Creed III wiki guide. (2014). Retrieved January 18, 2014, from IGN website: http://www.ign.com/wikis/assassins-creed-3/Animus_Database

Badges. (2014). Retrieved January 19, 2014, from Mozilla Wiki website: https://wiki.mozilla.org/Badges

Baer, R. H. (2005). *Videogames: In the beginning.* Springfield, NJ: Rolenta Press.

Bartle, R. (1996, April). *Hearts, clubs, diamonds, spades: Players who suit MUDs.* Retrieved July 22, 2013, from http://www.mud.co.uk/richard/hcds.htm

Bateman, C. (Ed.). (2009). *Beyond game design: Nine steps towards creating better videogames.* Boston, MA: Charles River Media/Cengage Technology.

Bergmann, J., & Sams, A. (2012). *Flip your classroom: Reach every student in every class every day.* Eugene, OR: International Society for Technology in Education.

Big Think interview with Nicole Lazzaro. (n.d.). Retrieved April 8, 2014, from Big Think website: http://bigthink.com/users/nicolelazzaro

Bill & Melinda Gates Foundation. (2014). Retrieved January 17, 2014, from http://www.gates-foundation.org

Bilton, N. (2013, September 15). Disruptions: Minecraft, an obsession and an educational tool. Retrieved December 8, 2013, from *New York Times* website: http://bits.blogs.nytimes.com/2013/09/15/minecraft-an-obsession-and-an-educational-tool/

Birnbaum, I. (2013, July 16). Behind Falskaar, a massive new Skyrim mod, and the 19-year-old who spent a year building it. Retrieved July 19, 2014, from *PC Gamer* website: http://www.pcgamer.com/2013/07/16/behind-falskaar-a-massive-new-skyrim-mod-and-the-19-year-old-who-spent-a-year-building-it/

Bissell, T. (2010). *Extra lives: Why video games matter.* New York, NY: Pantheon Books.

Bisz, J. (n.d.). The five simple game mechanics. Retrieved July 8, 2014, from Composition Games for the Classroom website: http://joebisz.com/compositiongames/Composition_Games_for_the_Classroom.html

Björn, Jeffrey, on why Toca Boca won't be selling to schools. (2014, March 17). Retrieved April 10, 2014, from gamesandlearning.org website: http://www.gamesandlearning.org/2014/03/17/bjorn-jeffrey-on-why-toca-boca-wont-be-selling-to-schools/

Boss level at Quest to Learn: Connected learning in a public school. (n.d.). Retrieved December 17, 2013, from Connected Learning website: http://connectedlearning.tv/case-studies/boss-level-quest-learn-connected-learning-public-school

Boss, S., & Krauss, J. (2007). *Reinventing project-based learning: Your field guide to real-world projects in the digital age.* Eugene, OR: International Society for Technology in Education.

Boyle, A. (2013, January 20). 10 most important board games in history. Retrieved December 22, 2013, from Listverse website: http://listverse.com/2013/01/20/10-most-important-board-games-in-history/

Brandt, R. (2011, October 15). Birth of a salesman. Retrieved December 14, 2013, from the *Wall Street Journal* website: http://online.wsj.com/news/articles/SB10001424052970203914304576627102996831200

Buck Institute of Education. (2014). Retrieved January 19, 2014, from http://bie.org

Caillois, R. (2001). *Man, play, and games* (M. Barash, Trans.). Urbana, IL: University of Illinois Press. (Original work published 1961)

Caillois, R. (2006). The definition of play: The classification of games. In K. Salen & E. Zimmerman (eds.), *The game design reader: A rules of play anthology* (pp. 122–155). Cambridge, MA: MIT Press. (Original work published 1962)

Campbell, C. (2013, December 10). YouTube video game shows hit with copyright blitz. Retrieved January 8, 2014, from Polygon website: http://www.polygon.com/2013/12/10/5198276/youtube-video-game-shows-hit-with-copyright-blitz

Campbell, J., & Cousineau, P. (1991). *The hero's journey: The world of Joseph Campbell: Joseph Campbell on his life and work.* San Francisco, CA: HarperSanFrancisco.

Catmull, E. E., & Wallace, A. (2014). *Creativity, Inc.: Overcoming the unseen forces that stand in the way of true inspiration.* New York, NY: Random House.

Center for Games and Impact. (2014). Retrieved January 18, 2014, from Arizona State University: Mary Lou Fulton Teachers College website: http://gamesandimpact.org/

Chai, B. (2011, July 28). Kill Screen hosts game night at the museum. Retrieved January 6, 2014, from the *Wall Street Journal* website: http://blogs.wsj.com/speakeasy/2011/07/28/moma-hosts-kill-screen-arcade-where-everybody-can-play/

Challenge based learning. (2014). Retrieved January 19, 2014, from https://www.challenge-basedlearning.org/

Chen, J. (2006). *Flow in games*. Retrieved January 4, 2014, from http://www.jenovachen.com/flowingames/flowing.htm

Chen, J., Lu, S.-I., & Vekhter, D. (n.d.). Zero-sum games. Retrieved January 13, 2014, from Game Theory website: http://www-cs-faculty.stanford.edu/~eroberts/courses/soco/projects/1998–99/game-theory/index.html

Chicago city of learning. (2014). Retrieved March 20, 2014, from http://explorechi.org

Class Dojo. (2014). Retrieved January 19, 2014, from http://www.classdojo.com

Clifton, D. (2013, November 26). New technology opens up world of learning for Marble Falls ISD students. Retrieved December 31, 2013, from the *River Cities Daily Tribune* website: http://www.dailytrib.com/2013/11/26/new-technology-opens-world-learning-marble-falls-isd-students/

Clowes, G. (2011). *The essential 5: A starting point for Kagan Cooperative Learning*. San Clemente, CA: Kagan Publishing.

Common core state standards initiative. (2014). Retrieved November 4, 2014, from http://www.corestandards.org

Crair, B. (2010, December 13). Brenda Brathwaite: Holocaust game designer. Retrieved December 24, 2013, from the *Daily Beast* website: http://www.thedailybeast.com/articles/2010/12/13/brenda-brathwaite-holocaust-game-designer.html

Creative Learning Exchange. (2013). Retrieved November 22, 2013, from http://clexchange.org

Csikszentmihalyi, M. (1990). *Flow: The psychology of optimal experience*. New York, NY: Harper & Row.

Cuban, L. (2001). *Oversold and underused: Computers in the classroom*. Cambridge, MA: Harvard University Press.

Davidson, C. (2012, February 21). Can badging be the zipcar of testing and assessment? Retrieved July 31, 2013, from DML Central website: http://dmlcentral.net/blog/cathy-davidson/can-badging-be-zipcar-testing-and-assessment

DeKoven, B. (2013). *The well-played game: A player's philosophy*. Cambridge, MA: The MIT Press.

Dell, A. G., Newton, D. A., & Petroff, J. G. (2012). *Assistive technology in the classroom: Enhancing the school experiences of students with disabilities* (2nd ed.). Upper Saddle River, NJ: Pearson.

Design squad teacher's guide. (2014). Retrieved February 15, 2014, from Design Squad Nation website: http://pbskids.org/designsquad/parentseducators/guides/teachers_guide.html

DeviantART. (2014). Retrieved January 19, 2014, from http://www.deviantart.com

Dirksen, J. (2012). *Design for how people learn*. Berkeley, CA: New Riders.

Disney Infinity. (2014). Retrieved January 15, 2014, from Disney website: https://infinity.disney.com/

Dixit, A., & Nalebuff, B. (n.d.). Prisoners' dilemma. Retrieved January 13, 2014, from Library of Economics and Liberty website: http://www.econlib.org/library/Enc/PrisonersDilemma.html

Doom WAD. (n.d.). Retrieved July 19, 2014, from Wikipedia website: http://en.wikipedia.org/wiki/Doom_WAD

Doty, M. (2013, December 10). Play "Frozen" find-it! Discover all the Easter eggs in Disney's blockbuster. Retrieved December 10, 2013, from Yahoo Movies website: http://movies

.yahoo.com/blogs/movie-news/play-frozen-discover-easter-eggs-disney-blockbuster-170605113.html

Duhigg, C. (2012). *The power of habit: Why we do what we do in life and business.* New York, NY: Random House.

Dunniway, T., & Novak, J. (2007). *Game development essentials: Gameplay mechanics.* Clifton Park, NY: Thomson Delmar Learning.

Ebert, R. (2010, April 16). Video games can never be art. Retrieved December 24, 2013, from Roger Ebert's Journal website: http://www.rogerebert.com/rogers-journal/video-games-can-never-be-art

The Edcamp Foundation. (2014). Retrieved August 29, 2014, from http://edcamp.org/what-is-edcamp/

Edwards, R. (2001, October 14). GNS and other matters of role-playing theory. Retrieved January 3, 2014, from The Forge website: http://www.indie-rpgs.com/articles/1/

Elias, G. S., Garfield, R., & Gutschera, K. R. (2012). *Characteristics of games.* Cambridge, MA: MIT Press.

E-Line Media. (2013). Retrieved December 10, 2013, from http://elinemedia.com

Epic Change. (2014). Retrieved January 18, 2014, from http://epicchangeblog.org

Farokhmanesh, M. (2014, June 10). Ubisoft abandoned women assassins in co-op because of the additional work. Retrieved July 7, 2014, from Polygon website: http://www.polygon.com/e3-2014/2014/6/10/5798592/assassins-creed-unity-female-assassins

Filament Games. (2014). Retrieved January 17, 2014, from http://www.filamentgames.com/

5 years of Doom. (n.d.). Retrieved July 19, 2014, from DoomWorld website: http://5years.doomworld.com/interviews/justinfisher/

Frum, L. (2012, October 19). American history unfolds in "Assassin's Creed 3." Retrieved January 18, 2014, from CNN website: http://www.cnn.com/2012/10/19/tech/gaming-gadgets/assassins-creed-3-history

Games and Learning. (2014). Retrieved January 21, 2014, from Games and Learning website: http://www.gamesandlearning.org

Games and Learning Society. (2013). Retrieved November 2, 2013, from http://www.gameslearningsociety.org/index.php

Games for Change. (2014). Retrieved January 18, 2014, from http://www.gamesforchange.org

Gannes, L. (2013, December 14). 15 million students learned to program this week, thanks to Hour of Code. Retrieved December 14, 2013, from All Things D website: http://allthingsd.com/20131213/15-million-students-learned-to-program-this-week-thanks-to-hour-of-code/

Gee, J. P. (2005). *Good video games and good learning.* Retrieved December 14, 2013, from http://www.jamespaulgee.com/sites/default/files/pub/GoodVideoGamesLearning.pdf

Gee, J. P. (2007). *What video games have to teach us about learning and literacy* (rev. ed.). New York, NY: Palgrave Macmillan.

Gee, J. P. (2010). Video games: What they can teach us about audience engagement. Retrieved April 17, 2014, from *Nieman Reports* website: http://www.nieman.harvard.edu/reports/article/102418/Video-Games-What-They-Can-Teach-Us-About-Audience-Engagement.aspx

Gee, J. P. (2012, March 29). Jim Gee on the use of video games for learning about learning. Retrieved January 18, 2014, from Spotlight on Digital Learning and Media website: http://

spotlight.macfound.org/blog/entry/jim-gee-on-the-use-of-video-games-for-learning-about-learning

Gee, J. P. (2013). *The anti-education era: Creating smarter students through digital learning.* New York, NY: Palgrave Macmillan.

Gerstein, J. (2013, February 11). Video games and social emotional learning. Retrieved January 4, 2014, from User Generated Education website: http://usergeneratededucation.wordpress.com/2013/02/11/games-and-social-emotional-learning/

Gilbert, B. (2011, June 23). Newell sees no distinction "between games and educational games." Retrieved July 28, 2013, from Joystiq website: http://www.joystiq.com/2011/06/23/newell-sees-no-distinction-between-games-and-educational-games/

Goldberg, D., & Larsson, L. (2013). *Minecraft: The unlikely tale of Markus "Notch" Persson and the game that changed everything.* New York, NY: Seven Stories Press.

Gray, P. (2014a). *Free to learn: Why unleashing the instinct to play will make our children happier, more self-reliant, and better students for life.* New York, NY: Basic Books.

Gray, P. (2014b, April 7). Risky play: Why children love it and need it. Retrieved April 15, 2014, from Freedom to Learn blog at *Psychology Today* website: http://www.psychologytoday.com/blog/freedom-learn/201404/risky-play-why-children-love-it-and-need-it

Green, R. (2014). About the game. Retrieved April 18, 2014, from *That Dragon, Cancer* website, http://thatdragoncancer.com/

Greenwald, T. (2013, March 19). How Jimmy Wales' Wikipedia harnessed the web as a force for good. Retrieved January 19, 2014, from *Wired* website: http://www.wired.com/wiredenterprise/2013/03/jimmy-wales-wikipedia/all/

Grundberg, S., & Hansegard, J. (2014, June 16). YouTube's biggest draw plays games, earns $4 million a year. Retrieved June 18, 2014, from the *Wall Street Journal* website: http://online.wsj.com/articles/youtube-star-plays-videogames-earns-4-million-a-year-1402939896

GTA V wiki: References to movies, TV, games and pop culture. (2014). Retrieved January 5, 2014, from IGN website: http://www.ign.com/wikis/gta-5/References_to_Movies,_TV,_Games_and_Pop_Culture

Harris, B. J. (2014). *Console wars: Sega, Nintendo, and the battle that defined a generation.* New York, NY: It Books.

Herr-Stephenson, B., Alper, M., Reilly, E., & Jenkins, H. (2013). *T is for transmedia: Learning through transmedia play.* Los Angeles, CA, and New York, NY: USC Annenberg Innovation Lab and the Joan Ganz Cooney Center at Sesame Workshop.

Higgins, C. (2013, November 7). SimCityEDU: Gaming in the classroom. Retrieved January 3, 2014, from *Mental Floss* website: http://mentalfloss.com/article/53544/simcityedu-gaming-classroom

Historia. (2014). Retrieved January 20, 2014, from http://playhistoria.com

Hoerr, T. R. (2013). *Fostering grit: How do I prepare my students for the real world?* Alexandria, VA: ASCD.

How to do a Let's Play. (2014). Retrieved January 18, 2014, from WikiHow website: http://www.wikihow.com/Do-a-Let's-Play

Huizinga, J. (1955). *Homo ludens: A study of the play-element in culture.* Boston, MA: Beacon Press. (Original work published 1938)

Hunicke, R., LeBlanc, M., & Zubek, R. (2004). *MDA: A formal approach to game design and game research.* Retrieved December 30, 2013, from http://www.cs.northwestern.edu/~hunicke/MDA.pdf

Impact guides. (2014). Retrieved August 30, 2014, from The Center for Games and Impact website: http://gamesandimpact.org/impact-guides/

Indvik, L. (2013, February 27). MoMA exhibit to feature "Pac-Man" and 13 other video game classics. Retrieved December 24, 2013, from Mashable website: http://mashable.com/2013/02/27/moma-video-games-exhibit/

Inform. (2014). Retrieved January 10, 2014, from http://inform7.com

Institute of Play. (2014). Retrieved April 27, 2014, from http://www.instituteofplay.org/about/context/glossary/

Interactive Fiction Community forum. (2014). Retrieved January 10, 2014, from http://www.intfiction.org/forum/

Interactive Fiction Competition. (2014). Retrieved January 10, 2014, from http://www.ifcomp.org

Jackson, S. (2010, February 2). PBS's *Frontline* airs *Digital Nation* tonight. Retrieved January 19, 2014, from Spotlight on Digital Learning & Media website: http://spotlight.macfound.org/blog/entry/pbss-frontline-airs-digital-nation-tonight/

Jenkins, H. (2006a). *Convergence culture: Where old and new media collide.* New York, NY: New York University Press.

Jenkins, H. (2006b). Reality bytes: Eight myths about video games debunked. Retrieved May 14, 2014, from the Video Game Revolution website: http://www.pbs.org/kcts/videogamerevolution/impact/myths.html

Jenkins, H. (2012, March 5). How to earn your skeptic "badge" [Blog post]. Retrieved from Confessions of an Aca-Fan: The Official Weblog of Henry Jenkins website: http://henry-jenkins.org/2012/03/how_to_earn_your_skeptic_badge.html

Jenkins, H., & Kelley, W. (Eds.). (2013). *Reading in a participatory culture: Remixing Moby-Dick in the English classroom.* New York, NY: Teachers College Press.

Kagan publishing & professional development. (2013). Retrieved April 3, 2014, from http://www.kaganonline.com/index.php

Kagan, S. (1998). *Teams of four are magic!* San Clemente, CA: Kagan Publishing.

Kagan, S. (2000). *Silly sports & goofy games* (C. Rodriguez, Illus.). San Juan Capistrano, CA: Kagan Publishing.

Kagan, S. (2004). *Silly sports and goofy games—the tenth reason to play: Brain-friendly instruction.* San Clemente, CA: Kagan Publishing.

Kamenetz, A. (2013, November 11). *SimCityEDU*: A video game that tests kids while killing the bubble test. Retrieved January 3, 2014, from Fast Company website: http://www.fastcompany.com/3021180/innovation-agents/simcityedu-a-video-game-that-tests-kids-while-killing-the-bubble-test

Kehrer, B. (2013, December 12). Mechanics are the message: Designing a game for change in 3 months. Retrieved January 17, 2014, from *Gamasutra* website: http://www.gamasutra.com/blogs/BrianKehrer/20131212/206517/Mechanics_are_the_Message_Designing_a_Game_for_Change_in_3_Months.php

Keirsey.com. (2014). Retrieved January 3, 2014, from http://www.keirsey.com

Keller, D., Ardis, P., Dunstan, V., Thornton, A., Henry, R., & Witty, B. (2007). Gaming, identity, and literacy. In C. L. Selfe & G. E. Hawisher (eds.), *Gaming lives in the twenty-first century: Literate connections* (pp. 71–86). New York, NY: Palgrave Macmillan.

Kelley, D., & Kelley, T. (2013). *Creative confidence: Unleashing the creative potential within us all.* New York, NY: Crown Business.

Kelly, K. (1994, January). Will Wright: The mayor of SimCity. Retrieved December 10, 2013, from *Wired* website: http://www.wired.com/wired/archive/2.01/wright.html?pg=2&topic=& topic_set=

Kent, S. L. (2001). *The ultimate history of video games: From Pong to Pokémon and beyond: The story behind the craze that touched our lives and changed the world.* Roseville, CA: Prima.

KerbalEdu. (2013). Retrieved December 10, 2013, from http://www.kerbaledu.com

Kim, A. J. (2012a, September 14). The player's journey: Designing over time [Blog post]. Retrieved December 29, 2013, from Amy Jo Kim website: http://amyjokim.com/2012/09/14/ the-players-journey-designing-over-time/

Kim, A. J. (2012b, September 19). Social engagement: Who's playing? How do they like to engage? [Blog post]. Retrieved April 8, 2014, from Amy Jo Kim website: http://amyjokim .com/2012/09/19/social-engagement-whos-playing-how-do-they-like-to-engage/

Kim, A. J. (2014a, February 28). Beyond player types: Kim's social action matrix. [Blog post]. Retrieved April 8, 2014, from Amy Jo Kim website: http://amyjokim.com/2014/02/28/ beyond-player-types-kims-social-action-matrix/

Kim, A. J. (2014b, March 4). DIY: Create your social action matrix. [Blog post]. Retrieved April 8, 2014, from Amy Jo Kim website: http://amyjokim.com/2014/03/04/diy-create- your-social-action-matrix/

Kim, A. J. (2014c, April 7). What makes games compelling? [Blog post]. Retrieved April 8, 2014, from Amy Jo Kim website: http://amyjokim.com/2014/04/07/what-makes-games-compelling/

Kim, A. J. (2014d, April 8). The player's journey. [Blog post]. Retrieved August 30, 2014, from Amy Jo Kim website: http://amyjokim.com/2014/04/08/the-players-journey/

Kim, A. J. (2014e, June 11). The co-op revolution: 7 rules for collaborative game design. Retrieved August 30, 2014, from Slideshare website: http://www.slideshare.net/amyjokim/ the-coop-revolution-7-rules-for-collaborative-game-design

Klein, E. (2013, September 9). Bring magic to your open house with augmented reality! Retrieved December 31, 2013, from Scholastic website: http://www.scholastic.com/ teachers/top-teaching/2013/09/bring-magic-your-open-house-augmented-reality

Klein, J. (2014, January 9). The participatory design culture and terms of badges. Retrieved January 19, 2014, from Jess Klein website: http://jessicaklein.blogspot.com/2014/01/ the-participatory-design-culture-and.html?m=1

Kohn, A. (1999). *Punished by rewards: The trouble with gold stars, incentive plans, A's, praise, and other bribes* (1999 ed.). Boston, MA: Houghton Mifflin.

Kohn, A. (1997). Why incentive plans cannot work. In S. Kerr (ed.), *Ultimate rewards: What really motivates people to achieve* (pp. 15–24). Boston, MA: Harvard Business School Press.

Kopfer, E., Osterweil, S., & Salen, K. (2009). *Moving learning games forward.* Retrieved December 14, 2013, from MIT Education Arcade website: http://education.mit.edu/ papers/MovingLearningGamesForward_EdArcade.pdf

Koster, R. (2005). *A theory of fun for game design.* Scottsdale, AZ: Paraglyph Press.

Kühn, S., Romanowski, A., Schilling, C., et al. (2011, November 15). The neural basis of video gaming. *Translational Psychiatry, 1*(53), 1–5. Retrieved December 10, 2013, from Nature.com website: http://www.nature.com/tp/journal/v1/n11/full/tp201153a.html

Kushner, D. (2012). *Jacked: The outlaw story of* Grand Theft Auto. Hoboken, NJ: John Wiley & Sons.

Lave, J., & Wenger, E. (1991). *Situated learning: Legitimate peripheral participation.* Cambridge, UK: Cambridge University Press.

Lazzaro, N. (2004, March 8). *Why we play games: Four keys to more emotion without story.* Retrieved April 20, 2014, from XEODesign website: http://www.xeodesign.com/xeodesign_whyweplaygames.pdf

Lazzaro, N. (2009). Understanding emotions. In C. Bateman (ed.), *Beyond game design: Nine steps toward creating better videogames* (pp. 3–48). Boston, MA: Charles River Media.

Learning Games Network. (2014). Retrieved January 17, 2014, from http://www.learninggamesnetwork.org

Lenhart, A., Kahne, J., Middaugh, E., Macgill, A. R., et al. (2008, September 16). *Teens, video games and civics.* Retrieved December 14, 2013, from Pew Internet & American Life Project website: http://www.pewinternet.org/~/media//Files/Reports/2008/PIP_Teens_Games_and_Civics_Report_FINAL.pdf.pdf

Let's Play Archive. (2013). Retrieved December 10, 2013, from http://lparchive.org

Lewin, K. (1947). Frontiers in group dynamics: concept, method and reality in social science; social equilibria and social change. Human Relations, 15–41. doi:10.1177/001872674700100103

Logo Foundation. (2011). What is Logo? Retrieved January 19, 2014, from http://el.media.mit.edu/logo-foundation/logo/index.html

LP guide for newbies. (2014). Retrieved January 18, 2014, from Wikia website: http://letsplay.wikia.com/wiki/LP_guide_for_newbies

Luckman, S., & Potanin, R. (2010). Machinima: Why think "games" when thinking "film"? In M. Knobel & C. Lankshear (eds.), *DIY media: Creating, sharing and learning with new technologies* (pp. 135–160). New York, NY: Peter Lang.

MacArthur Foundation. (2014). Retrieved January 17, 2014, from http://www.macfound.org/

Magdaleno, A. (2014, July 18). ESPN's "Dota 2" broadcast is a giant leap for e-sports. Retrieved July 19, 2014, from Mashable website: http://mashable.com/2014/07/18/esports-dota-2-espn/

Makebadges. (2014). Retrieved January 19, 2014, from http://www.makebadg.es/badge.html#

MaKey MaKey. (2014). Retrieved January 17, 2014, from http://www.makeymakey.com

Mashable. (2014). Retrieved January 18, 2014, from http://mashable.com/

Mass Effect 3 wiki. (2014). Retrieved January 19, 2014, from IGN website: http://www.ign.com/wikis/mass-effect-3/Paragon

McCormick, R. (2013, December 18). Smithsonian calls video games art, adds two to permanent collection. Retrieved December 24, 2013, from the Verge website: http://www.theverge.com/2013/12/18/5222932/smithsonian-adds-flower-halo-2600-to-permanent-collection

McGonigal, J. (2010, February). *Jane McGonigal: Gaming can make a better world.* Retrieved January 18, 2014, from TED website: http://www.ted.com/talks/jane_mcgonigal_gaming_can_make_a_better_world.html

McGonigal, J. (2011). *Reality is broken: Why games make us better and how they can change the world.* New York, NY: Penguin Press.

Millstone, J. (2012, May 5). National survey and video case studies: Teacher attitudes about digital games in the classroom. Retrieved February 7, 2014, from Joan Ganz Cooney Center at Sesame Workshop website: http://www.joanganzcooneycenter.org/publication/national-survey-and-video-case-studies-teacher-attitudes-about-digital-games-in-the-classroom/

Milton, S., Soares, P., & Maron, J. (2013). *Minecraft essential handbook.* New York, NY: Scholastic.

Mirani, L. (2014, April 3). Last year, 71 million people watched other people play video games. Retrieved April 5, 2014, from Quartz website: http://qz.com/195098/last-year-71-million-people-watched-other-people-play-video-games/

Mozilla Foundation and Peer 2 Peer University. (2012, August 27). *Open badges for lifelong learning.* Retrieved July 22, 2013, from MozillaWiki website: https://wiki.mozilla.org/images/5/59/OpenBadges-Working-Paper_012312.pdf

Mullich, D. (2013, September 28). Game-based learning. Retrieved January 6, 2014, from Slideshare website: http://www.slideshare.net/dmullich/game-based-learning-26636013

Nasar, S. (1998). *A beautiful mind: A biography of John Forbes Nash, Jr., winner of the Nobel prize in economics, 1994.* New York, NY: Simon & Schuster.

NationStates. (2014). Retrieved January 23, 2014, from http://www.nationstates.net

New Media Consortium. (2013a). *NMC horizon project shortlist: 2013 higher education edition.* Retrieved July 22, 2013, from http://www.nmc.org/pdf/2013-horizon-higher-ed-shortlist.pdf

New Media Consortium. (2013b). *NMC horizon report—2013 higher education edition.* Retrieved January 19, 2014, from http://www.nmc.org/publications/2013-horizon-report-higher-ed

NewSchools Venture Fund. (2014). Retrieved July 29, 2014, from http://www.newschools.org

Olson, C. K. (2010, January 16). Children's motivations for video game play in the context of normal development. *Review of General Psychology, 14*(2), 180–187. Retrieved December 14, 2013, from American Psychological Association website: http://www.apa.org/pubs/journals/releases/gpr-14-2-180.pdf

Papert, S. (1993). *Mindstorms: Children, computers, and powerful ideas* (2nd ed.). New York, NY: Basic Books.

Parker, I. (2013, March 26). Improv, robots, parkour and more: Boss level at Quest to Learn. Retrieved December 17, 2013, from Institute of Play website: http://www.instituteofplay.org/2013/03/improv-robots-parkour-and-more-boss-level-at-quest-to-learn/

Parlett, D. (2005). Rules OK, or Hoyle on troubled waters. Paper presented at the 8th annual colloquium of the Board Game Studies Association, Oxford, 2005. Retrieved December 14, 2013, from http://www.davpar.eu/gamester/rulesOK.html

Participatory design. (2014). Retrieved January 19, 2014, from Wikipedia website: http://en.wikipedia.org/wiki/Participatory_design

Persson, M. (2014, September 15). I'm leaving Mojang. Retrieved September 17, 2014, from Notch.net website: http://notch.net/2014/09/im-leaving-mojang/

Piaget, J. (1962). *Play, dreams and imitation in childhood*. New York, NY: Norton Library.

Piccione, P. A. (1980, July/August). In search of the meaning of *Senet*. *Archaeology*, 55–58.

Pink, D. H. (2009). *Drive: The surprising truth about what motivates us*. New York, NY: Riverhead Books.

PlayMaker School. (2013). Retrieved December 20, 2013, from http://www.playmaker.org

Poundstone, W. (1992). *Prisoner's dilemma*. New York, NY: Doubleday.

Razzouk, R., & Shute, V. J. (2012). What is design thinking and why is it important? *Review of Educational Research*, 82(3), 330–348.

Resnick, M. (2012, February 27). Still a badge skeptic. Retrieved July 31, 2013, from HASTAC website: http://www.hastac.org/blogs/mres/2012/02/27/still-badge-skeptic

Robinett, W. (2006). Adventure as a video game: Adventure for the Atari 2600. In K. Salen & E. Zimmerman (eds.), *The game design reader: A rules of play anthology* (pp. 690–713). Cambridge, MA: MIT Press.

Rufo-Tepper, R., Salen, K., Shapiro, A., Torres, R., & Wolozin, L. (2011). *Quest to learn: Developing the school for digital kids*. Cambridge, MA: MIT Press.

Salen, K., & Zimmerman, E. (2003). *Rules of play: Game design fundamentals*. Cambridge, MA: MIT Press.

Sandseter, E., & Kennair, L. (2011). Children's risky play from an evolutionary perspective: The anti-phobic effects of thrilling experiences. *Evolutionary Psychology*, 9(2), 257–284.

Schell, J. (2008). *The art of game design: A book of lenses*. Amsterdam: Elsevier/Morgan Kaufmann.

Schwartz, D. L., & Arena, D. (2009, August). *Choice-based assessments for the digital age*. Retrieved December 14, 2013, from Stanford University, School of Education website: http://aaalab.stanford.edu/papers/ChoiceSchwartzArenaAUGUST232009.pdf

Seedlings. (2014). Retrieved January 20, 2014, from http://seedlingsshow.com/

Senge, P. M. (2006). *The fifth discipline: The art and practice of the learning organization* (rev. ed.). New York, NY: Doubleday/Currency. (Original work published 1990)

SFMOMA presents less and more: The design ethos of Dieter Rams. (2011, June 29). Retrieved January 10, 2014, from San Francisco Museum of Modern Art website: http://www.sfmoma.org/about/press/press_exhibitions/releases/880

Shear, E. (2014, August 25). Letter from the CEO. Retrieved August 30, 2014, from Twitch website: http://www.twitch.tv/p/thankyou

Shechtman, N., DeBarger, A. H., Dornsife, C., Rosier, S., & Yarnall, L. (2013, February 14). *Promoting grit, tenacity, and perseverance: Critical factors for success in the 21st century*. Retrieved January 31, 2014, from Office of Educational Technology website: http://www.ed.gov/edblogs/technology/files/2013/02/OET-Draft-Grit-Report-2-17-13.pdf

Sheldon, L. (2012). *The multiplayer classroom: Designing coursework as a game*. Boston, MA: Course Technology/Cengage Learning.

Shirinian, A. (2011, July 8). Dissecting the postmortem: Lessons learned from two years of game development self-reportage. Retrieved April 13, 2014, from *Gamasutra* website: http://www.gamasutra.com/view/feature/134679/dissecting_the_postmortem_lessons_.php

Shuler, C. (2012). *Where in the world is Carmen Sandiego? The edutainment era: Debunking myths and sharing lessons learned*. New York, NY: Joan Ganz Cooney Center at Sesame Workshop.

Shute, V. J. (2014). Publications. Retrieved August 30, 2014, from Florida State University website: http://myweb.fsu.edu/vshute/publications.html

Shute, V. J. (2011). Stealth assessment in computer-based games to support learning. In S. Tobias, & J. D. Fletcher (Eds.), *Computer games and instruction* (pp. 503–524). Charlotte, NC: Information Age Publishers.

Shute, V. J., Ventura, M., & Torres, R. (2013). Formative evaluation of students at Quest to Learn. *International Journal of Learning and Media*, 4(1), 55–69.

Siddiqui, A. (2014, January 20). Playtime online: What does math have to do with games? Retrieved January 31, 2014, from Institute of Play website: http://www.instituteofplay.org/awsm/playtime-online/what-does-math-have-to-do-with-games/

Siwek, S. E. (2010). *Video games in the 21st century: The 2010 report*. Retrieved July 31, 2014, from Entertainment Software Association website: http://www.theesa.com/facts/pdfs/VideoGames21stCentury_2010.pdf

Squire, K. (2011). *Video games and learning: Teaching and participatory culture in the digital age*. New York, NY: Teachers College Press.

Stewart, B. (2011, September 1). Personality and play styles: A unified model. Retrieved January 3, 2014, from *Gamasutra* website: http://www.gamasutra.com/view/feature/134842/personality_and_play_styles_a_.php

Strauss, V. (2013, October 16). Howard Gardner: "Multiple intelligences" are not "learning styles." Retrieved December 25, 2013, from the *Washington Post* website: http://www.washingtonpost.com/blogs/answer-sheet/wp/2013/10/16/howard-gardner-multiple-intelligences-are-not-learning-styles/

Surge, V. (2009, June 10). Create paranormal images [Online forum post]. Retrieved from Comedy Goldmine website: http://forums.somethingawful.com/showthread.php?threadid=3150591&userid=0&perpage=40&pagenumber=3

Suttie, J. (2012, April 17). Eight tips for fostering flow in the classroom. Retrieved December 30, 2013, from Greater Good website: http://greatergood.berkeley.edu/article/item/eight_tips_for_fostering_flow_in_the_classroom

Takahashi, D. (2013, May 5). Valve's experimental psychologist discusses sweat detection and eye-tracking for games. Retrieved December 30, 2013, from Venture Beat website: http://venturebeat.com/2013/05/05/valves-experimental-psychologist-discusses-sweat-detection-and-eye-tracking-for-games/

TakingITGlobal. (2014). Retrieved January 18, 2014, from https://www.tigweb.org

Tassi, P. (2012, April 4). EA is the worst company in America, now what? Retrieved January 13, 2014, from *Forbes* website: http://www.forbes.com/sites/insertcoin/2012/04/04/ea-is-the-worst-company-in-america-now-what/

Tassi, P. (2013, July 19). The stunning video game resume that took 2,000 hours to make. Retrieved July 19, 2014, from *Forbes* website: http://www.forbes.com/sites/insertcoin/2013/07/19/the-stunning-video-game-resume-that-took-2000-hours-to-make/

Teacher Gaming. (2013). Retrieved December 8, 2013, from http://www.teachergaming.com

Thompson, C. (2013). *Smarter than you think: How technology is changing our minds for the better.* New York, NY: Penguin.

Toca Boca. (2014). A digital toy or a game—what is the difference? Retrieved January 23, 2014, from Toca Boca website: https://tocaboca.desk.com/customer/portal/articles/564124-a-digital-toy-or-a-game--what-is-the-difference-

Tools of the Mind curriculum. (2014). Retrieved February 20, 2014, from Tools of the Mind website: http://www.toolsofthemind.org/curriculum/

Tough, P. (2012). *How children succeed: Grit, curiosity, and the hidden power of character.* New York, NY: Houghton Mifflin Harcourt.

2014 essential facts about the computer and video game industry. (2014, April). Retrieved August 30, 2014, from The Entertainment Software Association website: http://www.theesa.com/facts/pdfs/ESA_EF_2014.pdf

Von Neumann, J., & Morgenstern, O. (2007). *Theory of games and economic behavior.* Princeton, NJ: Princeton University Press.

Vygotsky, L. S. (1997). *Educational psychology* (R. J. Silverman, Trans.). Boca Raton, FL: St. Lucie Press.

Waniewski, B. (2011, November 21). Designing a classroom game that can get kids excited about history. Retrieved January 20, 2014, from *The Atlantic* website: http://www.the-atlantic.com/national/archive/2011/11/designing-a-classroom-game-that-can-get-kids-excited-about-history/248614/

Wellings, J., & Levine, M. H. (2009). *The digital promise: Transforming learning with innovative uses of technology.* Retrieved December 14, 2013, from DML Central website: http://dml-central.net/sites/dmlcentral/files/resource_files/Apple.pdf

Well Played Journal. (2011, June 12). Retrieved April 26, 2014, from Carnegie Mellon Entertainment Technology Center website: http://press.etc.cmu.edu/wellplayed

Whalen, Z., & Taylor, L. N. (Eds.). (2008). *Playing the past: History and nostalgia in video games.* Nashville, TN: Vanderbilt University Press.

What is edu-LARP? (n.d.). Retrieved August 29, 2014, from Seekers Unlimited website: http://seekersunlimited.com/about-us/what-is-edu-larp/

Whitbourne, S. K. (2011, September 27). How videogames can promote empathy. Retrieved January 19, 2014, from *Psychology Today* website: http://www.psychologytoday.com/blog/fulfillment-any-age/201109/how-videogames-can-promote-empathy

White, D. (2014, January 3). Building educational games that get used in schools. Retrieved January 8, 2014, from *Gamasutra* website: http://www.gamasutra.com/blogs/DanWhite/20140103/208005/Building_Educational_Games_That_Get_Used_in_Schools.php

Wiggins, G. P., & McTighe, J. (2005). *Understanding by design* (2nd ed.). Alexandria, VA: Association for Supervision and Curriculum Development.

Wolpert-Gawron, H. (2011). *'Tween crayons and curfews: Tips for middle school teachers.* Larchmont, NY: Eye on Education.

Zieger, L., & Farber, M. (2012). Civic Participation Among Seventh-Grade Social Studies Students in Multi-User Virtual Environments. *Journal of Interactive Learning Research,* 23(4), 393–410.

INDEX

X

Xbox, 13, 15, 102, 111, 126, 129, 141, 147,
    169, 201, 211, 222
Xenos (game), 160, 241

Y

Youtopia, 7, 141, 144–146, 158
YouTube, 3, 22, 135, 139, 146, 197–199,
    201, 214, 219, 222, 240, 242, 244
Yowell, Connie, 162–163

Z

Zombies, Run! (game), 111, 119
Zone of Proximal Development, 33, 55, 88,
    132, 134
Zynga, 15, 180, 230–231
Zynga.org, 7, 224, 230–232, 242

new
literacies
ꟼ

AND DIGITAL EPISTEMOLOGIES

Colin Lankshear & Michele Knobel
General Editors

New literacies emerge and evolve apace as people from all walks of life engage with new technologies, shifting values and institutional change, and increasingly assume 'postmodern' orientations toward their everyday worlds. Despite many efforts to take account of such changes, educational institutions largely remain out of touch with the range of new ways of making and sharing meanings that increasingly mediate and shape the lives of the young people they teach and the futures they face. This series aims to explore some key dimensions of the changes occurring within social practices of literacy and the educational challenges they present, with a view to informing educational practice in helpful ways. It asks what are new literacies, how do they impact on life in schools, homes, communities, workplaces, sites of leisure, and other key settings of human cultural engagement, and what significance do new literacies have for how people learn and how they understand and construct knowledge. It aims to challenge established and 'official' ways of framing literacy, and to ask what it means for literacies to be powerful, effective, and enabling under current and foreseeable conditions. Collectively, the works in this series will help to reorient literacy debates and literacy education agendas.

For further information about the series and submitting manuscripts, please contact:

Michele Knobel & Colin Lankshear
Montclair State University
Dept. of Education and Human Services
3173 University Hall
Montclair, NJ 07043
michele@coatepec.net

To order other books in this series, please contact our Customer Service Department at:
(800) 770-LANG (within the U.S.)
(212) 647-7706 (outside the U.S.)
(212) 647-7707 FAX

Or browse online by series at:
www.peterlang.com